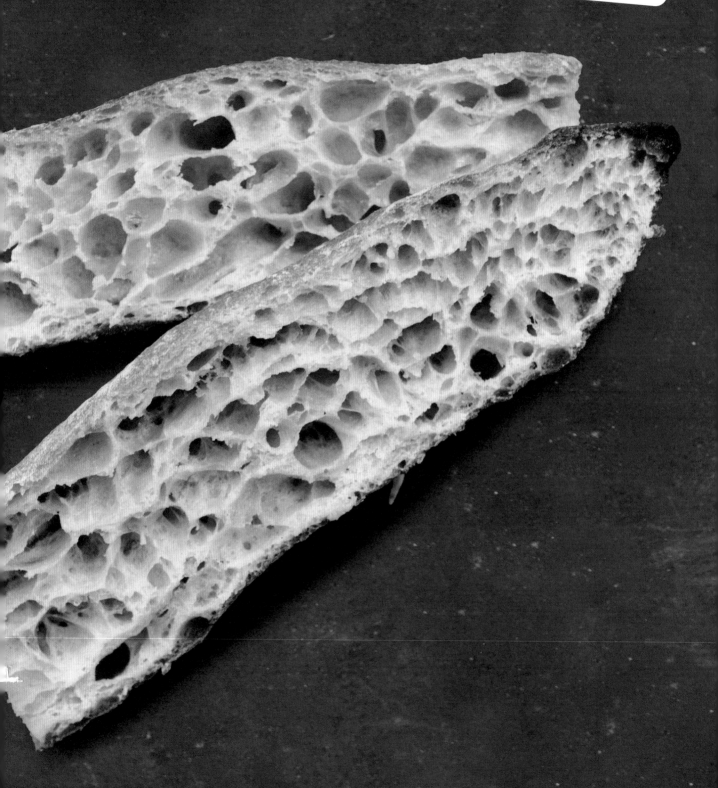

A

SLOW

RISE

A

Favorite Recipes from Four Decades of Baking with Heart

SLOW

Daniel Leader with Lauren Chattman and Amy Vogler
Photography by Joerg Lehmann

RISE

AVERY
an Imprint of
Penguin Random House
New York

AVERY

an imprint of Penguin Random House LLC
penguinrandomhouse.com

Photographs by Joerg Lehmann
Photograph on page 8 (top) from the *Woodstock Times*; photograph on page 8 (bottom) from the Bread Alone archive; photograph on page 13 by Lynne Gilson; photographs on pages 17, 75, 76–77 (top row: second and fourth from left, middle row: center and right, bottom row: second, third, and fourth from left), and 83 by Alekz Pacheco; photographs on pages 71 and 351 by Daniel Leader; photographs on pages 76–77 (top row: far left and third from left, bottom row: far left) from the Leader family archive; photographs on pages 76–77 (middle row: far left) and 81 by Mark Antman; photographs on pages 181, 183, 184–85, and 186 by Kate Devine; photograph on page 347 by Alfonso Cortes

Library of Congress Cataloging-in-Publication Data

Names: Leader, Daniel, author. | Chattman, Lauren, author. | Vogler, Amy, author.
Title: A slow rise: favorite recipes from four decades of baking with heart / Daniel Leader with Lauren Chattman.
Description: New York: Avery, an imprint of Penguin Random House, [2024] | Includes index.
Identifiers: LCCN 2023045864 (print) | LCCN 2023045865 (ebook) | ISBN 9780593421581 (hardcover) | ISBN 9780593421598 (epub)
Subjects: LCSH: Bread. | Cooking (Bread). | Sourdough bread. | LCGFT: Cookbooks.
Classification: LCC TX769.L3764 2024 (print) | LCC TX769 (ebook) | DDC 641.81/5—dc23/eng/20231207
LC record available at https://lccn.loc.gov/2023045864
LC ebook record available at https://lccn.loc.gov/2023045865

Printed in China
10 9 8 7 6 5 4 3 2 1

Book design by Ashley Tucker

To Julie,
thank you
for all you do

CONTENTS

The day before Bread Alone opened.

First week, trying to fine-tune the oven.

PROLOGUE

In mid-June 1973, I loaded my college possessions into a small U-Haul and drove from Greeley, Colorado, to Madison, Wisconsin. Encouraged by Paul Rea, my history professor at the University of Northern Colorado, to broaden my horizons, I had applied to transfer to the University of Wisconsin–Madison. Shockingly, in spite of my mediocre (if we're being generous) high school grades, and with just a year of college under my belt, I was accepted. As I turned onto Mifflin Street, looking for the number of my new apartment, I felt equally shocked and excited by the vibrant street life in front of my new home. I had spent the previous year at a very conservative rural state college. The tie-dyed, long-haired, guitar-carrying kids on the sidewalk here looked nothing like the clean-cut farm kids at my old school. Competing rock songs blared and vibrated from the rows of semi-detached houses, young people sang and danced on stoops, and the smell of marijuana wafted from every other open window. I had heard that Mifflin Street, like Telegraph Avenue in Berkeley, was the center of a counterculture that had sprung up in the late '60s as young people like myself protested the Vietnam War and embraced the civil rights movement. As I would soon learn, it was the site of large antiwar protests that had flared in Madison just four years earlier, in 1969. Every year since, the exuberant and sometimes out-of-control Mifflin Street Block Party has been held in honor of those demonstrations.

My new classes were galvanizing, and so was everyday life in my neighborhood. Like a magnet, the Mifflin Street Co-op, one of the first community-run co-ops in the US to sell bulk natural and organic foods, drew me in with its bins of oats and nuts, a new item called "yogurt," fresh local produce, and eggs. Unlike today's pricey natural foods stores, the co-op sold affordable food to its student and working-class clientele. It was at the co-op, a two-minute walk from my apartment, where I found the very first baking book I ever bought. *The Tassajara Bread Book*, by then unknown Zen monk and monastery baker Edward Espe Brown, was stacked in piles next to a bin of dark whole wheat flour. Ed's book called out to me with its cover, a simple sketch of a loaf of rustic-looking bread, coffee, jam, and morning buns. The drawing evoked for me memories of being in the kitchen with my grandmother as she sliced a homemade babka. I started reading it on my front porch as soon as I got home. Ed's gentle words and his conscious approach were both appealing and soothing. He described baking as a private refuge from the stresses of modern life. "Bread makes itself, by your kindness, with your help, with your imagination streaming through you, with dough under hand, you are breadmaking itself, which is why breadmaking is so fulfilling and rewarding."

I'd like to say that the moment I baked my first loaf I was hit with a premonition that I'd open an organic bakery one day. But at that point I was completely clueless as to what my future would hold. I was simply drawn to the process Ed described, and enjoyed his thoughtful words and instructions. Nonetheless, it was Ed's book that set me on my way. I have only vague memories of my first few attempts at his basic whole wheat loaf. But I do remember the very loud thud that one of the early examples—brick-like and under-risen—made when it accidentally landed on my kitchen floor. It was so dense and heavy that it could have served as a paperweight for one of my assignments. Undeterred, probably because at that point I had no idea what a "good" loaf really was, I kept trying. Loaf after loaf, I became fascinated with the transformation of light brown whole wheat flour into a soft and elastic dough. I felt satisfaction, warmth, and joy when I pulled a beautifully risen and caramel-colored bread from my small enamel oven. I remember feeling a broad inner smile after my first successful loaf.

The Zen belief in the primacy of learning, sharing, and teaching that undergirds Ed's baking practice inspired me as I began to make friends in my new community. Ed's insistence that "working to bake bread can renew our spirit, and with this work we renew the world, our friends and neighbors" rang true to my experience. "We are reconnecting with the earth, reconnecting with our common heritage, our shared life and livelihood—we have something to eat." Word started getting around as my friends tasted my early works in progress, and I slowly developed a reputation as the bread guy; it's still with me nearly fifty years later. When star Wisconsin history professor Harvey Goldberg, who spent half the year teaching at the Sorbonne in Paris and undoubtedly had eaten his share of French bread, asked a mutual friend if he could attend one of our dinners to sample my loaves, I was honored. I'd found a way of connecting with people whom I wanted to be around and respected: with an offer of good bread.

I'm the oldest of five kids, and like the other undergraduate philosophers I shot the breeze with on the stoops of our Mifflin Street apartments, I needed a part-time campus job for my spending money and to help my parents pay my out-of-state tuition bill. I had delivered the morning newspaper at 5 a.m. as a twelve-year-old, easily waking up early and getting right to work, even in Buffalo, where that might mean trudging through drifts of waist-high snow in the bitter cold. So I didn't mind the morning shift when I was offered a job in the campus dish room. At dawn each day, I descended deep into the bowels of Memorial Hall, donned a yellow rubber apron and tall waders (the getup looked like what the lobstermen wear here at my current home in Maine), and joined the crew that washed thousands of dirty dishes arriving by dumbwaiter from the various large dining halls above. One of my coworkers, an English major, recommended that I read *Down and Out in Paris and London* by George Orwell. We jokingly compared ourselves to the great author/*plongeur* as we scrubbed pots and sterilized countless plates and pieces of silverware, imagining we were cleaning up after artists and writers rather than the football team in our very hot, steamy, and overcrowded basement. We even signed up for a summer French intensive course so we could try communicating in French. This usually turned into cursing at each other. Intrigued by Orwell's descriptions of life as a Parisian dishwasher, I took courses in French literature, reading Anaïs Nin, Jean-Paul Sartre, Albert Camus, and Simone de Beauvoir. I read Hemingway's *A Moveable Feast* and spent countless hours daydreaming about Paris and French culture.

As I was studying, tinkering with Ed's recipe, and washing dishes, I became enchanted by another text I'd picked up at the co-op, *Living the Good Life* by Scott and Helen Nearing, who had recently visited campus. Not unlike Ed, who had retreated to the Zen center in Northern California for a life of contemplation, the Nearings left a cosmopolitan life in New York City to homestead in rural Vermont in a handmade stone house from 1934 to 1952, and eventually lived off their land in Harborside, Maine. In the late '60s, their book inspired a new generation of back-to-the-landers. I tucked their ideas about homegrown food and a simple and self-sustaining life in the back of my mind.

Early one morning in the dish room, my supervisor called me into the cavernous prep kitchen, also in the basement of Memorial Hall, and asked me if I wanted to become a breakfast cook. Although I'd never cooked in any sort of professional capacity, I found I had the knack. I already had the essential skill required, the ability to show up *on time* and seemingly *alert* at 5 a.m. The next day, I was preparing pancakes, bacon, and eggs for the masses. I learned to enjoy the setup and organization of my new kitchen life and the adrenaline rush of preparing large quantities of food on strict timelines. It helped in this fast-paced environment that I had a natural ability for multitasking. After a few months of this, my supervisor remarked to me that I was so good at making breakfast I should consider going to culinary school. Directionless and open to suggestion, I thought it was as good an idea as any other, and filed it away, probably in the same part of my brain where I stored everything I knew about Ed's whole wheat bread recipe along with the legend of the Nearings.

I mentioned cooking school to my Colorado mentor Professor Rea, whom I was in regular contact with, and he sent me a copy of *Ma Gastronomie* by Fernand Point, just published in English in 1974. Point, a legendary chef in France at that time, had trained a generation of great French chefs, including Paul Bocuse and Roger Vergé.

Whether he was making a roast beef stuffed with ham and truffles or frying an egg, he prized craft over speed, subtlety over style. Both my professor and the greatest chef in France thought that the study of cooking was a worthwhile, creative, and noble pursuit. So it came about, both gradually and then all of a sudden, that I saw my future in food. I applied to the Culinary Institute of America. Once again I was a transfer student, this time in Hyde Park, New York.

The Culinary Institute had moved recently from New Haven, Connecticut, into an old monastery overlooking the Hudson River. The school at that time was a mishmash of odd kitchens packed with used, donated equipment, and a far cry from the glittering showplace it is today. My instructors, mostly from Europe, were a mix of French, Spanish, Austrian, and German chefs and a few Americans. Each ran their kitchens and their classes as their private kingdoms and almost all acted like kings once the door was closed. While the sounds of the Grateful Dead and the smells of marijuana had been the constants of my life in Madison, in Hyde Park the background noise consisted of ear-shattering screams in French, Spanish, and German, and the marijuana smoke was replaced by the aromas of browning pastries and slowly cooking meats. The food was primarily French based and old school. At that time the CIA offered only a two-year associate's degree in culinary arts. The bakeshops, in an overlooked basement corner, were an afterthought and a second-tier culinary world. Baking in general was hardly an area of pride or focus, and students spent a mere six weeks during the two-year program on the subject. It didn't occur to me when I graduated to do anything but join the line at a kitchen in a French restaurant. Upon graduation I was lucky to get a job as a lunch cook at the oldest French bistro in New York City, Le Veau d'Or on Sixtieth Street, which had opened in the 1930s. And yet my interest in bread persisted, to the point where I'd join the bakers at a bakery in Little Italy after work, watching, learning, and helping until dawn, just to scratch that itch.

I've written previously about my travels through Europe and the impact that studying craft breadmaking in France, Germany, Italy, and Poland has had on my own baking. But until I retired recently from the day-to-day operations of Bread Alone, handing over CEO duties to my capable and visionary son Nels, I hadn't had time to consider these preprofessional experiences and the way early mentors helped me define the basic values of Bread Alone. I saw how buyers at the food co-op sought out local Wisconsin products at prices regular people could afford. I admired the co-op as a community hub where workers respected customers and vice versa. Ed Brown's encouraging voice and simple recipes convinced me I could learn to make bread, and to teach others. Fernand Point's definition of success as "the sum of a lot of small things done correctly" became my own. The college cafeteria tempered my romantic ideas about food, introducing me to the physical exertions and also

On my very first trip to France, I made a pilgrimage to la Pyramide and met chef Guy Thivard.

the camaraderie of the kitchen. The CIA gave me the skills to enter classical kitchens. The Nearings inspired me when I wanted to leave restaurants and become more self-reliant in my life and work. I built my first hearth oven by hand, using stones I collected from a stream near the Catskills property where I would begin my business. Is there anything more Nearing-ian than that?

As Bread Alone has reached its fortieth year, it's been fascinating to look back on these formative experiences, and to marvel at all the changes—in wheat farming, milling, sourdough baking, and artisan food production in general—that have taken place all around me across the decades. In this book, you'll read my reminiscences as I travel back in time to the North Dakota farm where I first encountered organic grain, and of my constant experimentation with a dozen different styles of sourdough growing in buckets in the original Bread Alone shop. I'll share with you what I'm doing in retirement these days, including fulfilling a yearslong dream of participating in the Grand Prix de la Baguette in Paris, and attending the International Symposium on Sourdough in Bolzano, Italy. And I'll even attempt to predict a bit of the future, as I collaborate with the grain scientists at the International Maize and Wheat Improvement Center (CIMMYT) in Mexico City, and advise would-be New York State farmers, millers, and bakers at the Grain Innovation Center at Hartwick College. When I first started baking, quality breads and pastries were available in only a few bakeries in large US cities. Today, thousands of home bakers show off incredible craft breads daily on Instagram. The recipes in this book are the result of every piece of knowledge and experience I've acquired over the years. With them, I want to acknowledge the sophistication of today's bakers while also staying true to my decades-long goal of making and teaching others how to make truly simple and soul-fulfilling food.

1.

INGREDIENTS

AND

EQUIPMENT

T HE AVAILABILITY OF HIGH-QUALITY BAKING IN-gredients has increased dramatically over the last few decades. Forty years ago, you used to have to look carefully on the supermarket shelf just to make sure you were buying flour that was unbleached and unbromated. Today, you can find organic dark rye, buckwheat, and ama-ranth flour as well as whole-grain millet, teff, and farro at many grocery stores, and easily order an outstanding selection of whole and milled grains and seeds from a small noncommodity mill not too far from your home.

Similarly, European-style butter, so much better for brioche, croissants, and cookies than American butter with its lower butterfat percentage, is easy to find. French sea salt, unparalleled in flavor and essential for making the best bread, is widely avail-able. And it seems that every neighborhood has a hobby farmer selling fresh eggs.

The recipes in this book call for a short list of ingredients. Take the time to seek out flour, whole grains and seeds, dairy, and salt of the highest quality and you will be re-warded with the best versions of these breads and pastries.

Ingredients

Wheat flour: Most of the bread in this book is made with at least a percentage of flour ground from wheat. Beyond "whole" and "white," the question is, *Which wheat flour is best for bread?* I don't endorse any one brand of flour, although I do strongly recommend using only unbleached, unbromated flours, and preferably ones that have been stone-ground from organic wheat. In my experi-ence, organic flours make better-tasting breads. Stone grinding, in contrast to com-mercial milling, removes less of the oily, vitamin-rich germ that adds flavor to and encourages fermentation in bread.

Bleaching is a way of chemically aging flour so that it will have more gluten-producing potential. Not only does this pro-cess remove natural beta-carotene pigments, which color and subtly flavor bread, but it can also inhibit fermentation in sourdoughs by killing the natural yeast. Unbleached flour is stored for three to eight weeks to allow it to oxidize naturally, giving it the same gluten-producing potential as bleached flour in the long run. Bromate (which is outlawed throughout Europe as a carcinogen) is also a gluten-maximizing additive. Large commercial bakeries often use bromated flour because bromate makes bread dough very extensible and thus easy for bakery machinery to handle. Home and artisan bakers are better off choosing unbromated flour with other gluten-friendly characteristics.

Most supermarket flour in the US is labeled as "all-purpose" or "bread." These classifications give a general idea of a flour's protein content and indicate the type of products they are best suited for. Generally, all-purpose flour has a protein content between 8 and 11 percent. It is suitable for cookies, muffins, and scones as well as softer pan breads and focaccia. Bread flour has a protein content between 12 and 14 percent, and is necessary for high-rising and crusty country-style breads. The recipes in this book that employ wheat flour will direct you to choose either all-purpose or bread flour, depending on how much strength the dough requires for a proper rise.

But looking at the classification of a bag of flour won't necessarily give you all the infor-

A bag of Farmer Ground Flour waiting to be opened at the bakery.

mation you need to make the best choice. For one thing, the protein content of a particular type of flour varies by brand. King Arthur's all-purpose flour has 11.7 percent protein, while Gold Medal's all-purpose flour has 9.8 percent protein. So to determine that you are buying the right flour for a particular recipe, it is crucial to look at the labeling or do some online research before you buy. Some brands, like King Arthur, advertise the protein content right on the front of the bag. Their organic bread flour proudly proclaims "12.7% gluten-forming protein content" on the upper-right-hand corner of the bag. Bob's Red Mill's artisan bread flour, in contrast, recommends a list of products—pretzels, baguettes, boules—on its label but doesn't list a specific number. You can discover on their website that their artisan bread flour averages 12 to 14 percent.

Home bakers often assume that more protein makes better bread, but I like a balanced flour, between 10.5 and 12.2 percent. In this range, you will get a dough that has enough strength to hold expanding gases within its cell walls to give the bread a high rise. At the same time, that bread will be soft enough to chew. Complicating the choice: all protein is not created equal. I have baked with 10.5 percent protein flours that have more strength than some 13 percent protein flours, because although there may be less protein in the 10.5 percent flour, that protein is of a higher quality.

If all this is confusing, don't despair. The reality is that the process of finding a flour you like can be one of trial and error. To start,

I recommend seeking out either unbleached and unbromated organic flour with a protein content suited to your recipe from a reputable source like Heartland Mill (heartlandmill.com) or Central Milling (centralmilling.com). These larger specialty mills supply some of the country's best artisan bakeries. They have been in business for decades and have built relationships with many larger family-owned farms, where wheat is grown specifically for them. They have the experience and equipment necessary to blend grain from different sources to come up with a consistent, and consistently excellent, product year after year. This quality and consistency will help you bake outstanding breads. As you gain experience using a particular flour with a particular recipe, you will be able to adjust—adding more or less water, kneading and turning more or less depending on how the dough develops—to get the exact result you seek.

Beyond flour from the larger specialty mills, there is an entire world of flour, relatively newly opened to consumers, outside the commodity system of which more mature and well-established brands, even organic ones, are a part. For bakers interested in supporting a local grain economy, noncommodity flour will be of particular interest. This is flour that small mills produce from grain they have exclusively purchased from nearby small farmers. I delve into this subject in some detail on pages 144–46. But at the very least, it is important to know that, unlike a bag of King Arthur flour, a bag of flour from Deep Roots Milling in Roseland,

Virginia, or Shagbark Seed & Mill in Athens, Ohio, might not have detailed information about protein on its label. Beyond that, these mills are each developing their own product mix, possibly using different varieties of wheat from season to season or batch to batch. Each of them has slightly different grinding and sifting systems, resulting in flours that are more or less refined and contain more or less bran and germ. Expect the unexpected when using a noncommodity flour: it might take more or less water than your trusty flour from Central Milling; its gluten might develop differently, resulting in a softer or bouncier dough. Don't expect to bake a perfect loaf the first time. When I developed the recipe for my 100% Whole Wheat Sourdough (page 147), I used whole wheat flour from Janie's Mill, and it took me four tries to figure out exactly how much water this flour could absorb and exactly how long I had to knead it. It was time well spent. In the end, I had a perfectly local loaf.

With the availability of moderately priced home mills, there is the option of grinding your own flour. If you are going to grind wheat berries, I would advise buying them directly from a mill, so you know what kind of wheat you are getting. There will definitely be a learning curve when it comes to discovering the right settings and extraction levels for the breads you want to bake. Personally, I prefer to buy wheat flour from a small mill and use my home mill to grind small quantities of alternative flours in order to diversify the ingredients in my breads.

If you find yourself ordering bulk quantities of organic flour or smaller quantities of noncommodity flour (artisan baking can be addictive), store them in airtight containers in the refrigerator or freezer. High-quality, minimally processed flour that still contains some germ oil will go rancid more quickly than commercial flour from which all oil has been removed. Remember to plan ahead and bring your flour to room temperature before you mix your dough, so that it will rise in the time range suggested in the recipe.

Buckwheat, rye, spelt, emmer, einkorn, khorasan, and other alternative-grain flours: The list of alternative-grain flours now available to consumers is long and intriguing. Feel free to substitute small amounts (no more than 40 percent) for wheat flour in breads of your choice to get a uniquely flavored loaf with a strong gluten structure.

Salt: I prefer the pure taste of sea salt in my breads. Table salt is flat tasting in comparison to sea salt, which is multidimensional in flavor. In addition, fine sea salt dissolves most easily into dough. I like Guérande, sea salt imported from France, for its delicious flavor.

Water: At the original Bread Alone location we use well water, filtered with ultraviolet rays to kill any bacteria, as mandated by the New York State Department of Health. We use this water to cultivate sourdough starters as well as to make bread dough. Because it comes from a well on our property and we

The Science and Marketing of "Ancient" Grains

For wheat breeders and scientists, "ancient" wheat refers to either the progenitors of the modern wheat or other wheat species. These include einkorn wheat (*Triticum monococcum*), emmer wheat (*Triticum dicoccon* Schrank ex Schübl), and spelt (*Triticum spelta*). These species have not been subjected to extensive genetic improvements over the last several hundred years.

When wheat scientists talk about "modern" wheat, they are referring to bread wheat (*Triticum aestivum*) and durum wheat (*Triticum durum* Desf.). Bread wheat is the most cultivated wheat in the world and accounts for 95 percent of global wheat production. Durum wheat is grown mainly to make pasta. These species have been subject to more intensive breeding programs, especially after World War II.

But for consumers, the term *ancient*, along with the less scientific *heirloom* and *heritage*, are often used (and misinterpreted) for marketing purposes and to justify a higher price. On packages of einkorn, emmer, and khorasan (or Kamut, as it has been trademarked) flour, *ancient* refers to the fact that these grains were grown by early farmers thousands of years ago. But just because their history can be traced back to ancient times doesn't mean that they are healthier or better for baking than modern grains. Studies by scientists affiliated with the International Maize and Wheat Improvement Center (CIMMYT) show that there is very little difference between "ancient" and modern wheat when it comes to vitamins and minerals, and modern wheat takes the advantage when it comes to fiber. Nutritionally speaking, whole grains, whether ancient or modern, are going to be healthier than refined grains, whatever their pedigree.

Heirloom and *heritage* are somewhat interchangeable terms for grain that was grown in the more recent past and has been handed down through several generations. Often, consumers will assume that grain that carries either of these labels is more "authentic" than modern grain because it hasn't been manipulated by scientists to affect its productivity or other characteristics. But just because a wheat is labeled "heirloom" or "heritage" doesn't mean it hasn't been subject to human intervention in the form of selective breeding, as when a farmer might choose seeds from the year's best plants to use in next year's crop. Nor does it mean that the variety has not evolved on its own in response to environmental conditions. The Turkey Red wheat brought to this country by Ukrainian immigrants in the nineteenth century has certainly adapted over time to the growing conditions of the Great Plains, evolving to favor plants that thrive in that particular location.

Landrace is a more complicated concept, generally referring to a local variety of a species with distinctive characteristics and arising from development and adaptation over time to conditions of a defined ecogeographical area and under the influence of local human culture. Sometimes it refers to a variety of wheat that has been grown in a particular location for generations, developing a "terroir" because of particular soil and farming traditions as much as the characteristics of the variety. But *landrace* can also refer to a type of modern wheat that has developed over time because of the practice of growing a dozen or more varieties of wheat in the same field, allowing them to cross-pollinate and resulting in the natural selection of certain traits to predominate eventually. And ancient grains, grown in the same location over time, can also be considered landraces.

test it frequently, I can be sure it doesn't contain a lot of chlorine or high mineral levels that could kill the yeast in a sourdough culture before the culture has had time to become well established. When we mix it into bread dough, the dough rises reliably and the clean taste of wholesome grain predominates. If your water is particularly hard or chlorinated, you might consider using bottled spring water in your starters and your breads. It's not just the question of minerals inhibiting fermentation. If you don't like the taste of your tap water, you might not like the way it flavors your bread.

Yeast: Some of the recipes in this book call for small amounts of **instant dry yeast**, otherwise known as bread machine yeast, because it is the most convenient to use and most commonly available to home bakers. Unlike traditional active dry yeast, instant dry yeast does not need to be dissolved in water. So you can just add it to the flour when mixing the dough. It will become fully hydrated during kneading. I've tried every brand out there, and they all work, but I prefer SAF brand yeast for its consistency, liveliness, and flavor. You can buy instant dry yeast in small envelopes and keep them in a cool, dry pantry. Or you can buy yeast in a larger container, which is more economical and handy if you bake a lot. After you open the box or jar, transfer the yeast to an airtight container and refrigerate or freeze it.

If you'd like, you can substitute traditional **active dry yeast** in an equal amount. Just moisten it in the water (or in a very few cases, milk) before adding the flour. Once the yeast particles are thoroughly wet, the dough can be mixed right away. It is a myth that dry yeast needs to sit in liquid until it bubbles, in order for you to check that it is "working." Unless it has been contaminated by moisture, dry yeast will raise bread many months and even years beyond the sell-by date printed on the package.

One type of yeast that you should definitely avoid is **rapid-rise**. This is dry yeast that has been packaged with a lot of yeast foods and enzymes to accelerate fermentation. Rapid-rise yeast was first developed for commercial bakers who wanted to save time and money. Using this yeast, they could skip the first rise and immediately divide and shape the dough as soon as it was mixed. In contrast, experienced craft bakers prefer to use a small amount of yeast and give their dough a slow rise to develop its flavor.

Seeds, pulses, and whole grains: In my previous books, I primarily used seeds and whole grains to add texture to breads. These days, I am just as likely to grind them, along with dried beans, for use in a fermented nutritional supplement (see page 154 for more on this technique). I predict that we will see more and more bakers grinding and fermenting a variety of seeds, pulses, and grains in the future, to add nutrients to their breads and to encourage farmers to grow a diversity of crops to better feed the world. I buy organic seeds, pulses, and whole grains at my local food co-op and store them in the freezer to maintain their freshness.

Butter: European butter has a butterfat content of at least 82 percent, compared to US butter, which generally contains just 80 percent butterfat. More butterfat means more flavor, so I go with European butter at the bakery and in these recipes.

Eggs: The recipes in this book call for large eggs, which weigh about 55 grams. Shell color is unimportant, but you should seek out organic eggs from a local source for the freshest, most wholesome flavor.

Dried fruit and nuts: Buy unsulfured dried fruits and raw nuts, preferably organic. Soak dried fruits in water, drain, and pat dry before using, so they don't rob moisture from the dough. In some cases, I call for toasting nuts and cooling them before mixing them into bread dough, to bring out their full flavor.

Equipment

Digital scale: All professional bakers weigh ingredients rather than measure them by volume, because it is the surest way to wind up with uniform-quality breads, batch after batch. If you buy only one new piece of equipment for bread baking, make it a digital scale that will show the weight of your ingredients in ounces and in grams. A tare function, so you can zero out the scale before adding a new ingredient, is very helpful. I use a Polder digital scale imported from Switzerland. It weighs up to 2 kilograms (4 pounds 4 ounces), more than enough for the breads in this book. I prefer to weigh ingredients by grams rather than ounces, for the sake of precision. This is especially true when measuring small quantities that won't register in ounces but will in grams.

Instant-read thermometer/oven thermometer: In my first book I was a fanatic for measuring the temperature of everything: the water, the flour, the dough, the oven. I had to know that every batch of dough at every moment of its journey would be the same temperature as the last. This consistency is just not that important at home as it is in a professional setting. When you have a batch of dough that weighs hundreds of pounds, it might take hours for it to warm up or cool down just a degree or two, completely throwing off the day's baking schedule. If you are mixing a batch of dough that weighs just 2 pounds, it will reach optimum room temperature in 20 to 30 minutes even if it is 67° or 87°F (19° or 30°C) when mixed. If you are just baking a bread or two a day, you can simply adjust to accommodate the rate of fermentation.

Still, an instant-read thermometer comes in handy sometimes. I prefer to start with a relatively cool dough, which takes longer to rise than a warm one. A longer rise allows the dough to develop more flavor. So I mix my dough with cool (70° to 78°F / 21° to 25.5°C) rather than warm water to encourage a slower fermentation. At this point in my life, I can tell by touch the temperature of the water, but if you are just starting out, you can use the thermometer for this purpose.

You can also take the temperature of your dough at various points, to give you an idea of how slowly or quickly it is going to rise.

When you are ready to bake, use an oven thermometer to make sure that your oven is actually at the temperature you've set it for. Some ovens run hot, and some run cold. If yours isn't accurate, it will affect the baking times in the recipes.

One way to test the doneness of bread is by taking its internal temperature with the instant-read thermometer. To do this, flip the bread over so you don't mark the top with a hole, and insert the thermometer into the middle (for pan loaves, carefully lift the bread halfway out of the pan and insert the thermometer into the center). Softer, enriched breads like brioche (page 289) will be done at around 190°F (90°C). But the large majority of the breads in this book are better when cooked to a higher temperature of 200° to 205°F (90° to 95°C).

To be honest, I never judge a bread's doneness this way, and I did not test the recipes in this book using an instant-read thermometer. Take your bread's temperature if your bread has baked for the recommended amount of time but you are worried that it isn't done yet. But don't use temperature alone as a guide when deciding to take bread out of the oven. The visual clues provided in each recipe, along with your taste and eventually your experience with a particular bread and how long you've baked it in the past, are better gauges. Some people like their loaves with crusts on the pliant side. If that describes you, you might want to bake

your bread a few minutes less than someone who likes extra-chewy hard crusts. Sometimes, a bread made from a particularly wet dough will register an internal temperature of 205°F (95°C), but may still need an additional 5 or 10 minutes in the oven, not so much to get hotter but to dry out.

Electric mixer: A KitchenAid Pro Line stand mixer was used to test the recipes in this book. It has a powerful motor that is essential for kneading highly hydrated doughs and is well worth the investment, since it will last a lifetime. I also really enjoy my Ankarsrum mixer, a Swedish workhorse that can knead up to 11 pounds of dough. It's pricey, about $800, and not for everyone. But if you are making a lot of bread and are in it for the long haul, you might consider treating yourself to one. New to the market is a professional-style mini double-arm mixer with a 7-kilogram capacity from Star Pizza, which kneads slowly and gently.

Heated seedling mat: I'm really proud of this discovery, which I made during the chilly first winter in my Maine kitchen. Cultivating a sourdough starter in a 65°F (18°C) room was taking weeks. When I placed my starter on an inexpensive seedling mat and set the temperature to 74°F (23°C), I saw it fully mature in five days.

Sourdough incubator: New to the market, this gadget, made by Goldie, consists of a glass cover that sits on a heating disk. You place your jar of sourdough under the cover and the disk will maintain the starter's temperature between 75° and 82°F (23.5° and 27°C), growing your sourdough quickly and reliably in a matter of hours. Brod & Taylor makes a similar device with exact temperature settings that looks like a mini refrigerator.

Clear 2-quart straight-sided container with lid: Put your kneaded dough in a clear container and mark the container so that when the dough reaches the mark, you will know it has risen adequately. The lid will keep the dough moist as it expands. King Arthur sells dough-rising buckets with quart markings on the sides to make these judgments simple.

Glass measuring cups: A 2-cup glass measuring cup is just the right size for feeding your sourdough before adding it to bread dough. Cover it with plastic or beeswax wrap (see below) and you can easily watch your starter double in volume in 6 to 8 hours.

Dough proofing box: Placing your dough in a plastic dough proofing box, rather than in a rounded bowl, will make turning your dough easier and more efficient. The flat, rectangular shape of the box makes it possible to stretch your dough all the way to the edges before turning, encouraging maximum gluten development. I like the dough proofing box made by Challenger for its sturdy construction and airtight seal.

If you live in a cold climate, you might invest in a heated proofing box like the one made by Brod & Taylor (as an added benefit, the Brod & Taylor model doubles as a slow cooker). This appliance is every bit as consistent as our space-age, computer-controlled retarder proofers at the bakery, creating and maintaining a warm, draft-free environment for consistent and repeatable results.

Hand sheeter: Brod & Taylor also makes a 12-inch-wide (30 cm) hand sheeter that is wonderful for rolling out croissant dough with precision. With ten thickness settings ranging from 1 mm to 17.5 mm, it can also handle cookie, pie, and tart doughs as well as pizza dough, pasta dough, and fondant to cover cakes. At $600, it is quite the investment for the home baker, but is worth considering if you bake a lot and crave pastry shop results.

Beeswax wrap: A reusable, and thus more sustainable, choice than plastic wrap for covering dough as it ferments.

Bowl scraper: A handleless plastic spatula with a rounded edge that is useful for scraping dough from an oiled bowl onto the countertop. If you don't have one, use a large rubber spatula with a handle.

Bench scraper or taping knife: A bench scraper is a rectangular steel blade about 4 inches by 5 inches (10 by 12 cm) with a handle on the long edge. I use it to lift soft or sticky doughs during kneading as well as to cut dough into pieces. It is also great for scraping up excess dough that sticks to the counter. Just as effective, if not better, is a plasterer's taping knife with a steel blade with a perpendicular handle (look for one at the hardware store), which smoothly scrapes up the stickiest doughs.

Loaf pan: Some of these breads are baked in 8½ by 4½-inch (21.5 by 11 cm) loaf pans. Use light-colored metal, not ceramic, for the most effective heat conduction and most well-developed crust.

Banneton or shallow bowl: Bannetons are canvas-lined baskets that help dough rounds maintain their shape as they rise. Even with regular home use, they'll last a lifetime. They don't require much maintenance. Just shake them after every use to remove excess flour and store in a dry place. I don't know anyone who's bought one who has regretted the expense. If you're just starting out and don't want to make this investment right away, shallow bowls lined with floured kitchen towels work just as well.

Transfer peel: When a bread is shaped, it is traditionally placed seam side down in a proofing basket. A transfer peel is a piece of wood, plastic, or even heavy cardboard that the shaped loaf is turned out onto, seam side up. It is then turned again onto the peel to be seam side down, ready to be transferred to the baking vessel.

Baking peel or rimless baking sheet: A baking peel is a thin, flat wooden or metal sheet with a long handle attached. Use it to slide loaves onto the baking stone. Alternatively, use a rimless stainless steel baking sheet.

Parchment paper: I use parchment paper to cover the peel or baking sheet before placing loaves on top of it for the final rise. Then I slide the loaves, still on the parchment, onto the baking stone. This way, I don't have to worry that my risen dough will stick to the peel and possibly deflate as I'm attempting to get it into the oven. I also use pleated parchment paper to simulate a *couche*, a traditional linen support for baguettes that helps them maintain their shape as they rise. You can also place rounded dough on top of parchment, let it ferment, score it, and then lift it, still on the parchment, into a preheated cast-iron Dutch oven. And of course, lining baking sheets with parchment before baking croissants and cookies will save you some cleanup time.

Lame, razor blade, or sharp serrated knife: Special bread-slashing knives called *lames* are sold online and cost less than $10. Their very sharp blades easily cut through sticky dough. But a single-edged razor blade or very sharp serrated knife will as well.

Cast-iron Dutch oven or baking pan: A preheated Dutch oven (or baking pan, which is similar but has a flat bottom and a domed top) not only conducts heat beautifully into the bottom and sides of a loaf and keeps it soft with steam when covered during the first minutes of baking, but it also helps produce a perfectly round bread, which doesn't always happen when you turn dough out of a banneton. I also own a Challenger bread pan, which is even heavier than a Dutch oven and holds a lot of heat. Its oblong shape is good for ovals and snub-nose loaves. If you are going to invest in a Challenger, also buy the company's oven mitts, which will protect your hands and arms as you handle the pan.

Cast-iron skillet: When using a pizza stone or steel, it's important to generate steam in the oven. The most effective way to do so at home is to slip some ice cubes into a cast-iron skillet that's been heating in the oven along with the baking stone. When the ice hits the hot metal, it quickly turns to steam, keeping the crust soft for those first crucial minutes so the bread can expand to its maximum potential. I don't recommend other methods like using a water spritzer bottle (you tend to lose a lot of heat from the oven when you keep the oven door open to spray the breads) or tossing ice cubes right onto the oven floor (carelessly aimed ice cubes have been known to shatter oven light bulbs).

Baking stone or steel: An absolutely essential piece of equipment for making baguettes and other breads not baked in a cast-iron baking pan or Dutch oven. A baking stone made of fire-tempered brick will conduct heat instantly and efficiently right into the bottom of the loaves, mimicking the heat of a professional hearth oven. A baking steel is also a good option, but it takes longer to reheat if you are baking two or more loaves one after the other. Buy a large rectangular stone or steel. Smaller round ones are meant for pizza and won't be able to accommodate larger breads.

Wire rack: Transfer just-baked breads to heavy wire racks to cool. The racks, elevated from the counter, allow air to circulate all around the loaves so the bottoms don't get soggy. Buy the largest size you can find to accommodate the larger breads in this book.

Home mill: Even though I primarily use flour from a local mill, I am devoted to my Mockmill, a German brand of home mill that's become popular here in the US (see page 158). It allows me to grind small quantities of grains and seeds to add to my starters and doughs, vastly expanding the flavors and nutrients I can add to my bread.

Rolling pin: A handleless French-style rolling pin is my preference. An untapered pin is best for evenly rolling out laminated doughs.

Baking sheets: I prefer baking sheets made from heavy-duty steel, which bake evenly without scorching.

Tart pans: Buy these with fluted edges and removable bottoms. Choose light-colored metal, since dark pans tend to burn delicate pastry.

Pie plates: Glass is the best material, encouraging even baking and allowing you to view the bottom of your pie.

2.

ESSENTIAL

TECHNIQUES

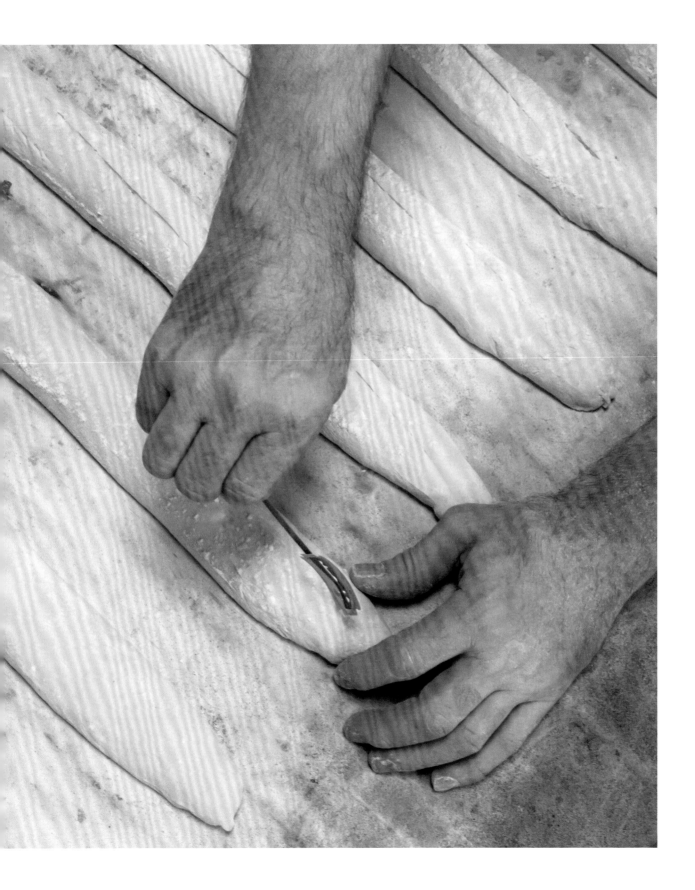

T THE RISK OF SOUNDING LIKE THE OLD-timer that I am, I'll share my memory of vigorously and athletically hand-kneading dough in my college apartment kitchen: I had a large earthenware bowl in which I'd mix my ingredients together with a wooden spoon until the water was fully absorbed by the flour. I'd scrape the dough out of the bowl and onto the Formica kitchen table in my apartment. Then I'd knead it, pulling the top edge of the dough up and folding it over to meet the bottom edge, and then pressing the dough firmly into the tabletop with the heel of my hand, repeating this motion nonstop for 10 to 15 minutes. On hot summer days, I would break into a sweat. I get tired just thinking about it. Fashions in kneading have changed, and these days I'm more likely to build structure in my dough, with less strain on my muscles, with a powerful mixer.

As I'll discuss in the next chapter, developing sensitivity to your dough, knowing what it needs at different moments during the process, is crucial. But so are a few essential techniques, including kneading, that will encourage your dough to rise into a tall, beautifully shaped loaf with a crisp, burnished crust and a shiny, bubbly crumb structure. Some of them I've practiced for years. Others are relatively new additions to my routine. In general, I've been moving to-ward a slower, quieter, gentler way to make bread. Here are key ways I'm getting good results in my home kitchen today:

Autolyse

In some cases, the first step in developing gluten is simply combining your flour and water and letting it stand for 30 minutes to 2 hours. Salt and leavener are mixed in after this step is completed. French bread scientist Raymond Calvel, who popularized the practice in the 1970s, believed that over-kneading led to overoxygenated, less flavorful bread. This was recently reinforced when I took an intensive class at Les Ambassadeurs du Pain (see page 154), where most mechanical kneading is limited to 3 to 4 minutes.

During autolyse, gluten bonds begin to form all on their own, strengthening the dough without any effort on the part of the baker or the electric mixer, which reduces kneading time later on. At the same time, enzymes in the flour are activated, breaking down some of the dough's protein and causing the dough to become smoother and stretchier, or more extensible, in professional baker parlance. The ability of dough to stretch without tearing is essential for a smooth dough and a well-risen loaf. Most wheat-based doughs benefit from autolyse.

Mixing, Stretching, Folding

Salt and starter (also called the levain) or yeast are added to the dough after autolyse, or directly to flour and water if you are skipping the autolyse step. After stirring to moisten all ingredients, you can develop the dough in several different ways.

You might turn the mixture onto the countertop and gently stretch it and fold it in on itself multiple times to strengthen it. You might use an electric mixer fitted with a dough hook to knead it until it is smooth and cohesive. Both are types of kneading that will result in gluten development. You will be able to watch the dough, and feel it under your fingertips, as it transforms from a rough, inert ball into a smooth and stretchy mass.

With highly hydrated doughs, you will want to take the additional step of stretching and folding the dough one to three times to strengthen and stabilize it. After transferring the dough to a container with a lid or a bowl and letting it ferment for an hour or so, spray or drizzle it lightly with water, pat it into a rectangle, and fold from the top and then the bottom like a business letter. Slide both hands under the dough and fold from left then right like a letter. Let the dough rest again as long as your recipe directs, and then mist or drizzle with water again and fold from top to bottom and then left to right, once again letting it rest at room temperature as directed. Repeat this folding as directed. These stretches and folds will give your dough a good balance of strength, extensibility, and stability.

Bathing the Dough

Not all, or even most, of the breads in this book have an open crumb with large holes, but the ones that do employ the French technique of *bassinage*, which translates as "bathing the dough," to achieve this structure. The idea is to hold back some water during the initial kneading, since a less-hydrated dough will form a stronger gluten network more effectively than a very wet dough. Once this gluten network is established, the remaining water is drizzled into

My Favorite Baking Timeline

Professional baking is a 24-7 business, and at Bread Alone some kind of human activity is being performed every minute of every day. At home, I have things to do other than refreshing my sourdough, kneading, shaping, and baking bread. Luckily, when I'm making one loaf at a time, my bread crafting truly is more wait than work.

For sourdough breads, I follow a basic schedule that allows enough time for my dough to develop structure and flavor while I go about my business.

DAY 1

Late evening: I take my ripe levain out of the refrigerator and mix some of it with fresh flour and water according to the recipe I'll be making. I'll heat some water in a glass measuring cup and then place my starter alongside this hot water in my microwave oven (without turning the oven on) so it can develop in a warm and moist environment. It will be ready to use 6 to 8 hours later.

DAY 2

I'll mix my dough, using my active starter. Then I'll let it ferment for 2 to 4 hours, again depending on the recipe, giving it a fold every hour or so.

When the dough is properly fermented, I'll place it, either in bulk or shaped, depending on the recipe, in the refrigerator overnight to slow its fermentation and allow it to develop flavor.

DAY 3

When I wake up, I'll remove the dough from the refrigerator and let it either proof slightly if it is shaped, or I'll let it warm up and then shape it for its final proof. This will take 1 to 3 hours, depending on the weight of the dough and the temperature in my kitchen. I'll also preheat the Dutch oven.

the dough during the last few minutes of kneading, resulting in a dough that has 3 to 8 percent more water than it could have absorbed if all the water had been added at once, and one that is marvelously extensible. A dough that is strong and stretchy in equal measure is one that can achieve that coveted open crumb texture during baking.

Refrigerating the Dough

Retarding is the baker's word for refrigerating your dough after you've let it ferment on the countertop for a few hours, lengthening fermentation. It is a way to use temperature to your advantage. In the cool of the refrigerator, fermentation slows down significantly, allowing the dough to develop flavor without the danger of overproofing. I generally don't leave the dough in the fridge for more than 24 hours.

Preshaping and Shaping

Preshaping and shaping give you two more chances to develop your dough's strength and extensibility before it goes into the oven. Preshaping, during which you loosely shape an amorphous piece of dough into a log or round, will result in some tightening of its gluten structure. Giving the dough a rest for 10 to 15 minutes allows the gluten to relax so that you can easily get it into final shape without tightening it up again. Very soft, high-hydration doughs will need some help keeping this final shape unless they are placed in couches or bannetons.

Each recipe in this book provides shaping instructions to give your bread the shape you see in the corresponding photo. But you shouldn't feel pressure to follow these instructions. If you'd rather shape your boule into a bâtard, go ahead and do so. If you'd rather bake your bread on a traditional baking stone than in a Challenger bread pan or Dutch oven, that's great. It is best to follow the steps I've given for breads baked in a tra-

Oven Setup

IF USING A DUTCH OVEN OR CAST-IRON BAKING PAN: About 1 hour before baking, position one oven rack in the center. Place the Dutch oven or cast-iron baking pan on the center rack. Preheat the oven as directed in the recipe.

IF USING A STONE OR STEEL: About 1 hour before baking, position one oven rack on the lowest rung and the other in the center. Set a cast-iron skillet on the lower rack and the stone or steel on the center rack. Preheat the oven as directed in the recipe.

ditional loaf pan, but otherwise shaping can be adjusted to suit your preference and the equipment you have on hand.

Scoring

One way or another, your dough is going to expand in the oven. When you score it, you take control of that expansion, or *oven spring*, encouraging it to expand along certain lines and with a certain design. Scoring, if done thoughtfully, can actually help your dough reach its maximum volume. If I know my dough is a bit underproofed, I will make deeper cuts than usual, to encourage oven spring. If I suspect it is overproofed, I score more conservatively, so as not to risk the dough's collapse. When scoring, quickly insert the tip of the blade into the dough where the first cut will be, running it across the surface of the loaf, making a single straight cut about ¼ inch (6 mm) deep. Repeat with the desired number of cuts.

As with shaping, each recipe will direct you to score according to its corresponding photo. Again, feel free to experiment, scoring a different pattern if you so desire.

Steaming

Adding steam to the oven during baking will keep the surface of your dough moist and flexible, which is essential for achieving maximum volume during the first 10 minutes of baking. I do this in one of two ways. Either I'll preheat a cast-iron skillet on the rack underneath my preheating baking stone, dropping some ice cubes into the skillet when I slide the bread onto the stone, or I'll bake my bread in a preheated Dutch oven or cast-iron baking pan, keeping the lid on for the first portion of the bake, to allow steam released by the dough when it hits the hot pot to circulate around the bread. Steaming not only encourages volume but produces a bread with a crisp, shiny crust. Breads baked without steam, in contrast, will have leathery, dull crusts, and no one wants that.

Flour Mix for Proofing in a Banneton

It's convenient to have a combination of wheat and rice flour at the ready, for dusting your banneton and proofing cloth to help prevent soft doughs from sticking. Dusting with wheat flour alone is risky, because the moisture released from the dough during a long period in the refrigerator can give it a glue-like consistency. Including some rice flour keeps the dusting mixture nice and slippery. I like to use a mix of 50 percent rice flour and 50 percent wheat flour.

Boules and Bâtards

Here are detailed instructions on how to shape your dough into a boule or a bâtard, the two shapes I use most frequently throughout this book.

SHAPING AND BAKING A BOULE (ROUND)

Preshape into a round. Gather the edges and bring them together to make a round bundle. Turn the dough seam side down. Cup your hands over the round, making tight circles as you bring the round toward you, bringing any rough pieces of dough underneath. Continue until the round is smooth and the top is taut. Dust the top with flour and cover with a clean kitchen towel. Let sit for 10 minutes.

To shape the boule, repeat the steps taken for the preshaping, cupping your hands over the round and then moving them in tight circles to create a tight ball with a taut skin around it. Transfer seam side up to a banneton lightly dusted with flour or to a medium bowl lined with a kitchen towel dusted generously with flour. Alternatively, line the basket or a bowl with parchment paper (or even a hairnet) and transfer the boule seam side down. Cover with an inverted box and proof as directed in the recipe.

Meanwhile, see Oven Setup on page 33 and preheat to the temperature in the recipe instructions.

IF BAKING IN A DUTCH OVEN: When it comes time to transfer the boule, using heavy-duty oven mitts or potholders, remove the very hot Dutch oven from the oven. Place it on a heatproof surface and remove the lid. Carefully turn the boule onto a transfer peel (see page 26), score, and then place into the Dutch oven. Alternatively, if the boule was proofed seam side down, score, lift the boule still on the parchment, and set in the Dutch oven.

Replace the lid, return the Dutch oven to the middle rack, and bake as directed.

IF BAKING ON A STONE OR STEEL: Carefully turn the boule onto a peel, score, and slide onto the baking stone; or lift the boule still on the parchment onto a peel, score, and then transfer to the stone. Carefully and quickly add 1 cup of ice cubes to the hot skillet to create steam, and close the oven door. Bake as directed.

SHAPING AND BAKING A BÂTARD

Preshape into a round. Gather the edges and bring them together to make a round bundle. Turn the dough seam side down. Cup your hands over the round, making tight circles as you bring the round toward you, bringing any rough pieces of dough underneath. Continue until the round is smooth and the top is taut. Dust the top with flour and cover with a clean kitchen towel. Let sit for 10 to 20 minutes.

To shape the bâtard, turn the round seam side up and gently press out any air bubbles, while pressing and stretching the dough into a rectangular shape. Fold the bottom half of the dough up and over about two-thirds of the dough, then fold the top down to cover the first fold completely. Press along the bottom edge of the dough to seal.

Turn the dough, now in a log shape, seam side down. Place your hands together, palms down, in the middle of the log. Using light, even pressure, roll the log back and forth as you spread your hands apart. Repeat two or three times until the bâtard is the desired length. The ends can be tapered more by increasing downward pressure at the tips as you roll.

Set the bâtard on a lightly floured dusted linen or large kitchen towel or baker's cloth. Gather the linen gently against the sides of the bâtard, using rolling pins or something similar to support the sides. Cover with an inverted box and proof as directed in the recipe.

Meanwhile, see Oven Setup on page 33 and preheat to the temperature in the recipe instructions.

IF BAKING IN A CAST-IRON BAKING PAN: When it comes time to transfer the bâtard, using heavy-duty oven mitts or potholders, remove the very hot cast-iron baking pan from the oven. Place it on a heatproof surface and remove the lid. Carefully turn the bâtard onto a transfer peel (see page 26) and then onto a baking peel (optional to line the peel with parchment paper). Score, then slide into the cast-iron pan or lift the bâtard still on the parchment and set in the cast-iron pan.

Replace the lid, return the pan to the middle rack, and bake as directed.

IF BAKING ON A STONE OR STEEL: Carefully turn the bâtard onto a transfer peel (see page 26) and then onto a baking peel (optional to line the peel with parchment paper). Score and slide onto the baking stone. Carefully and quickly add 1 cup of ice cubes to the hot skillet to create steam, and close the oven door. Bake as directed.

3.

A GUIDE
TO THE
ESSENTIAL
SOFT SKILLS
OF BAKING

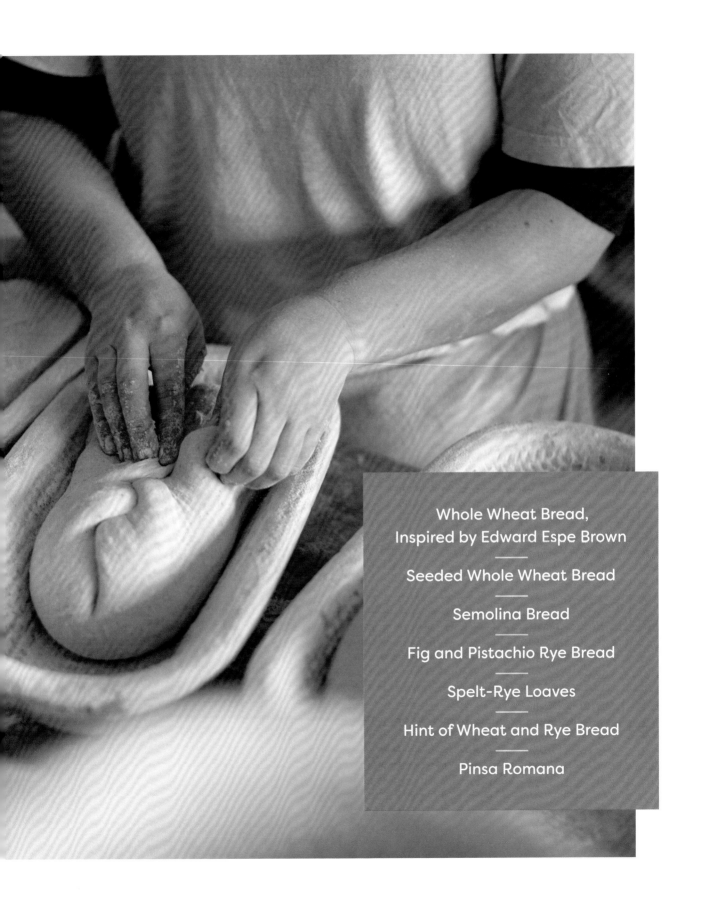

THE FIRST TIME I WENT TO PARIS, SEVERAL YEARS before I opened Bread Alone, I invited myself into a bakery to shadow the *boulanger* as he made his baguettes. I'll never forget the moment when he pulled the first breads from the oven and placed them into a willow panier. "Listen," he commanded, "it only lasts a few seconds." The long golden- and caramel-colored loaves began making a quiet and crisp crackling sound. "The sweet song of love from the baguette," he called it. Just as I had felt myself changed when I baked my first loaf from the *Tassajara Bread Book*, I noticed that this baker, who had been making baguettes since his apprenticeship long ago, was newly and visibly affected by the fruit of his labor as he held it gently in flour-coated hands, inhaled its scent, paused to take the moment in, and smiled as he listened to its music. Sharing one of his small secrets with me seemed to add to his pleasure, amazement, and feeling of accomplishment.

Of course, there is a scientific explanation for these noises. As a baked bread drops in temperature when it is removed from the oven, its crust contracts. The crackling is the sound of tiny fissures forming as a result of this contraction. This sound, I learned later, can change subtly depending on the quality of the crust. Understanding bread science is important. But all the great bakers I know, including this one, place great value on their in-the-moment knowledge of and responsiveness to their bread. And nearly all of them want to share their joy and excitement in the process.

In baking, there is always an element of the unknown, and even a bit of magic. As much as professional bakers try to eliminate variables by scaling ingredients to the gram, mixing their dough to a precise temperature for equally precise lengths of time, proofing dough in temperature-controlled boxes or rooms, and using a pH meter to measure the acidity of sourdough, they will all tell you that no two bakes are ever exactly the same. So they cultivate a profound sensitivity to the dough, but also to the temperature in the room, the humidity in the air, the strength and absorbency of the flour, the subtle changes in the dough as it ferments during the process of crafting a loaf of bread.

Sometimes this awareness is put to practical use: If I notice that flour from a new shipment is absorbing more water than flour from the last shipment from the same mill, I might make a note and add as much as 5 percent more water to my dough, thus ensuring that this batch of breads will have a similar rise and crumb structure as the last. But other times, this awareness is a reward in and of itself. My goal is not necessarily to pull a ten out of the oven, which doesn't happen every time I bake. Even if I ultimately give my bread a score of seven or eight, I have practiced the skills of seeing, feeling, smelling, and even hearing my bread, and I feel happy and satisfied. I've come to enjoy and appreciate the imperfections and idiosyncrasies of each bake. When I watch yet another baker's Instagram reel displaying the bubbly interior of a just-baked baguette, I understand the excitement of such a seemingly mundane moment. Today's baguette isn't going to look just like yesterday's, and that is part of the thrill. If my wife comes home while I have bread in the oven, we enjoy its aroma together. If she enters the kitchen when it is ready to slice (and she al-

ways seems to enter at this moment), I am happy to see her and take in her delight as she tastes what I have baked . . . and then I start the series of steps again.

I recognized this tactile, spiritual approach to baking when I first read Ed Brown's book. He describes his introduction to breadmaking at the Zen monastery kitchen as "love at first touch," and goes on to describe baking not as a series of tricky technical maneuvers but as a moment-by-moment sensory communion. As he gives in to this experience, he feels free: "No more worry about not being perfect." Ultimately, baking is about connection and sharing, not perfection. So many people, all over the world, discovered this during the pandemic.

Right after our wedding, Julie and I went to Paris together for the first time and visited Meilleur Ouvrier de France recipient Joël Defives at his bakery, Boulangerie Baptiste. Joël participates in a centuries-old French program called Les Compagnons du Devoir, which sends young bakery apprentices from bakery to bakery in order to acquire knowledge and skills from multiple masters. As Julie and I toured Joël's immaculate shop, we met his four current compagnons as well as a twenty-four-year-old graduate of the program who had returned to the bakery for a visit. He spoke passionately to me about his experience, which gave him the practical knowledge he needed to bake anything from the classic French bread and pastry repertoire, but also gave him a deep appreciation for age-old traditions and a desire to someday pass along what he knows to another generation.

As a student and teacher, I felt a strong kinship with this young man. In tribute to Ed Brown, Joël, and all the bakers who have taught me not just technique and science but what I have come to call the "soft skills" of baking—observation, sensitivity, patience, generosity—I took a look at that first whole wheat bread recipe that I baked from his book and, inspired by that wholesome, simple loaf, developed the yeasted bread recipes that follow. As I learned from their experience, I hope you can learn something from mine.

Before I present these breads to you, I'd like to outline the essential soft skills I used to create them. You can learn a lot from watching YouTube videos demonstrating bassinage, stretch and fold, shaping, and scoring, but it is truly in the repetition of a recipe, when you are tuned in to a dough's development at a particular moment while recalling with your senses all your previous experiences with that type of dough, that you not only learn and grow as a baker but gain the most pleasure and satisfaction from crafting a loaf of bread.

Setup

I remember the first few nights I spent working with a couple of Bernard Lebon's bakers in a basement of his bakery near Place des Petits-Pères. They arrived at midnight, and they spent the first fifteen minutes just getting things aligned: lighting the ovens, cleaning the peels, placing a small bowl of flour on the work table so it would be there when they needed it for shaping the dough, unrolling the couche cloths for the baguettes, checking the levain, setting the stage before that night's bread performance. They were constantly in motion, and yet their movements were calm and purposeful as they oiled pans and arranged and lightly floured bannetons. Their routine was well practiced and clearly disciplined but far from robotic. At every moment they were also evaluating and tuning in to their environment and their equipment (was all the debris from yesterday swept from the bottom of the oven?), their ingredients (was their sourdough sufficiently fermented?), the temperature of the flour, and their environment (was it raining outside, contributing to humidity in the shop, even though the bakeshop was two floors below street level?).

Mise en place at home can be similarly focused. Place your Dutch oven in the oven first thing, so you won't forget to preheat it. Or if you store your flour in the freezer, weigh it out before you do anything else, so it can come to room temperature. Get all your bowls and baking tools ready. I like to line them all up on the left side of my work surface. Get your mill out and mill your flour if that is part of your routine. Get all your ingredients ready and organized. Inhale the scent of your flour, which may smell nutty or like fresh hay, butter, or honey. Place your fingers under the tap as your water runs to gauge its temperature before you add it to your flour. Like breathing exercises or meditation, setting up in a deliberate manner will not only contribute to the success of your bake but can be a calming pleasure in and of itself.

Pre-ferments and Starters

The recipes in this chapter employ whole wheat sponges—small quantities of flour, water, and yeast mixed together and added to the dough hours later to lend superior flavor, texture, and shelf life to the finished bread. Deeper into the book, you'll find recipes with sourdough starters. Preparing a pre-ferment or starter hours before or the day before baking is a way of practicing patience, one of the most essential soft skills.

It is also an opportunity to observe and experience the proliferation of yeast and the development of flavor components like lactic acid at different stages. I remember a Polish baker who showed me how he prepared his rye starter in ceramic vats. He would stick his hand into a vat after one hour, then three hours, then five hours, pointing out the differences in taste and texture as it aged. You, too, should examine your pre-ferment or starter before you use it. Note its increase in volume, its cell structure. Sponges and starters are teeming with live yeast and bacteria and are somewhat unpredictable because their activity depends on their environment. Is your starter less bubbly than it was the last time you used it? Maybe your kitchen was a few degrees colder overnight. Did your sponge rise and then fall while you were sleeping? If you are worried that it's not active enough, you might add an extra gram of yeast to your final dough or another 2 percent starter if it seems sluggish. Before you proceed, take a moment to inhale your starter's aroma, identifying wheatiness, yeastiness, tartness, sweetness.

Blending, Kneading, Folding

I recently watched master whole-grain baker Arnd Erbel make a few spelt loaves in his bakery in Dachsbach, Germany. Arnd bakes exclusively with freshly ground flour, whose properties he says change from batch to batch, season to season. He spoke to me about the unknown qualities hidden in each bag and the excitement he feels as he adds water to a new flour for the first time. He seldom pays attention to the numbers that accompany the grain—its protein and ash content, its falling number (which measures the amount of preharvest sprouting occurring in the grain while on the stalk in the field)—in part because his flour is very fresh and his mill doesn't test each batch. Instead, he relies on what he observes when he first mixes flour and water together and as it develops. His little tests—checking on the dough's hydration at 5 minutes, 10 minutes, 30 minutes; evaluating the dough each time he folds it in on itself to judge its increasing strength, elasticity, and extensibility—are rudimentary versions of tests performed at mills to ascertain the properties of batches of flour. But his tests take into account the conditions in his bakeshop at the moment that he is kneading, and are more personal and accurate because of this additional information.

You, too, can learn to rely on your senses to evaluate your flour, and evaluate your dough as you knead or fold. Never walk away from your mixer, and not just because it might inch its way off the counter while you have your back turned. Instead, stand by and check on the dough every 2 to 4 minutes, noting how long it takes for the flour to absorb the water. In just a few minutes, you'll be able to see signs of elasticity and feel the very undeveloped gluten network coming into being.

Stop the mixer periodically and press on the dough with your thumbs to get a sense of its developing elasticity. Is it significantly softer or firmer than the dough you kneaded last week when you were using a different bag of flour? The dough will tell you whether it can absorb more water in the next few minutes.

Folding the dough periodically will not only build strength and elasticity but give you the opportunity to evaluate and be in tune with it as it develops. After a couple of hours and just a couple of folds, you will witness the dough transform from a fragile and unstable mass to a cohesive, smooth, and stable dough able to hold a shape. As you transfer the dough to a container to proof, feel it for stretchiness and extensibility. If it is especially soft or sticky, fold it in on itself once again at this point before covering it and letting it rise.

Proofing

After your dough has developed, it will do most of the work of fermenting on its own while sitting in a warm, draft-free spot in your kitchen. Again, patience is key. Observe it frequently, at least once an hour, so you can judge when it has reached the proper volume for folding and shaping. If you place it in a clear, straight-sided container and mark the spot where your dough was when it began to ferment, it will be easy to see. Note the speed of fermentation—your dough won't necessarily ferment at the same rate that is indicated in your recipe, depending on the temperature of your room and your dough at the beginning of fermentation. Practice patience as you let the dough develop fully. Through the sides of the clear container, you will see the beginnings of a cell structure and can get a sense of the strength of the dough. Some recipes require folding at various stages of the fermentation process, and this is always a good time to reexamine and reconnect with your dough.

If the dough is in a storage container, with slightly damp hands, pat the dough into a rectangle and fold from the top and then the bottom like a business letter. Slide both hands under the dough and fold from the left and then the right like a letter. If the dough is in a bowl, the dough can be folded like a letter as above in the bowl or turned out onto a damp work surface for folding.

If you are watching the dough regularly, you will see it expand, forming a gentle dome. In many recipes, the breads are preshaped, shaped, and then allowed to relax and expand for 30 minutes to an hour before baking. Observing fermentation over many bakes will give you the experience to know when it is time to get breads in the oven.

Shaping

Shaping is a completely tactile skill that requires experience and muscle memory. No matter how many photos and videos and in-person demonstrations you see, you will never learn to shape bread until you've done it yourself, paying close attention to the feel of the dough and how it transforms as it comes in contact with your hands.

The goal with shaping is to give the dough structure and form without deflating its delicate cell structure or overworking the dough. The key is to shape the dough as quickly as possible. In general, form the dough into a very loose round. This preshaping will get the dough into basic shape. Letting the dough stand for 10 to 15 minutes after pre-shaping allows the gluten strands to strengthen without damaging the cell structure. When bringing the dough to its final shape, use a gentle touch. It isn't about perfection; it's about feeling the dough beneath your hands and understanding how much or how little pressure you need to apply to create the surface tension that will allow the dough to maintain its form.

On my first visit to Altamura in southern Italy, I marveled at the skill but also the sensitivity of an experienced baker, who was quickly shaping one *filone* (an Italian-style bâtard) after another in just a few seconds on a rustic wooden table. I watched him carefully and saw that he dealt with each piece of dough a little bit differently, applying a bit more pressure to the ends of one, giving an extra roll or two to another, instinctively understanding, by feel, what each piece of dough needed to become a *filone*. It's that constant calibration, that individualized reaction, that experienced bakers have developed over time. It's mesmerizing to watch, and when you see it, you will want to get your hands on some dough ASAP.

Scoring

When I met my friend and world-renowned baking expert Didier Rosada years ago, and we first baked side by side, he was shocked by my self-taught baguette scoring technique. While Didier had learned to shape and score baguettes from master bakers in his hometown of Toulouse in France, I had just sort of guessed at how scoring was done and then kept doing it that way. Instead of making cuts from top to bottom, I was scoring from bottom to top, causing my cuts to open in reverse. I was cutting ¼ inch (6 mm) too deep, said Didier, and the angle was wrong. These mistakes, taken together, were preventing my loaves from expanding to reach their full potential. Scoring, Didier taught me, is not solely about beautifying the bread. It is about evaluating the state of the dough just before it is ready to go into the oven, how much tension there is in the dough, how strong and developed it is, and making cuts that will allow it to rise and expand optimally. Sometimes proofed baguettes stand up tall and round; sometimes they are a little bit flat. Depending on how they look and feel, you'll score the bread slightly differently. If the dough is very elastic and developed, I'll make shallow cuts, because I know that these baguettes don't need as much room to expand. If they are less developed, I'll make deeper cuts, to coax them higher in the oven. Use your judgment, which will improve over time. If you score your bread off-center, or make cuts that are too shallow or too deep, you might be disappointed with its looks. But you will not have ruined the loaf! Be proud of its imperfections and think about what you might do differently next time.

Baking

As you bake one loaf after another, pay attention to how your particular oven behaves and where its hot spots (or cool spots) are. This will teach you where to position your bread in the oven and when to turn your loaf or cast-iron pot, if necessary, for even cooking. Probably more importantly, observe the differences in the way similar loaves bake in different vessels or on a stone. If you are using a Challenger bread pan, for example, you might notice that it holds heat so well that the bread bakes more quickly than it would on a stone. With this knowledge, you can adjust baking times accordingly. Learn to use the baking times in recipes as a general guide rather than as a strict instruction.

You might think your journey is over once you get your loaf into the oven. But there are still plenty of details to note and moments to enjoy. For me, there's a huge amount of suspense. How much oven spring will I get? How will my scoring open up? Will the bread have that explosive quality that I'm hoping for? If I'm using a new flour from a small, local mill, my bread will most likely be subtly or even dramatically different, rising more or less, caramelizing to a different hue, perfuming the kitchen with an entirely new aroma. You can make some good guesses depending on how your dough has behaved up until this moment, but you won't know for sure until it is fully baked. I never just put the dough in the oven, set the timer, and walk away. Even though there isn't any action I can take, I love to check on it every 5 or 10 minutes through the oven window, noting its transformation, marking the moment when I can detect its scent. What tones of honey, caramel, and brown will the baked loaf exhibit? To check for doneness, I might take its internal temperature, but I will also thump lightly on the underside of the loaf, listening for that telltale hollow sound.

If my bread exhibits that longed-for baking exuberance, I celebrate. If it's a little bit flat, I think back on whether my sourdough was less developed than it could have been, whether my refrigerator was colder overnight, whether the dough needed an extra fold. I file all these questions away in the memory bank and continue to enjoy the sight, aroma, and sweet song of my imperfect loaf, until it has cooled enough to eat.

Whole Wheat Bread

INSPIRED BY EDWARD ESPE BROWN

Like a favorite piece of music, the melody of Ed Brown's whole wheat loaf has played in my head on and off for years. I'm sentimental about that bread because it was the first one I made on my own. But I also have distinct memories of its delicious aroma and flavor. These memories compelled me to pick up the phone and talk to him as I began to write this book. I wanted to find out what he was up to and what his relationship with bread was today. We had an incredibly lovely conversation, which helped me pinpoint just what it was about that loaf that gave me so much pleasure and spurred me on in my baking journey.

Ed still teaches—both Zen meditation and bread baking. He explained to me, "In Zen, you don't just get enlightened; you have the thought of awakening enlightenment in others and so on. So if I'm going to make bread, I want to teach people, and I want them to share their knowledge and inspiration, and so forth." That has certainly come to pass. So many bakers my age started with Ed's book, continued to study and learn, and have passed on their knowledge to the next generation. But it was something else Ed said that summarized the most important lesson I took away from his book: "Finally, Buddhism is about liberation or freedom. Liberation means if you want to make bread, make bread. You don't say, 'I could never do that.' No, you decide. That's implicit in Zen too: create the life you choose."

Anyone can choose to make bread, and I am living proof of this. I wanted to make bread, I made some, and then I made a choice to make bread for others. Start with a simple loaf and decide where you want to go with it. You might choose to make it over and over again for the rest of your life. Or it might become a starting point for a more varied journey.

Reflecting on the recipe itself, I know exactly why I responded to it at the time. First of all, it was simple. I could easily understand the steps and perform them in the course of an afternoon. Second, it employed whole wheat flour. Today we take for granted the variety of flours available in the supermarket and online, but in the 1970s, whole wheat flour was still a novelty. Tasting a bread made with this unsifted flour was truly like tasting wheat for the first time. It made such a strong impression on me that I became an instant convert to whole-grain baking.

In books and online, we are inundated with complex, multilayered sourdough bread recipes. And while I deeply appreciate those recipes and techniques, I also understand the appeal of the simplest breads. Customers, readers, and friends frequently ask me for a bread recipe that can be made without the commitment that sourdough requires. The ideal whole-grain loaf they describe—wholesome, kid-friendly, good for sandwiches and toast—reminds me very much of that first Ed Brown recipe I baked in college. Nothing complicated, just a flavorful, healthy bread that I could enjoy throughout my week. This is why I responded to Ed's recipe years ago.

I went back and baked the old recipe. It smelled just as wonderful as I remembered. Because it was made with 100 percent whole wheat, it contained all the vitamins, minerals, nutrients, and

RECIPE CONTINUES

fiber that wheat has to offer. The whole wheat flour that I buy from my local mill is fresher and more flavorful than what I used to buy at the Mifflin Street Co-op, so the bread's flavor was better than I remembered. But I couldn't resist making a few adjustments to suit my tastes and maybe to entice my grandchildren to ask for the bread.

Ed's original recipe contained a short-fermented sponge with a lot of yeast. I've cut the yeast by more than half and let the sponge ferment overnight. Two grams might seem like a minuscule quantity, but when it has 8 to 12 hours to feed and multiply, it will raise the bread very effectively. A tiny amount of honey or diastatic malt powder (ground malted barley that contains enzymes that convert flour starch to sugar) encourages yeast activity. The long fermentation enriches the bread's flavor. The first thing you taste and smell will be wheat, not yeast, which tends to dominate when used in larger quantities in quickly fermented dough.

The slightly bitter bite from the tannins in whole wheat can be a tough sell to children, especially if they've only encountered white breads. Commercial white breads often contain large amounts of sugar or other sweeteners. Even if they don't, their starches quickly turn into sugars on the tongue, which explains why kids love to gnaw on plain bagels. To balance the bitterness of the wheat bran in the flour, I added some mashed sweet potato to my dough. It gives the bread a pleasant but not cloying sweetness, adds moisture, and contributes to a longer shelf life.

If you are like me, no matter where your bread-baking journey takes you, you will always have use and affection for a recipe that speaks to life's simple, practical, and fulfilling pleasures. Thanks to Ed Brown, this is mine.

Makes 1 or 2 loaves, 800 grams each

Start to finish:
about 15 hours

Gathering ingredients and preparing the dough, day one:
about 10 minutes

Proofing: **overnight**

Mixing and proofing, day two: **4½ hours**

Baking:
40 to 45 minutes

Ingredients	Metric	
	One 800-gram loaf	**Two 800-gram loaves**
DAY ONE		
water (70° to 78°F / 21° to 25.5°C)	275 g	550 g
honey or diastatic malt powder	16 g	32 g
whole wheat flour	178 g	355 g
milk powder	7.5 g	15 g
instant dry yeast	2 g	3 g
DAY TWO		
whole wheat flour	217 g, plus more for dusting (optional)	435 g, plus more for dusting (optional)
fine sea salt	10 g	20 g
unsalted butter, melted	32 g	64 g
roasted sweet potato, peeled and mashed	120 g	240 g
vegetable oil, for brushing the loaf pan(s)		

1. In the bowl of a stand mixer, weigh all the day one ingredients: the water, honey, flour, milk powder, and yeast. Using either the paddle attachment or a spoon, mix the ingredients together. Cover the bowl tightly, preferably with beeswax wrap. Let sit at room temperature overnight.

2. The next day, very lightly drizzle a tablespoon or two of water into a rectangular plastic storage container with a lid or a large bowl. Brush with a pastry brush to coat.

3. In the bowl of the stand mixer that has the day one ingredients, weigh the day two flour, salt, and melted butter. Fit the mixer with the dough hook and mix on the lowest setting for about 1 minute.

   Add the mashed sweet potato. Mix on the Stir setting for about 1 minute, then increase the speed to low to medium-low and mix until the dough is combined and smooth, about 15 minutes, stopping as needed to scrape the sides and bottom of the bowl.

4. Transfer the dough to the storage container or the bowl. Cover the container with the lid or the bowl tightly with beeswax wrap. Let sit to proof at room temperature for 1 hour. Fold from top to bottom and then left to right. Let rest at room temperature until doubled in volume, another 1½ hours.

5. Brush a traditional loaf pan, 8½ by 4½ by 2½ inches (21.5 by 10 by 6 cm), lightly with oil. If making two loaves, brush a second loaf pan.

6. If making two loaves, using a bowl scraper or dough cutter, divide the dough in half. Press half the dough into an 8-inch (20 cm) square. Make a groove across the middle of the square with the side of your hand and fold the dough over itself, pressing lightly on the edges to seal. With the seam side down, roll the rectangle back and forth on a lightly floured countertop until it is the same length as your loaf pan. Repeat with the remaining dough, if making two loaves. Set in the prepared pan(s).

   Cover the pan(s) with an inverted box or plastic tub and let sit at room temperature to proof until risen just above the top of the pan, 1½ to 2 hours.

RECIPE CONTINUES

7. About 1 hour before baking, position one oven rack on the lowest rung and the other in the center. Place a cast-iron skillet on the lower rack of the oven.

Preheat the oven to 400°F (200°C).

8. Close to baking time, fill a medium bowl with about 1 cup of ice cubes to have ready to add to the skillet to create steam.

Dust the top of the loaf lightly with whole wheat flour, if using. With sharp, pointed scissors, make rows of ¼-inch-deep (3 cm) cuts at a 45-degree angle across the top of the bread to create a spiky effect, if desired.

Slide the pan(s) onto the middle rack, pour the ice cubes into the skillet to produce steam, and close the door.

Bake until the bread is a rich caramel brown, 40 to 45 minutes.

9. Transfer the pan(s) to a wire rack for about 15 minutes, then invert onto the rack to cool completely. The bread may need to be loosened by running a spatula or knife around the edges.

Seeded Whole Wheat
Bread, PAGE 52

Whole Wheat Bread

Seeded Whole Wheat Bread

As much as I love the simple Whole Wheat Bread (page 47), I really appreciate the flavor and texture that seeds contribute to this variation. I specify certain seeds below, but feel free to use any combination you like as long as the total weighs 90 g for one loaf or 180 g for two. In addition, the soaked seeds provide extra moisture, for an especially tender and long-keeping loaf.

Makes 1 or 2 loaves, about 1 kilogram each

Start to finish:
about 15 hours

Gathering ingredients and preparing the dough and soaker, day one: **about 45 minutes**

Proofing: **overnight**

Mixing and proofing, day two: **4½ hours**

Baking:
40 to 45 minutes

Ingredients	Metric	
	One 1-kilogram loaf	Two 1-kilogram loaves
DAY ONE		
water (70° to 78°F / 21° to 25.5°C)	235 g	470 g
honey	14 g	28 g
whole wheat flour	150 g	300 g
milk powder	6 g	12 g
instant dry yeast	2 g	3 g
MIXED SEED SOAKER		
sunflower seeds or millet	30 g	60 g
flaxseeds, golden or brown	30 g	60 g
white sesame seeds	15 g	30 g
chia seeds or teff	15 g	30 g
boiling water	180 g	360 g
DAY TWO		
whole wheat flour	185 g	370 g
fine sea salt	9 g	18 g
unsalted butter, melted	27 g	54 g
roasted sweet potato, peeled and mashed	102 g	204 g
vegetable oil, for brushing the loaf pan(s)		
mixed seeds, for rolling the dough	50 g	100 g

1. In the bowl of a stand mixer, weigh all the day one ingredients: the water, honey, flour, milk powder, and yeast. Using either the paddle attachment or a spoon, mix the ingredients together. Cover the bowl tightly, preferably with beeswax wrap.

Weigh and combine the sunflower seeds, flaxseeds, sesame seeds, and chia seeds for the soaker in a medium bowl and pour the boiling water over them. Cover tightly. Let both sit at room temperature overnight.

2. The next day, very lightly drizzle a tablespoon or two of water into a rectangular plastic storage container with a lid or a large bowl. Brush with a pastry brush to coat.

3. In the bowl of the stand mixer that has the day one ingredients, weigh the day two flour, salt, and melted butter. Fit the mixer with the dough hook and mix on the lowest setting for about 1 minute.

Drain any excess water from the seed mixture. Add the seeds and the mashed sweet potato to the bowl. Mix on the Stir setting for about 1 minute, then increase the speed to low to medium-low until the dough is combined and smooth, 15 to 20 minutes, stopping as needed to scrape the sides and bottom of the bowl.

4. Transfer the dough to the storage container or the bowl. Cover the container with the lid or the bowl tightly with beeswax wrap. Let sit to proof at room temperature for 1 hour. Fold from top to bottom and then left to right. Let rest at room temperature until doubled in volume, another 1½ hours.

5. Brush a traditional loaf pan, 8½ by 4½ by 2½ inches (21.5 by 10 by 6 cm), lightly with oil. If making two loaves, brush a second loaf pan.

6. If making two loaves, using a bowl scraper or dough cutter, divide the dough in half. Press the dough into an 8-inch (20 cm) square. Make a groove across the middle of the square with the side of your hand and fold the dough over itself, pressing lightly on the edges to seal. With the seam side down, roll the rectangle back and forth on a lightly floured countertop until it is the same length as your loaf pan.

Sprinkle the seeds on the work surface or on a large plate. Moisten the loaf lightly with water, roll the loaf in the seeds, and set in the prepared pan. Repeat with the remaining dough, if making two loaves.

RECIPE CONTINUES

Cover the pan(s) with an inverted box or plastic tub and let sit at room temperature to proof until risen just above the top of the pan, 1½ to 2 hours.

7. About 1 hour before baking, position one oven rack on the lowest rung and the other in the center. Place a cast-iron skillet on the lower rack of the oven.

Preheat the oven to 400°F (200°C).

8. Close to baking time, fill a medium bowl with about 1 cup of ice cubes to have ready to add to the skillet to create steam.

Slide the pan(s) onto the middle rack, pour the ice cubes into the skillet to produce steam, and close the door.

Bake until the bread is a rich golden brown, 40 to 45 minutes.

9. Transfer the pan(s) to a wire rack for about 15 minutes, then invert onto the rack to cool completely. The bread may need to be loosened by running a spatula or knife around the edges.

Semolina Bread

This makes a lovely, dense, golden-crumbed loaf. Semolina flours can vary in how finely they are milled. Flour milled in Italy tends to be double milled and sifted. Local semolinas from smaller mills might be coarser and contain more of the whole grain. I prefer the finely milled Italian semolina. This is a large loaf. If you'd prefer to bake two smaller bâtards, just divide the dough in half equally before shaping and proceed as directed.

Makes 1 bâtard, about 900 g

Start to finish:
12 to 14 hours

Gathering ingredients and preparing the dough, day one:
about 1½ hours

Proofing: **overnight**

Proofing, day two:
2 hours

Baking:
40 to 45 minutes

Ingredients	Metric
fine semolina flour	250 g, plus more for dusting
bread flour	250 g
water	400 g
instant dry yeast	1 g
fine sea salt	10 g
white sesame seeds, for rolling the dough	50 g

1. In the bowl of a stand mixer, weigh the semolina flour, bread flour, and water. Fit the mixer with the dough hook and mix on low speed until well combined, about 5 minutes. Cover the bowl tightly, preferably with beeswax wrap. Let sit at room temperature for 1 hour.

2. Sprinkle the yeast and salt over the top and mix into the dough on low to medium-low speed for about 5 minutes. Cover the bowl tightly. Let sit at room temperature overnight.

3. The next day, lightly dust the work surface with semolina flour. Preshape the dough into a round (see page 35). Dust the top with flour and cover with a clean kitchen towel. Let sit for 10 minutes.

4. To shape into a bâtard, turn the round seam side up and gently press out any air bubbles, while pressing and stretching the dough into a rectangular shape. Fold the bottom half of the dough up and over about two-thirds of the dough, then fold the top down to cover the first fold completely. Press along the bottom edge of the dough to seal.
   Turn the dough, now in a log shape, seam side down. Place your

RECIPE CONTINUES

hands together, palms down, in the middle of the log. Using light, even pressure, roll the log back and forth as you spread your hands apart. Repeat two or three times until the bâtard is the desired length, tapering the ends by increasing downward pressure at the tips.

Set the bâtard on a flour-dusted linen or large kitchen towel. Gather the linen gently against the sides of the bâtard, using rolling pins or even rolled kitchen towels to support the sides.

Brush the surface of the bâtard lightly with water and then sprinkle with the sesame seeds.

Cover with an inverted box or plastic tub and let sit at room temperature to proof until slightly pillowy and risen, 1½ to 2 hours.

5. Meanwhile, set up the oven: Position one oven rack on the lowest rung and the other in the center. If using a cast-iron baking pan with a lid, set it on the center rack. If using a stone or steel, set it on the center rack and set a cast-iron skillet on the lower rack. Preheat the oven to 500°F (260°C).

6. If using a stone or steel, close to baking time, fill a bowl with about 1 cup of ice cubes to have ready to add to the skillet to create steam.

Carefully turn the bâtard onto a transfer peel and then a baking peel. With a lame, a single-edged razor blade, or a serrated knife, score the loaf with three cuts on the diagonal.

Slide the bâtard onto the stone or steel, pour the ice cubes into the skillet to produce steam, and close the door.

If using a cast-iron baking pan with a lid, use heavy-duty oven mitts or potholders to remove the pan from the oven. Place it on a heatproof surface and remove the lid.

Carefully turn the bâtard onto a transfer peel and then a baking peel. With a lame, a single-edged razor blade, or a serrated knife, score the loaf with three cuts on the diagonal. Slide the loaf into the pan.

Return the lid to the pan and the pan to the center rack.

7. For both baking methods, immediately lower the oven temperature to 450°F (230°C).

If baking on the stone or steel, bake until the loaf is a rich golden brown, slightly darker where scored, 40 to 45 minutes.

If baking in the cast-iron pan, bake for 20 minutes. Remove the lid and bake until the loaf is golden brown, 20 to 25 minutes more. Transfer to a wire rack and let cool completely.

Fig and Pistachio Rye Bread

I first ate bread studded with pistachios and figs in the South of France. This simplified version, baked not in a loaf pan but on a stone or in a cast-iron baking pan, gives it the chewy crust. It has the same sweetness, richness, and texture of the original, making it a good choice for a European-style breakfast with some cheese or cured meat. This is a large loaf. If you'd prefer to bake two smaller rounds, just divide the dough in half equally before shaping and proceed as directed.

Makes 1 rectangular loaf, about 1.3 kilograms

Start to finish:
16 to 20 hours

Gathering ingredients and preparing the dough, day one:
about 30 minutes

Proofing: **overnight**

Mixing and proofing, day two: **6 hours**

Baking:
40 to 45 minutes

Ingredients	Metric
DAY ONE	
water (70° to 78°F / 21° to 25.5°C)	100 g
honey	15 g
whole or dark rye flour	100 g
instant dry yeast	1 g
DAY TWO	
whole wheat flour	175 g, plus more for dusting
bread flour	175 g
water (70° to 78°F / 21° to 25.5°C)	230 g
fine sea salt	8 g
dried figs, roughly chopped	175 g
unsalted pistachios, coarsely chopped	80 g

1. In the bowl of a stand mixer, weigh all the day one ingredients: the water, honey, rye flour, and yeast. Mix together with a wooden spoon. Cover the bowl tightly, preferably with beeswax wrap. Let sit at room temperature overnight.

2. The next day, very lightly drizzle a tablespoon or two of water into a rectangular plastic storage container with a lid or a large bowl. Brush with a pastry brush to coat.

3. In the bowl of the stand mixer that has the day one ingredients, weigh the day two whole wheat flour, bread flour, water, and salt. Fit

RECIPE CONTINUES

the mixer with the dough hook attachment and mix on the Stir setting for about 30 seconds to begin to incorporate the ingredients, then increase the speed to low to medium-low and mix until combined, 2 to 3 minutes. Add the figs and pistachios and mix on medium-low speed until incorporated, 1 to 2 minutes more.

4. Transfer the dough to the storage container or the bowl. Cover the container with the lid or the bowl tightly with beeswax wrap. Let sit to proof at room temperature for 2 hours. Fold from top to bottom and then left to right. Let rest at room temperature until doubled in volume, another 2 hours.

5. Dust a piece of parchment paper with whole-wheat flour.

Dust the work surface with flour.

Turn the dough out onto the work surface. Lightly press and pull the rounded corners as needed to create a straighter-sided rectangle measuring about 7 by 9 inches (18 by 23 cm). Transfer the rectangle to the parchment.

Lift and gather the parchment on the sides, using rolling pins or even rolled kitchen towels to support the sides. Cover with an inverted box or plastic tub and let sit at room temperature to proof until pillowy and slightly risen, about 1½ hours.

6. Meanwhile, set up the oven: Position one oven rack on the lowest rung and the other in the center.

If using a cast-iron baking pan with a lid, set it on the center rack.

If using a stone or steel, set it on the center rack and set a cast-iron skillet on the lower rack.

Preheat the oven to 450°F (230°C).

7. If using a stone or steel, close to baking time, fill a medium bowl with about 1 cup of ice cubes to have ready to add to the skillet to create steam.

Remove the supports from the sides of the loaf and with a lame, a single-edged razor blade, or a serrated knife, score the loaves with one long cut from the top left corner to the bottom right corner and then with four or five small fanned cuts on both sides of the central diagonal cut.

Slide the rectangular loaf, still on the parchment, onto the stone or steel, pour the ice cubes into the skillet to produce steam, and close the door.

If using a cast-iron baking pan with a lid, use heavy-duty oven mitts or potholders to remove the pan from the oven. Place it on a heatproof surface and remove the lid.

Remove the supports from the sides of the rectangular loaf. With a lame, a single-edged razor blade, or a serrated knife, score with one long cut from the top left corner to the bottom right corner and then with four or five small fanned cuts on both sides of the central diagonal cut. Lift the loaf, still on the parchment, by the edges of the parchment and carefully transfer to the pan.

Return the lid to the pan and the pan to the center rack.

8. If baking on a stone or steel, bake until the loaf is a rich golden brown, 40 to 45 minutes.

If baking in the cast-iron pan, bake for 20 minutes. Remove the lid and bake until the loaf is a rich golden brown, 20 to 25 minutes more.

9. Transfer to a wire rack and let cool completely.

Spelt-Rye Loaves

We get many requests from people with wheat sensitivities for a bread that is more digestible than whole wheat. While spelt does contain gluten, its particular gluten proteins are weaker than those of wheat. In addition, it contains fewer fructans, the carbohydrates in wheat that cause stomach problems for some. I developed this recipe for these people, although I must say that I enjoy the earthy, pleasantly musty aroma of spelt so much that I make this bread simply because I love it.

Makes 4 small square loaves, about 200 grams each

Start to finish:
about 16 hours

Gathering ingredients and preparing the dough, day one:
about 30 minutes

Proofing: **overnight**

Mixing and proofing, day two: **5 hours**

Baking: **40 minutes**

Ingredients	Metric
DAY ONE	
water (70° to 78°F / 21° to 25.5°C)	350 g
honey	40 g
white spelt flour	200 g
whole or dark rye flour	50 g
instant dry yeast	2 g
DAY TWO	
white spelt flour	250 g, plus more for dusting
fine sea salt	10 g
unsalted butter, melted	30 g

1. In the bowl of a stand mixer, weigh all the day one ingredients: the water, honey, spelt and rye flours, and yeast. Using either the paddle attachment or a spoon, mix the ingredients together. Cover the bowl tightly, preferably with beeswax wrap. Let sit at room temperature overnight.

2. The next day, very lightly drizzle a tablespoon or two of water into a rectangular plastic storage container with a lid or a large bowl. Brush with a pastry brush to coat.

3. In the bowl of the stand mixer that has the day one ingredients, weigh the day two spelt flour, salt, and melted butter. Fit the mixer with the dough hook and mix on the lowest setting for about 1 minute,

RECIPE CONTINUES

then increase the speed to low to medium-low and mix until the dough is combined and smooth, about 10 minutes, stopping as needed to scrape the sides and bottom of the bowl.

4. Transfer the dough to the storage container or the bowl. Cover the container with the lid or the bowl tightly with beeswax wrap. Let sit to proof at room temperature for 1 hour. Fold from top to bottom and then left to right. Let rest at room temperature until doubled in volume, another 1½ hours.

5. If the dough is in a storage container, with slightly damp hands, pat the dough into a rectangle and fold from the top and then the bottom like a business letter. Slide both hands under the dough and fold from left then right like a letter.

If the dough is in a bowl, the dough can be folded like a letter as above in the bowl or turned out onto a damp work surface for folding. Cover and let rest at room temperature for 2 hours more.

6. Meanwhile, after 1½ hours, set a baking stone on the middle rack and preheat the oven to 400°F (200°C). Alternatively, plan on baking the loaves on parchment paper on a baking sheet.

7. Dust the work surface and a linen or, if using a baking sheet, a large piece of parchment paper (the size of the baking sheet) with spelt flour. Turn the dough out onto the work surface and let it expand naturally to a rectangle, about 7 by 9 inches (18 by 23 cm). Lightly press and pull the rounded corners as needed to create a straighter-sided rectangle. Using a metal bench scraper or a chef's knife, divide the dough into four equal pieces. Transfer to the linen or parchment.

Lift and gather the linen or parchment between the pieces, adding support to the sides. Cover with an inverted box or plastic tub and let sit at room temperature to proof until pillowy and slightly risen, about 30 minutes.

8. Close to baking time, fill a medium bowl with about 1 cup of ice cubes to have ready to add to the skillet to create steam.

If baking on a baking stone, using a transfer peel, invert one or two of the squares at a time from the linen onto a parchment-lined peel. Dust the top with additional flour, if needed. With a lame, a single-edged razor blade, or a serrated knife, score the loaves with one straight cut from the top right corner to the lower left corner, and then with three cuts on the opposite diagonal.

Slide the breads onto the stone, still on the parchment paper, pour the ice cubes into the skillet to produce steam, and close the door.

If baking on a baking sheet, lift the loaves, still on the parchment, onto the baking sheet, pull on the corners of the parchment to flatten it, score the loaves as directed above, and slide the baking sheet into the preheated oven, pouring the ice cubes into the skillet to produce steam.

Bake until the loaves are a rich golden brown, about 40 minutes.

9. Transfer to a wire rack and let cool completely.

Hint of Wheat and Rye Bread

This is my version of a bread made with the "no-knead" technique made incredibly popular by Jim Lahey. I have a preference for whole grains, so I include whole wheat and rye flours in my loaf. I find that gently kneading the dough for just 5 minutes, rather than not at all, produces the kind of open crumb not often associated with whole-grain breads. Letting it proof overnight at cool room temperature develops the flavor as well as the texture of the dough.

Makes 1 boule, about 800 grams

Start to finish:
about 11 hours

Gathering ingredients and preparing the dough:
1½ hours

Proofing: **overnight**

Proofing, day two:
1½ hours

Baking: **45 minutes**

Ingredients	Metric
bread flour	400 g, plus more for dusting
whole wheat flour	50 g
whole or dark rye flour	50 g
water	390 g
instant dry yeast	1 g
fine sea salt	12 g

1. In the bowl of a stand mixer fitted with the hook attachment, weigh and mix together the bread flour, whole wheat flour, rye flour, and water. Mix until well combined, about 5 minutes. Cover the top of the bowl tightly, preferably with beeswax. Let sit at room temperature for 1 hour.

2. Sprinkle the yeast over the top and mix into the dough, using a spatula to fold the dough from the outer edges of the bowl to the center, 3 to 4 minutes. Cover the top of the bowl tightly. Let sit at room temperature for 15 minutes.

3. Sprinkle the salt over the top and mix into the dough, folding again with a spatula as described above for another 2 minutes.

4. Very lightly drizzle a tablespoon or two of water into a plastic, rectangular storage container with a lid or a large bowl. Brush with a pastry brush to coat. Transfer the dough to the container with the lid or to the bowl covered tightly with beeswax wrap. Let sit at room temperature overnight.

RECIPE CONTINUES

5. Lightly dust the work surface with bread flour.

To preshape the dough into a round, gather the edges and bring them together to make a round bundle. Turn the dough to be seam side down. Cup your hands over the round, making tight circles as you bring the round toward you, bringing any rough pieces of dough underneath. Continue until the round is smooth and the top is taut. Dust the top with flour and cover with a clean kitchen towel. Let sit for 10 minutes.

To shape the boule, repeat the steps taken for the preshaping, cupping your hands over the ball and then moving them in tight circles to create a tight ball with a taut skin around it. Transfer to a banneton/basket lightly dusted with flour seam side up or to a medium bowl lined with a kitchen towel dusted generously with flour seam side up. Alternatively, line the basket or bowl with parchment paper (or even a hairnet) and transfer the boule, seam side down.

Cover and let sit at room temperature to proof until the dough is pillowy and slightly risen, about 1½ hours.

6. Meanwhile, set up the oven: Position one oven rack on the lowest rung and the other in the center.

If using a Dutch oven, set it on the center rack.

If using a stone or steel, set it on the center rack and set a cast-iron skillet on the lower rack.

Preheat the oven to 500°F (260°C).

7. If using a stone or steel, close to baking time, fill a medium bowl with about 1 cup of ice cubes to have ready to add to the cast-iron skillet to create steam.

Carefully turn the boule onto a peel. (Or lift the boule still on the parchment onto the peel.) Dust with flour and then with a lame, a single-edged razor blade, or a serrated knife score the loaf with four cuts in a box pattern, creating a square in the center.

Slide the boule onto the stone or steel, pour the ice cubes into the skillet to produce steam, and close the door.

If using a Dutch oven, use heavy-duty oven mitts or potholders to remove the Dutch oven from the oven. Place it on a heatproof surface and remove the lid.

Carefully turn the boule onto a peel, and then into the Dutch oven. (Or lift the boule still on the parchment and set in the Dutch oven.)

Dust with flour and then with a lame, a single-edged razor blade, or a serrated knife score the loaf with four cuts in a box pattern, creating a square in the center.

Return the lid to the Dutch oven and the Dutch oven to the center rack.

8. For both baking methods, bake at 500°F (260°C) for 20 minutes.

If baking on the stone or steel, after the 20 minutes, without opening the oven, lower the oven temperature to 450°F (230°C) and bake until a rich golden brown, about 20 minutes more.

If baking in a Dutch oven, after the 20 minutes, lower the oven temperature to 450°F (230°C), remove the lid from the Dutch oven, and bake until golden brown with caramel and dark caramel tones on the cut edges, 20 to 25 minutes more.

9. Transfer to a cooling rack and cool completely.

Pinsa Romana

After I first tasted the Roman-style pizza at Forno Campo de' Fiori in Rome, where I had spent a few days at that bakery learning how it was made, I developed a Roman pizza recipe for my book *Local Breads*. Hundreds of pizzas later, I was satisfied that I couldn't do any better than this chewy but airy delight.

Then recently, several European bakers that I know began talking about a new pizza style spreading like melted mozzarella across Italy and southern France. Called *pinsa*, from the Italian word for "to press," this bubbly pie is made with rice flour in addition to wheat flour, which gives it a crust that is eggshell delicate but also eggshell crisp, and an interior that is light and bubbly.

This is a great recipe for gaining confidence with long fermentation, practicing some soft skills, and staying open to new ways of making breads. After mixing the dough, you let it double completely, and then you refrigerate it overnight, or for up to 24 hours. Not only does this give you the flexibility of baking your pinsa whenever you want to eat it (pinsa is best enjoyed right from the oven), but it will also give you a chance to notice the differences between 18 and 24 hours of fermentation.

Depending on where I am, I bake pinsa either on a pizza stone or in my Challenger bread pan (my AGA stove in Maine can't accommodate my favorite stone), in which case I divide the dough into three pieces instead of two and bake them one at a time. The dough pieces can also be baked on a grill or grill pan.

As far as toppings go, I stick to classics like olive oil with salt and rosemary, pine nuts, and basil, or a little bit of grated Parmesan and zucchini blossoms. Whatever you choose, don't overpower the delicate dough with heavy toppings. A sprinkling of shredded mozzarella will be better than a half pound.

Makes 2 pinsa, about 500 g each

Start to finish:
14 to 30 hours

Gathering ingredients and preparing the dough, day one:
2½ hours

Proofing: **overnight**

Proofing, day two:
1½ to 2 hours

Baking:
10 to 20 minutes

Ingredients	Metric
00 flour	510 g
brown or white rice flour	60 g, plus more for dusting
spelt flour	30 g
instant dry yeast	3 g
water (70° to 78°F / 21° to 25.5°C)	484 g
fine sea salt	12 g
extra-virgin olive oil, plus more for brushing the dough	12 g
flaky sea salt, for sprinkling	
all-purpose flour, for dusting	
sauce and toppings of your choice (optional; see headnote)	

RECIPE CONTINUES

1. Very lightly drizzle a tablespoon or two of water into a rectangular plastic storage container with a lid or a large bowl. Brush with a pastry brush to coat.

In the bowl of a stand mixer or in a large bowl if mixing by hand, weigh the 00 flour, rice flour, spelt flour, yeast, and 384 grams of the water. Fit the mixer with the dough hook and mix on low to medium-low speed until the flours are moistened and the dough is shaggy, about 3 minutes. There will still be dry areas. Cover and let rest at room temperature for 15 minutes.

2. Add the fine sea salt and mix on low to medium-low speed. Stream in 20 grams of the remaining 100 grams water and mix for 2 minutes, thoroughly scraping down the sides and bottom of the bowl to get all of the gummy bits off until the bowl is clean. Repeat three times, adding 20 grams of water at a time. Add the final 20 grams, mix for 2 minutes, scrape the bowl, and then turn the mixer to medium-high and mix for 3 more minutes. Last, with the mixer still running, stream in the olive oil and mix on medium until combined, 2 to 3 minutes more.

3. Transfer the dough to the storage container or the bowl. The dough will feel wet and fragile. Don't worry. As it sits it will gain strength. Right away, fold from top to bottom and then left to right, repeating twice for a total of six folds. Cover the container with the lid or the bowl tightly with beeswax wrap. Let rise at room temperature for 1 hour, then fold again. Repeat one or two more times, depending on the strength of the flour, folding and letting it rise for another 2 hours.

4. Refrigerate at least overnight, but preferably for 24 hours.

5. Lightly dust the countertop with flour. Quickly invert the bubbly dough onto the counter. You should have a sloppy rectangle measuring approximately 8 by 12 inches (20 by 30 cm). Dust the top with flour. Spread a clean large kitchen towel out onto the counter. Dust with a mixture of 50 percent rice flour and 50 percent all-purpose flour (see page 34) and make a pleat down the center the long way. Use a dough knife to cut the dough into two skinny rectangles measuring about 4 by 12 inches (10 by 30 cm) each. Place each dough piece on top of the kitchen towel, on either side of the pleat. Cover with another towel and let stand for 75 minutes.

6. Meanwhile, set up the oven: Position one oven rack on the lowest rung and the other in the center.

Set a cast-iron skillet on the lower rack. Line a baking peel or rimless baking sheet with parchment paper. Alternatively, the pinsas can be baked on parchment paper–lined or lightly oiled baking sheet(s).

Preheat the oven to 525°F (275°C), or 500°F (260°C) if that is your oven's highest setting.

7. About 15 minutes before baking, with your fingertips, dimple the tops of the dough pieces every 1½ inches (4 cm). Transfer one of the rectangles to the lined peel or baking sheet. Cover the remaining rectangle with the towel.

Close to baking time, fill a medium bowl with about 1 cup of ice cubes to have ready to add to the skillet to create steam. Slide the rectangle, still on the parchment, onto the stone or steel, pour the ice cubes into the skillet to produce steam, and close the door.

Bake until the dough is beginning to puff up with some golden brown spots, 10 to 12 minutes, depending on the temperature of your oven.

8. Carefully remove the pinsa from the oven and sprinkle with flaky sea salt. If adding toppings, skip the sea salt and arrange the sauce, cheese, or any other ingredients on top. Return the pinsa to the oven and bake until the dough is golden brown, the toppings are warmed through, and/or the cheese has melted, about 8 minutes. Depending on your oven, you might want to turn the oven to broil to toast the cheese for 1 to 2 minutes, keeping a watchful eye so as not to let it burn. Repeat with the remaining rectangle, baking the second loaf as directed above then sprinkling with sea salt or adding other toppings as desired before returning to the oven.

4.

BREAD

ALONE

PAST, PRESENT, AND FUTURE

Bread Alone
Farm Bread Revisited

TOP ROW, FROM LEFT: First expansion at Bread Alone; Sharon in front of the Bread Alone ovens; Nels's early training as CEO, Bread Alone at Union Square Greenmarket.

MIDDLE ROW: Tom Olivieri, André Lefort, Dan, and John Zydell; muffins at the bakery; Nels.

BOTTOM ROW: Roy Wood; head of production Athénaïs Boeffard; at the Lake Katrine cafe; lunch at Lake Katrine.

I COME FROM A FAMILY OF SCRAPPY SMALL-business owners. My grandfather emigrated from Ukraine in 1915, and by 1920 he was making money manufacturing burlap bags in Buffalo, New York. When burlap went the way of the horse and buggy, his two sons-in-law successfully transitioned the company to manufacturing plastic bags. My other grandfather, a postal worker, moonlighted selling table pads door-to-door. I had an uncle who began his career after World War II, scavenging for glass to recycle. When he found a warehouse filled with bottles and the owner wouldn't sell them unless he bought the building, too, he agreed and went into commercial real estate, eventually building one of the largest privately held real estate companies in the US. Another uncle ran a small printing company, and yet another owned an automotive garage he took over from his father. My grandfathers and uncles financed and grew their businesses in inventive ways (all legal, they assured me). As a boy, I observed their small-business fearlessness, grit, persuasiveness, and determination.

After leaving the University of Wisconsin and completing my culinary studies, I thought of myself as an intellectual, a cook, and a free spirit. But in hindsight I can see that the entrepreneurial air I breathed as a kid was just as much of an influence on my career trajectory as my education has been. In the early 1980s, I was cooking at the Water Club and moonlighting at night at D&G Bakery on Mulberry Street in Little Italy, one of the few places in New York where old-world artisans were using traditional techniques and coal-fired ovens to make rustic loaves. The process was brutally physical. Large batches of dough were divided by hand and preshaped in shallow wooden boxes, which were stacked one on top of another. After preshaping, we unstacked the boxes, shaped the breads, and then placed them back into the boxes, which we stacked again for proofing. We loaded the proofed loaves in and out of the coal-fired oven with a very long, sixteen-foot oven peel. It was exhausting, but exhilarating. On weekends, I took field trips to a few places out of town that had wood-fired ovens, like Baldwin Hill Bakery in Phillipston, Massachusetts, where owner Hy Lerner, a doctor turned baker, made desem-style whole wheat bread (a mild sourdough popular in Holland) from freshly milled flour, and to O Bread in Shelburne, Vermont. Nearby, Jules and Helen Rabin baked handmade sourdough bread in a large wood-fired backyard brick oven that they built themselves. I began to covet a wood-fired oven of my own.

At this point, I was married to my first wife, Lynne, and we had two small children, Liv and Nels. To get the kids out of our tiny apartment on West Ninetieth Street on the weekends, we bought an unwinterized house in the Catskills town of West Shokan, choosing the location because I was familiar with the area from my time at the CIA, and because the house was affordably priced at $24,000. There was a shuttered garage on the country road approaching the house, and when we saw a For Sale sign outside, we called the owner, Hal Anderson, and made a deal to purchase the place for another $20,000. We borrowed $10,000 from the Holy Order Federal Credit Union on Hertel Avenue in my hometown of Buffalo. The loan was cosigned by my dad and uncle. We quit our jobs in the city. We painted the walls and concrete floor of the one-thousand-square-foot space. We built my wood-fired oven, modeled after the oven at Baldwin Hill. We bought a wooden work table and a horizontal mixer similar to the one I had used at D&G. All of a sudden we were in business.

It was October 1983, and we were so new to the area that we didn't realize that the Catskills basically shut down on November 1 every year, as soon as it gets cold. Still, our timing wasn't terrible. Americans were just starting to pay attention to and pay money for organic products. The first Whole Foods opened in Austin, Texas, in 1980, and began its expansion to Houston and Dallas in 1984. We were able to sell a couple hundred loaves a day to locals and winter weekenders as well as to a few grocery stores and restaurants nearby. After baking in the morning, I would pack the family Mazda hatchback with bags of bread and make deliveries. Our initial menu was small: a peasant bread modeled on a D&G loaf that included some wheat bran, a Norwegian-style rye and whole wheat bread, a whole wheat–walnut boule, a raisin-pumpernickel loaf, and baguettes.

The bakery was gaining a following, and thanks to the low cost of flour (about 22 cents per pound, translating to $1.50 a loaf wholesale; today, flour can cost $1 per pound, and our larger loaves are priced from $5.99 to $7.49), we were able to make just enough money to pay our bills and support our little family. I had to admit that my homemade oven wasn't as reliable as it should have been.

That, combined with a Patricia Wells article in the *New York Times* about the best bakeries in Paris, compelled me to travel to France in search of information, better equipment, and advice from real bakers who were actually trained in the craft of making authentic old-world breads.

The trip was transformational. Until this time, I had been under the impression that the method I had learned at D&G—reserving some dough from the night before and adding it to the next day's dough—was sourdough baking. Seriously. Remember, in 1983, there were no sourdough baking books, no Facebook groups about natural starters, no Instagram accounts or YouTube channels devoted to the craft.

I arrived in Paris just as a group of young bakers was attempting to rescue traditional French bread from encroaching industrialization. Basil Kamir, a former music promoter turned pain au levain master, took me under his wing and taught me his method of cultivating wild yeast. He put some whole wheat flour in a paper bag. Then he made a stiff little ball of dough from some flour and water and buried it in the flour in the bag. The next day, he'd remove the ball, trim off the hard skin that had formed around it, add more flour and water to the dough ball, and return it to the bag of flour. After he had repeated the process for ten or so days, he trimmed the tough skin from the ball and assured me it was teeming with natural yeast and would explode with an earthy, acidic, and fermented aroma when the starter was ripe. I brought this stiff sourdough starter

back from France, and I began to use it to develop my first real sourdough bread recipe, for pain au levain. After baking bread in Basil's vintage brick oven and experiencing what a really good oven could produce, I shook hands with the legendary mason André Lefort to come to Boiceville to build two for me. With the necessary knowledge and equipment, we significantly upped our bread game.

Later that year, another *New York Times* story changed our lives. Nancy Harmon Jenkins's 1989 piece about Bread Alone is a quaint reminder of how basic the average reader's knowledge about baking was at that point. Forget about discussions of stone milling, kneading and stretching techniques, or how professional bakers shape boules and baguettes. There isn't a single mention of sourdough. Instead, Nancy focused on the sights and smells at the bakery, and our simple (because we were broke!) lifestyle. The recipe included at the end of the story isn't even for bread. It's for a lentil stew I cooked while being interviewed. At that point, the *Times* assumed that their readers had little interest in making a Bread Alone baguette at home.

And yet Nancy managed to capture every important aspect of our business: our reliance on organic grain, our belief that long fermentation is essential in building flavor, our investment in European hearth ovens for producing superior breads, and our commitment to selling reasonably priced loaves directly to consumers at our shops and greenmarkets, creating a community of

Back to the Basics At a Catskills Bakery

By NANCY HARMON JENKINS

BOICEVILLE, N.Y.

IN the office of Bread Alone, a bakery in the Catskills village of Boiceville, about 90 miles north of Manhattan, there is a color photograph of two smiling men standing waist-deep in a sunny North Dakota wheat field, an "America the Beautiful" kind of scene that brings "amber waves of grain" immediately to mind.

One of the men is Daniel Leader, who with his wife and partner, Lynne Gilson, owns the bakery. The other is Marshall Kargas, one of the main suppliers of grain for the 17,000 pounds of flour that Bread Alone uses every two weeks.

Bread Alone bakes the gamut of breads, from elegant French baguettes to hearty, peasant-style four-grain mixtures. All are made from the flour of organically grown grains, and all are baked in an enormous wood-fired brick oven that was built 18 months ago under the supervision of André LeFort, a master oven builder from France.

The bread, which is sold at the bakery and at two New York City Greenmarkets, as well as to restaurants and retail shops in New York and New England, is extraordinary, with the crisp, friable crust and the dense, moist crumb of the best European versions. Mr. Leader credits its quality to a number of factors, including the long, slow rising of the

dough — it takes a minimum of five and a half to six hours — and the traditional method of baking: loaves are cast directly on the floor of the masonry oven, with its combination of intense, even heat and steam.

But much of the credit, Mr. Leader says, goes to the quality of the flour, especially that made from hard red spring wheat like Mr. Kargas's. This wheat is stone-ground, and part of the bran is sifted off to make a powdery cream-colored flour that feels like grainy silk and releases a nutty aroma.

"I love those fields," Mr. Leader said, showing off the photograph of him and Mr. Kargas. "When you walk through them, you start partridges and pheasants — imagine, partridges and pheasants in a wheat field."

This is not, he explained, typical of most American wheat fields, where the combined use of pesticides and chemical fertilizers have tended to eradicate the insects that game birds feed on. "When I walk through a regular wheat field," Mr. Leader said, "the ground is hard and unyielding. It's cracked and dry. When I walk through that wheat field" — he pointed again at the picture of Mr. Kargas's wheat — "the earth gives under my feet like a sponge. It's alive."

This passion for the products of organic growing, and a sense of stewardship for the land itself, animates the lives of both Mr. Leader and Ms. Gilson. Five years ago, both

Continued on Page C10

The New York Times/Mark Amenan

Daniel Leader, framed by racks of baguettes at his bakery, Bread Alone, where only organically grown grains are used.

---

bread lovers where there was none before. It's hard to overstate how important the article was to the future of the business. Immediately, high-end markets like Balducci's and Fairway wanted to open wholesale accounts.

Within hours of the story's publication, the bakery phone started ringing with calls from a half-dozen editors, offering contracts for a Bread Alone book. Within the week, I had agreed to write one for legendary cookbook editor Maria Guarnaschelli. Her enthusiasm, even in the face of my inexperience as a baker and a writer, spurred me on.

Maria told me in our first planning session to write only about what I know. The problem was I didn't know much: just what I had learned visiting other bakers, traveling to a couple of wheat farms in North Dakota, Kansas, and Montana, and talking to our miller at Little Bear Trading Company in western Wisconsin. I took her advice, writing about these encounters and including the recipes I had practiced through trial and error. Readers in 1993 were eager to learn about baking bread using wholesome ingredients and European techniques. There really hadn't been anything like *Bread Alone*, which was both a bread baking manual and the very personal story of the bakery. I won my first IACP Award. I was shocked by the book's success and excited by the doors in the food world that it opened for me.

That's not to say that it was all smooth sailing. We added on to the original bakery to make space for a cafe, hoping to improve our bottom line by selling coffee and cookies. The profit margin on a loaf of bread was and is pitifully small. I'll never forget the day I was standing in the checkout line at my local Grand Union when I overheard one shopper ask another, "Have you been to that bread bakery in Boiceville?" His companion remarked, "Yeah, I feel sorry for that guy. He'll never make it."

Yet we hung on. We opened cafes in more populated locations like Rhinebeck and Woodstock. Our greenmarket business grew, from Wednesdays in Union Square to multiple days of the week at forty-five different locations. Sharon Burns-Leader joined Bread

Alone as baker and eventually co-owner in the early 1990s, and we worked together side by side every step of the way as we tracked advances in organic farming and specialty milling, purchased state-of-the-art German baking equipment to increase our production without sacrificing handcrafted quality, and hired and trained dozens of new employees in best bread-baking practices.

By 2010, Bread Alone was producing about eight thousand loaves a day. Sometimes we felt like our success was killing us. Sharon and I were running the bakery 24-7, trying to meet the demand. We had outgrown the original space to the extent that we had no room to cool the just-baked breads. Our solution was to pull one of our trucks up to the loading dock, fill it with wire racks, and let the breads cool in there. We still considered ourselves scrappy small-businesspeople, doing whatever it took to keep it all going.

So we were surprised and flattered when Nels, at the time a student at NYU's Stern School of Business, told us he wanted to use the bakery as a case study for a class project. He trekked up to the Catskills with a bunch of his classmates, and they analyzed what we did. I was a proud dad when Nels and his group won the prize for Business Modeler of the Year. More than that, it was extremely energizing to read their report on how we might grow a small, family-branded business. The fact that the Stern School of Business thought we had a future gave us a boost. I was even more surprised when, a year later, Nels asked to meet me near Washington Square Park to say he wanted to join the business. "Are you doing it for me, or for yourself?" was my response. I didn't want my son to come and work with me out of a sense of obligation and because I was getting older. "I'm doing it for both of us" was his reply. So Sharon and I welcomed him with open arms.

Nels had grown up around the bakery, absorbing the business's fundamental values. He respected our commitment to organic ingredients, which has always been as much about preserving the planet as it has been about making healthy and delicious bread. He understood our mission to feed our customers wholesome food at a reasonable price. In graduate school, Nels acquired the analytical and professional skills to help us take the business to the next level while strengthening the ideals that made us who we are. He set new goals, insisting that we could grow the company carefully, thoughtfully, and exponentially, supporting more organic farmers and feeding more of our community than I had thought possible. In our early days, we bought 7,000 pounds of flour a week. Today, we are getting 150,000 pounds.

Nels spearheaded the design and construction of Bread Alone's new artisan baking facility in Kingston, New York, with a Heuft thermal oil oven system imported from Germany that uses a single natural gas burner to bake hundreds of breads each hour. A 196-kilowatt solar array on the roof supplies electricity for the pumps and motors that circulate heat around the ovens. In Boiceville, at Bread Alone's original location,

we are now operating the country's first carbon-neutral bakery, with two oven systems, one running on electricity from a thousand solar panels and one that uses scrap wood from local lumber.

Our bread is better than ever, not only because of the sixty-plus years of craft experience that Sharon and I have, but because Nels has supported Sharon's work with local grain initiatives to source some of our flour closer to home and has nurtured new talent. He's even asked some of our young bakers to revise and update a couple of original Bread Alone recipes, taking into consideration new techniques.

Finally, we are no longer scrappy. But we are still Bread Alone.

So, in 2019, I retired from the day-to-day running of the bakery, handing over CEO duties to my son. I bought a house by the ocean in Castine, Maine. I married my best friend, Julie Bohan, under a tent outside the village art museum. I still check in at Bread Alone occasionally and drive down to Kingston once a month to say hi to everyone in person. Almost as soon as I bought my house, I installed a cream-colored AGA oven, which I'd been dreaming about for years. For the first time since I was a college student, I am baking bread at home. Without the pressures of production, finances, and managing employees, I am purely enjoying it. My last book, *Living Bread*, was a collection of recipes from Europe's best artisan bakers. Since its publication in 2019 and my retirement, I've been able to nurture the connections I've made with all kinds of people who have reached out to me to talk about grain science, home milling, sourdough, and so many other issues that interest both professionals and home bakers these days. Bread Alone is my legacy, and this book tells my story—past, present, and near future—through my recipes.

Bread Alone Boiceville today, powered by the sun.

Bread Alone Farm Bread Revisited

This is an updated version of one of the first breads we made at Bread Alone. I've always gravitated toward cracked grains and seeds. Originally, I simply added cracked rye and wheat berries to the dough, which gave the bread an almost crunchy texture. Eventually, we started to hydrate the berries in boiling water, so they were much softer going in. Now the bread is chewy rather than crunchy.

The dough, which is rather soft, benefits from being mixed in a stand mixer. If you are going to knead by hand, do so firmly and expect to give it an extra turn during fermentation to build structure.

Ever evolving, this bread now includes abundant walnut pieces, and the slightly yielding texture of the nuts gives the bread a wonderful richness. During the summer, when I have plentiful fresh, soft sprigs of rosemary from my garden, I add 1 tablespoon of chopped herbs. This is a large loaf. If you'd prefer to bake two smaller rounds, just divide the dough in half equally before shaping.

Makes 1 bâtard, about 1.3 kilograms

Start to finish: **3 days**

Gathering ingredients and preparing the starter, day one:
10 minutes

Proofing the starter:
overnight

Gathering ingredients, autolyse, and mixing the dough, day two:
1 hour 20 minutes

Folding, proofing, and resting the dough:
6 hours

Refrigerating the dough:
overnight

Proofing, day three:
1½ hours

Baking: **40 minutes**

Ingredients	Metric
RYE STARTER, DAY ONE	
dark rye flour	60 g
water (70° to 78°F / 21° to 25.5°C)	60 g
Sourdough Starter (page 98)	10 g
SOAKED RYE AND WHEAT, DAY ONE	
cracked wheat	50 g
cracked rye	50 g
boiling water	80 g
DOUGH, DAY TWO	
bread flour	300 g, plus more for dusting
whole wheat flour	100 g
dark rye flour	100 g
water (70° to 78°F / 21° to 25.5°C)	370 g, plus more as needed
fine sea salt	10 g
walnut halves, lightly toasted	50 g

RECIPE CONTINUES

1. **PREPARE THE RYE STARTER:** In a small bowl, weigh the rye flour, water, and sourdough starter. Stir together until well incorporated. Cover the bowl tightly, preferably with beeswax wrap.

   SOAK THE RYE AND WHEAT: Weigh the cracked wheat and rye in a medium bowl. Pour in the boiling water. Cover the bowl tightly, preferably with beeswax wrap.

   Let both the starter and soaked rye and wheat sit at room temperature overnight.

2. **FOR THE AUTOLYSE:** In the bowl of a stand mixer or in a large bowl, weigh the bread flour, whole wheat flour, rye flour, and 350 g of the water. Fit the mixer with the paddle attachment and mix on low speed (or with a spatula if in a large bowl) until a rough, shaggy dough forms, 3 to 4 minutes, scraping the bowl as necessary to incorporate any loose pieces. Cover and let stand for 1 hour.

3. Very lightly drizzle a tablespoon or two of water into a rectangular plastic storage container with a lid or a large bowl. Brush with a pastry brush to coat.

4. **MAKE THE FINAL DOUGH:** Add the rye starter and the soaked rye to the dough. Attach the dough hook to the stand mixer and mix on low to medium-low speed until incorporated, 4 to 5 minutes.

   Add the salt to the bowl and mix until distributed, 2 to 3 minutes. This is a slightly sticky dough.

5. Spread the walnuts and the remaining 20 g water in the storage container or put in the bottom of the bowl. Transfer the dough to the storage container or bowl, pressing the dough into the nuts. Lightly brush the top of the dough with 1 tablespoon of water. Cover the container with the lid or the bowl tightly with beeswax wrap. (The walnuts and additional water will continue to incorporate and evenly distribute with the folds.)

   Let sit at room temperature for 1 hour.

6. If the dough is in a storage container, with slightly damp hands, pat the dough into a rectangle and fold from the top and then the bottom like a business letter. Slide both hands under the dough and fold from left then right like a letter.

RECIPE CONTINUES

If the dough is in a bowl, the dough can be folded like a letter as above in the bowl or turned out onto a damp work surface for folding.

Add a little water to the bowl and dough as needed to keep the dough from sticking. Cover and let rest at room temperature for 1 hour.

7. Fold from top to bottom and then left to right. Let rest at room temperature for 1 hour.

8. Repeat the folds again and let rest at room temperature for 1 hour.

9. Repeat the folds one last time and let rest at room temperature for 3 hours.

10. Lightly dust the work surface with bread flour and turn out the dough.

To preshape the dough, gather the edges and bring them together to make a round bundle. Turn the dough seam side down. Cup your hands over the round, making tight circles as you bring the round toward you, bringing any rough pieces of dough underneath. Continue until the round is smooth and the top is taut. Dust the top with flour and cover with a clean kitchen towel. Let sit for 10 minutes.

11. To shape into a bâtard, turn the round seam side up and gently press out any air bubbles, while pressing and stretching the dough into a rectangular shape. Fold the bottom half of the dough up and over about two-thirds of the dough, then fold the top down to cover the first fold completely. Press along the bottom edge of the dough to seal.

Turn the dough, now in a log shape, seam side down. Place your hands together, palms down, in the middle of the log. Using light, even pressure, roll the log back and forth as you spread your hands apart. Repeat two or three times until the bâtard is the desired length, tapering the ends by increasing downward pressure at the tips.

Dust a linen or large kitchen towel with flour and place it on top of a baking sheet. Set the bâtard on the baking sheet (for ease of moving it into the refrigerator to rest overnight). Gather the linen gently against the sides of the bâtard, using rolling pins or even rolled kitchen towels to support the sides.

Cover so the beeswax wrap is not pressed directly against the dough but is secure around the edges. Refrigerate overnight.

12. Remove the bâtard from the refrigerator. Cover with an inverted box or plastic tub and let sit at room temperature to warm up and proof until slightly pillowy, about 1½ hours.

13. Meanwhile, set up the oven: Position one oven rack on the lowest rung and the other in the center.

If using a cast-iron baking pan with a lid, set it on the center rack.

If using a stone or steel, set it on the center rack and set a cast-iron skillet on the lower rack.

Preheat the oven to 500°F (260°C).

14. If using a stone or steel, close to baking time, fill a medium bowl with about 1 cup of ice cubes to have ready to add to the skillet to create steam.

Carefully turn the bâtard onto a transfer peel and then a baking peel. With a lame, a single-edged razor blade, or a serrated knife, score the loaf with a large S-shaped cut from the top to the bottom, and then add a few smaller slashes on the side.

Slide the bâtard onto the stone or steel, pour the ice cubes into the skillet to produce steam, and close the door.

If using a cast-iron baking pan with a lid, use heavy-duty oven mitts or potholders to remove the pan from the oven. Place it on a heatproof surface and remove the lid.

Carefully turn the rectangular loaf onto a transfer peel and then a baking peel. With a lame, a single-edged razor blade, or a serrated knife, score the loaf with a large S-shaped cut from the top to the bottom, and then add a few smaller slashes on the side. Slide the loaf into the pan. Return the lid to the pan and the pan to the center rack.

15. For both baking methods, bake at 500°F (260°C) for 20 minutes.

If baking on the stone or steel, after 20 minutes, without opening the oven, lower the oven temperature to 450°F (230°C) and bake until the loaf is a rich golden brown, slightly darker where scored, about 20 minutes more.

If baking in a cast-iron baking pan, after 20 minutes, lower the oven temperature to 450°F (230°C), remove the lid, and bake until the loaf is a rich golden brown, slightly darker where scored, about 20 minutes more.

16. Transfer to a wire rack and let cool completely.

5.

SOURDOUGH

FOR

EVERYONE

Miche Reconsidered

———

Polenta Bread

———

Lefort Levain

———

Buckwheat Triangle

———

Baltic Dark Rye

———

Black Bread with Raisins

———

24-Hour Slow-Baked
Pumpernickel

I N 1993, I PUBLISHED MY FIRST SOURDOUGH recipe in *Bread Alone*. My early readers marveled at this bread made without commercial yeast, as did I. The general public had little knowledge of what seemed to be a magical and unknown process. I had learned the technique from my mentors in France. In the US, it was practiced by just a handful of young artisans, among them Steve Sullivan at Acme Bread in Berkeley, California; Herman Lerner at Baldwin Hill Bakery in Phillipston, Massachusetts; and Jules and Helen Rabin at Upland Bakers in Plainfield, Vermont.

San Francisco sourdough, a bread long marketed to tourists, was cloaked in mystery. There were *no books* in English that I knew of at that time that revealed the steps for making a natural starter.

If you had told me forty years ago that somewhere around 2020 hundreds of thousands of bakers worldwide would become obsessed with sourdough baking, posting pictures on Instagram, joining sourdough Facebook groups, and asking for sourdough advice on Reddit threads, not only would I have asked, "What is Reddit?" but I would have scoffed that an obscure technique practiced by old-school European *boulangers* and just a handful of American pros might become part of our common vocabulary and a food phenomenon.

Unbelievably, that's where we are today, and I couldn't be more surprised or thrilled.

Interest in sourdough has exploded not just because so many people were sheltering in place during the pandemic and looking for projects to fill their time but also because they discovered the joy that comes from making truly great and delicious bread at home.

Sourdough Science, in Short

Sourdough's popularity is part of a larger interest in homemade fermented foods like kimchi, yogurt, and kombucha. Not only do these foods have well-documented health benefits, but they also develop layers of wonderful flavor during the fermentation process that make them uniquely delicious. As many have recently discovered, craft baking with a natural starter is a tremendously comforting, creative, satisfying, and nutritious activity in both the best and worst of times.

You don't have to understand the science of fermentation to make your own natural yeast starter for raising bread—for thousands of years before the discovery of microbes, people across cultures successfully baked sourdough bread with no scientific information at all. (Medieval illuminated manuscripts from the thirteenth century depict monks sliding naturally fermented dough into beehive ovens.) In fact, none of my early mentors ever spoke about the science behind making levain, but they certainly knew how to create a delicious and effective sourdough. Their focus was always on careful observation and patience. If you looked closely and waited long enough, you would eventually see, smell, and taste the proof that your sourdough was alive and active enough to raise bread.

However, just a little bit of knowledge about how natural yeast proliferates might take the mystery and anxiety out of the process. I wrote extensively about the subject in my previous books. So here I'll be brief.

Fermentation is the term for the breakdown of molecules in organic substances by yeast and bacteria. When yeast and bacteria get to work on milk, they feast on its sugars, thickening and flavoring the milk and transforming it into yogurt, buttermilk, or cheese. By a similar process, yeast and bacteria transform grape juice's sugars into a tangy and sometimes effervescent alcoholic beverage we know as wine.

The transformation of moistened flour into a tart and bubbling sourdough starter happens in the same way. Wild yeast lives in flour and the air. When water is mixed into flour, it triggers enzymes present in both the flour and the wild yeast to begin to break down the flour's starches into simple sugars. The yeast feeds on these simple sugars, producing carbon dioxide, which causes the mixture to bubble. The well-fed yeast multiplies rapidly, and with care and under the right conditions, the sourdough culture becomes a powerful leavener. Once a healthy wild yeast colony is established in a bowl of flour and water, some of it is added in precise amounts to bread dough, causing the dough to ferment and rise on the countertop and in the oven—*without any commercial yeast at all.*

Sourdough gets its name from the acids that build up in the culture during fermentation. These acids are not produced by yeast, but by bacteria called lactobacilli that exist in the environment alongside yeast and feed off sugars in the dough. As they feed and multiply, these lactobacilli produce organic acids, including lactic and acetic acids, that flavor the bread.

If You've Made One Sourdough, You Can Make Them All

My early knowledge of sourdough techniques came strictly from personal experience. Visiting Kaufman's, a big commercial bakery in Buffalo, with my grandfather was a special adventure. An old Russian baker there showed us a little artisan section in the back of the shop where he kept some liquid rye sourdough in an earthenware crock, and used it to bake extra-dark ten-kilogram rye breads once or twice a week. In France, I watched Max Poilâne feed the firm starter he used to create the giant miches he learned to make from his father. I remember my first trip to Italy, where I encountered the firm *lievito madre* that raises *pane di Altamura*. I saw semolina starters in southern Italy, and very soft levain-type starters in Genzano. I was impressed by the elaborate rye and spelt starter systems I encountered in Germany. When I first saw the liquid sourdough machines manufactured by the German baking equipment company Isernhager in the '90s, I ordered one for Bread Alone, blown away by the idea that a machine with temperature controls could be preprogrammed to stir and blend when no one was in the bakery.

Every encounter with sourdough was different from the last, and no two bakers' techniques were the same. Each baker seemed to have a subtly distinct method for building, maintaining, and using a culture. Some bakers used firm sourdough exclusively, were strict about hydration levels, and always fed their cultures once and fermented them in exactly the same place in the bakery. Other bakers would do multiple feedings before they deemed their culture ready and were more haphazard and varied in their timing and hydration levels, based on weather and temperature.

Bakers get attached to their cultures. When I asked my friend Fabrice Guéry, an expert baker who works at the fine French mill Suire, to help me bake breads for the photo shoot for my last book, he arrived with a small container of his own starter. It gave him the confidence (not that he needed it, considering his unbelievable skill) to use unfamiliar formulas in a high-stress setting.

For a long time, I viewed every culture as different from the next, and believed that we needed a large array of them in the bakery, made with different grains and at a variety of hydrations, to make authentic European-style loaves. I used to drive the staff crazy insisting on maintaining six different starters at Bread Alone—spelt, rye, einkorn, semolina, whole wheat, and white. But as I learned more about the science of sourdough, I understood that these cultures were more alike than different. Each one contained a yeast colony that produced the carbon dioxide that could make bread dough rise. Each one was flavored with tangy and delicious lactic and acetic acids, by-products of the friendly bacteria proliferating in sourdough. It was easy enough to use one type of sourdough culture to make a variety of starters. If I wanted a spelt starter for my spelt bread, I could simply refresh a little bit of my liquid wheat starter with spelt flour. If I wanted to bake buckwheat miches with a firm buckwheat starter, I could quickly make this starter by refreshing my liquid starter with buckwheat flour and half as much water as I'd add for a liquid version.

Today at Bread Alone, we keep just three separate starters—white, whole wheat, and rye—going continuously, and use them to make any variation we'd like. In my home refrigerator, I keep just one type of sourdough, a simple liquid levain that I will explain how to make below and use to mix every variety of starter in the recipes in this book.

Reasons to Try Sourdough

Sourdough bread is lower on the glycemic index than bread made with commercial yeast: Research shows sourdough has higher levels of resistant starch than other breads, especially when made with whole grains. It takes the body longer to digest these carbohydrates, preventing blood sugar spikes that can lead to type 2 diabetes.

Sourdough bread is more nutritious: Phytic acid, a substance found in plant seeds including wheat berries, prevents the body from absorbing minerals. During long sourdough fermentation, however, phytic acid breaks down, improving the bioavailability of these minerals.

Sourdough bread is easier to digest: Wheat gluten contains proline and glutamine, amino acids that are indigestible and can cause stomach pain in people with gluten intolerance. During sourdough fermentation, lactobacilli break down these amino acids, making wheat bread more digestible for many.

Sourdough bread tastes better: Fermentation is immensely important in flavoring bread dough. As yeast and lactobacilli feed off the starches in flour, they produce a variety of acids, alcohols, aldehydes, and esters that give bread its complex aroma and taste. The longer you ferment your dough, the more complexly flavorful it will be. By adding sourdough culture to your dough instead of commercial yeast, you are adding days' and weeks' worth of flavor development.

Making a sourdough starter is easier than you think: While sourdough bread has developed a reputation and mystique as an "advanced" type of recipe, the first step in making it, cultivating a starter, requires no experience, knowledge, or technique. In my mind, it takes more discipline than skill. When we first started making pain au levain at Bread Alone, I knew nothing about sourdough science and had never cultivated a sourdough starter on my own. I simply followed the steps I had been shown in France, repeating the feeding of my culture daily, until I saw that it had doubled in volume in 8 hours.

Simply Sourdough

Over the course of my career, I have encountered dozens of ways to cultivate sourdough. I've seen recipes that employ yogurt, grape skins, raisins, potato peels, and other ingredients to initiate a culture. I've watched as bakers in southern Italy fed their sourdough and stored it in inherited earthenware crocks placed in holes in the ground to keep the culture cool. I've purchased high-tech

Dispatch from the Eighth Annual Sourdough Symposium

Today, sourdough exists on the cutting edge of science, studied by a group of researchers from around the world who are investigating how this type of natural fermentation can improve the healthfulness of wheat breads and other cereal products, and help create a more sustainable, less wasteful grain economy. Many of these researchers gather every three years for a symposium on the subject. In June 2022, the Eighth International Symposium on Sourdough took place at the Free University of Bozen in Bolzano, Italy, chaired by sourdough eminence Dr. Marco Gobbetti, a professor of food microbiology and the author of the *Handbook on Sourdough Biotechnology*.

The conference's motto was "Resilience, Sustainability and Wellness." Presenters made detailed, convincing cases that sourdough is not simply a part of bread's heritage but an essential ingredient in our future diet. On the subject of resilience, Kati Katina of the University of Helsinki addressed the increasing demand, in the face of wheat shortages, for alternative crops like legumes, and described how the fermentation of wheat alternatives might make them more palatable. "Tailored bioprocessing," as she calls this type of fermentation, can minimize off flavors in baked goods made with bean flour, improving their acceptability and usability and allowing them to become staple food items in our daily diets. Erica Pontonio of the University of Bari presented related research, outlining how the sourdough fermentation of hempseed renders this previously unexploited ingredient suitable for fortifying both gluten-free and wheat breads.

Sustainability was also thoroughly covered. In a paper on fermentation and zero-waste strategies for the cereal industry, Carlo Giuseppe Rizzello of the Sapienza University of Rome noted that germ and bran are by-products of milling that traditionally have been used as animal feed or considered waste. Leftover bread is one of the planet's major food-waste products. Fermented with sourdough, however, these cereal by-products and surplus breads, rich in minerals, vitamins, and beneficial bioactive compounds, can be added to baked goods to enhance their overall nutritional profile while eliminating waste.

Not surprisingly, wellness in this age of gastric distress was a crucial subject of investigation. While bakers and consumers have long suspected that sourdough wheat breads are more easily digestible than breads raised with commercial yeast, researchers Lilit Ispiryan and Elke Arendt from University College Cork presented data indicating that a potent sourdough culture containing specific strains of yeast and lactic acid bacteria actually expresses FODMAP-degrading enzymes, rendering wheat breads low FODMAP and offering choices beyond gluten-free bakery products to people with gluten sensitivity. Applicable to an even wider swath of the population, a survey of thirty years of data by Georgia Chatonidi of KU Leuven in Belgium provides persuasive evidence that eating sourdough bread suppresses appetite through lowering glucose response, resulting in increased satiety, weight control, and longevity.

I was thrilled to hear cold, hard scientific confirmation of what I and so many other sourdough enthusiasts have long suspected—that sourdough bread is good for the body and the planet, and that sourdough technology can and should be used to feed the world. Thrillingly, this research is still in its infancy. Sourdough already makes the world a better place. Only time will tell how it may be used in new and innovative ways to improve our health and quality of life.

sourdough tanks manufactured in Germany after seeing bakers there control a culture's rate of fermentation and level of acidity to the minute.

In my journey back to home baking, I've left behind the tanks and other professional tools. In doing so, I've struggled with the same challenges that my nonprofessional readers have reported over the years. What is the best vessel for my incipient culture? Are flour and water really all that I need? Should I give up if my culture shows no signs of life after a week? If my kitchen is cold, how can I hurry the process along? How can I minimize food waste, and what can I do with the discard? For this book, I've walked in your shoes, using all my experience to come up with the simplest, quickest, and most foolproof method for growing a healthy sourdough culture in a home kitchen.

My favorite easy-to-maintain culture is a highly hydrated liquid sourdough, jump-started with some whole wheat flour and then fed daily with white flour. Almost pourable in consistency, it is easy to make and nourish, just by stirring with a spoon.

The first step is simple: feed the flora naturally existing in flour by mixing it with water. I use tap water, but if your water is especially hard or extremely chlorinated, you might want to use bottled spring water, since minerals and chlorine may inhibit the growth of yeast and lactobacilli. I add some whole wheat flour to white flour, to invigorate the culture. Whole wheat flour naturally contains more microorganisms than white

flour, and more nutrients in the form of minerals contained in wheat bran. But after this first feeding, white flour will do.

Every day after this, for up to three weeks but generally much faster than this, you'll mix a portion of this developing culture with fresh flour and water, to feed the hungry microbes that are multiplying within it. (You'll discard the remaining culture, so you don't wind up with buckets of the stuff by the end of the process.) You'll notice increasing activity as the days go by. There will be larger bubbles dotting the surface of the culture. It will rise, at first slightly, and later on voluminously. It will develop a tart and fruity flavor. Because of the uniqueness of your starter's environment, it will reach maturity at its own pace. Don't worry if it hasn't doubled by the end of day four, or even after a couple of weeks. Continue to feed it and observe it to determine when it is ready to use. Your patience will be rewarded with a natural starter that you've made with your own two hands.

The Creation, Care, and Feeding of Your Sourdough

The following is a guide for cultivating a liquid starter from scratch. Do your best to keep the starter in the 70° to 74°F (21° to 23°C) range to encourage fermentation. If you live in a very warm climate, store your sourdough in a cool, draft-free place in your kitchen, and be aware that it will ferment more quickly than it might in a cooler place. If your schedule prevents you from feeding your culture on time every once in a while, don't worry. A missed feeding may slow down the development of your starter, but won't harm it. It's not unusual for a starter to appear practically inert for a number of days before suddenly springing up in its container. A mature culture will double in volume in 6 to 8 hours. Yours may reach this stage after just a few days, or may take an additional week or two to achieve peak power.

While patience is key, and your starter will improve in strength as weeks and even months go by, there is a cheap and easy way to hurry it along. Seedling heat mats with temperature controls are available online for as little as $12. Set up your mat on a countertop, place your culture on top of the mat, and let it sit on the warm surface as it develops. Warmed at a constant 74°F (23°C), it will be ready to use in as few as four days after its initial feeding.

After that, you can use your potent liquid sourdough to make whatever kind of sourdough starter you'd like: a firm wheat starter like the ones traditionally used in French bakeries to make country-style boules, a starter made with rye flour that is used in German and Scandinavian whole-grain breads, or one made with spelt, einkorn, or emmer if you're inclined to use an older or ancient variety of wheat.

Initiating the Culture

To initiate a culture, combine 50 grams whole wheat or rye flour, 50 grams bread flour, and 100 grams water in a clean, clear straight-sided 400- to 600-ml container. Cover, set it on your kitchen countertop or on a heated seedling mat if desired, and let it stand for 24 hours.

Nourishing the Culture

Every 24 hours, uncover the container and observe the culture. Note any changes from the previous day. Then discard all but 100 grams of the culture, leaving that portion in the container. (See page 104 for ways to use the starter discard if you don't want to throw it away.) Stir 50 grams bread flour and 50 grams water into the remaining starter, cover it, and place it back on the counter or heated seedling mat. Continue to feed it this way once a day. Your culture may show signs of life after a day or two, with a few small bubbles on the surface. As the days go by, it will get bubblier and more fragrant. If the culture has doubled in volume during the previous 6 to 8 hours, if it has a nutty and pleasantly sour flavor, if it has a consistently bubbly structure (look through the clear sides of the container to see this), if it has a bubbly surface with some little cracks, then it is ready to raise bread. At this stage, the culture becomes a starter.

Maintaining the Starter

Your mature starter can be used right away, but it can also be kept covered in the refrigerator for up to one week. After a week, remove it from the refrigerator, feed it as described above, discarding all but 50 grams and adding 50 grams fresh flour and 50 grams fresh water. Let it sit on the countertop for a couple of hours, and refrigerate again. This way, you will always have an active starter waiting for you when you are ready to bake.

Using the Starter to Bake a Bread

Each of the recipes in this book calling for a sourdough starter instructs you to measure out some of your ripe starter, to feed that portion with a specific amount of flour and water, and to let it stand to ferment for a while before adding it to your bread dough. At the same time that you do this, give 50 grams of the remaining starter a fresh feeding, let it sit on the countertop for a few hours, and refrigerate until you are ready to bake again, up to one week.

If you bake regularly, whether it is every day, twice a week, or once a month, you will become accustomed to the rhythm of refreshing your starter as necessary so you never run out. But if you do run out—say you take a cruise around the world for six months and have no way of feeding it, or your partner accidentally throws it in the garbage when cleaning out the refrigerator—don't panic. A new and equally powerful starter is simple enough to cultivate now that you know how to do it.

Making a Firm Sourdough Starter

By varying the amount of water you use to initiate and then feed your culture, you can cultivate sourdoughs of different consistencies. When I first went to France years ago, a claylike firm starter was the norm, simply because it was easier to control the fermentation of a firm starter than a fast-fermenting liquid one. As technology

Speed-Fermenting Your Starter

At the bakery, we have a temperature-controlled room where we ferment our sourdoughs at 74°F (23°C), so they rise reliably in 6 to 8 hours. When I moved to Maine, I was dismayed to see that my sourdough was taking much longer to rise in my 65°F (18°C) kitchen. The solution to this problem was simple. I improvised a proofing box by boiling some water in a Pyrex measuring cup in the microwave, and then setting my just-fed and covered starter alongside the still-hot water inside the microwave. I was amazed at how quickly it rose in the warm, moist environment. Whenever it's chilly or I'm in a rush, I'll use this technique to revive a starter.

Baltic Dark Rye, PAGE 124

made possible a temperature-controlled environment within the bakery, liquid sourdoughs, almost pourable in consistency, became popular. Both firm and liquid sourdoughs are common in artisan bakeries today.

Hydration affects the kind of acid produced during fermentation. The extra water in a liquid levain promotes lactic acid production, while a stiff sourdough culture promotes the production of acetic acid. Thus, liquid sourdough will develop a milder acidic flavor in dough that is perfect for mild breads with a high percentage of white flour. Firmer sourdough will have a stronger flavor that complements assertively flavored rye or whole wheat flour in whole-grain bread recipes.

So you will notice that recipes in this book that call for mostly or all white flour also call for liquid sourdough. Breads that contain 40 percent or more whole wheat or rye generally call for a firm starter. No need to worry—the directions in these recipes will instruct you on how to convert some of your liquid sourdough into a firm starter made with whole wheat flour.

To convert your liquid sourdough into a firm starter for use in any other recipe, follow these simple steps:

In a small bowl, combine 20 grams liquid starter with 100 grams whole wheat flour and just 60 grams water. Knead this mixture, still in the bowl, repeatedly folding the dough over and then pressing it with

your palm, until just smooth. Cover it and let it stand on the countertop or on a seedling mat until doubled in volume, 6 to 8 hours. Weigh out what you need for your recipe and use immediately, or cover and refrigerate for up to 1 week.

Making a Spelt, Semolina, Emmer, Einkorn, Rye, or Buckwheat Starter

While I could certainly use my standard liquid sourdough, made with sifted bread flour, in any type of bread recipe, I will generally convert some of that starter to match the predominant flour in the bread I'm planning to bake. I've grown to appreciate the subtle difference in flavor I get when the sourdough is curated for the bread I'm making.

As with recipes calling for a firm starter, the recipes in this book that require a starter made with an alternative flour will instruct you on how to convert some of your liquid sourdough into either a liquid or firm starter made with spelt, semolina, emmer, einkorn, rye, or buckwheat.

To convert your liquid sourdough into a liquid spelt, semolina, emmer, einkorn, rye, or buckwheat starter for use in any other recipe, follow these simple steps:

In a small bowl, combine 20 grams liquid starter with 100 grams flour of your choice and 100 grams water. Stir until mostly smooth, cover it, and let it stand on the countertop or on a seedling mat until doubled in volume, 6 to 8 hours. Weigh out what you need for your recipe and use immediately, or cover and refrigerate for up to 1 week.

To convert your liquid sourdough into a firm spelt, semolina, emmer, einkorn, rye, or buckwheat starter for use in any other recipe, follow these simple steps:

In a small bowl, combine 20 grams liquid starter with 100 grams flour of your choice and just 50 grams of water. Knead this mixture, still in the bowl, repeatedly folding the dough over and then pressing it with your palm, until just smooth. Cover it and let it stand on the countertop or on a seedling mat until doubled in volume, 6 to 8 hours. Weigh out what you need for your recipe and use immediately, or cover and refrigerate for up to 1 week.

How to Use
Your Leftover Starter

As you cultivate your sourdough, and as you maintain it over the weeks, months, and years, you will surely have some undeveloped (not bubbly), overdeveloped, or just excess culture that must be discarded when it is time to feed only a portion of the culture as part of the process. That's a lot of dough to throw in the trash.

In a bakery setting, leftover starter is not an issue. We plan our production to accommodate it, adding a little of it into whatever breads we are mixing so it doesn't go to waste. You can do the same at home. In general, the leftover liquid sourdough that you add should not be more than 20 percent of the total weight of the flour in the recipe you are using. If your starter is mature, you won't have to add any yeast. If it's under- or overdeveloped, you'll need to add some yeast to help your bread rise. It's a good idea to have a go-to recipe for leftovers, so that you can learn over time how your sourdough, at any stage, will perform. No matter what the condition of the leftover starter, it is sure to contain some acetic and lactic acids that will add flavor to your bread.

Here is my favorite recipe for leftover starter: waffles.

Sourdough Discard Waffles

Makes about 10 waffles

This batter is great because most of it is mixed together the night before. You might wonder why the recipe calls for both milk and buttermilk. I like the tangy flavor that some buttermilk gives the waffles, but I find that adding a little bit of regular milk prevents them from being too sour.

When you add your eggs and other ingredients in the morning, assess the consistency of the batter, which should be almost liquid, like a thick pancake batter. Add a little extra milk or extra flour as necessary to achieve this result.

Ingredients	Metric
leftover unfed starter (sourdough discard; see above)	200 g
all-purpose flour	125 g, plus more as needed
whole wheat flour	125 g
sugar	20 g
whole milk	125 g
buttermilk (any fat content)	125 g
eggs	110 g (2 large)
melted unsalted butter, cooled slightly	60 g, plus more for greasing
fine sea salt	5 g
baking soda	5 g

1. The night before you plan on enjoying your waffles: In a large bowl, weigh the starter, all-purpose flour, whole wheat flour, sugar, milk, and buttermilk. Mix together until smooth. Cover the bowl tightly, preferably with beeswax wrap. Let sit at room temperature overnight.

2. The next morning, preheat a waffle iron. Add the eggs, butter, salt, and baking soda to the waffle base. Adjust the consistency of the batter if necessary, so it is pourable like pancake batter, by adding a little bit more milk or all-purpose flour.

3. Lightly butter the waffle iron. Spoon batter for the first waffle onto the iron, close, and cook until golden. Repeat with the remaining batter.

Miche Reconsidered

We have been making a miche (the French term for a large round loaf) with a firm whole wheat sourdough at Bread Alone for nearly forty years. As other grains became available, we used our basic formula to experiment, substituting spelt, buckwheat, and/or einkorn for some of the whole wheat flour to add some complexity to the miche's flavor profile. Here is our well-balanced multigrain iteration. To unlock the flavor potential of these grains, we decreased the amount of sourdough we used and increased fermentation time, letting it sit overnight at cool room temperature (at home, I like to ferment my dough in the basement). You just wouldn't get the same magnification of these grains' distinctive qualities with a 6-hour proof as you will with a full 14 hours.

Makes 1 rectangular loaf, about 900 grams

Start to finish: **3 days**

Gathering ingredients and preparing the starter, day one:
10 minutes

Proofing the starter:
overnight

Gathering ingredients, autolyse, and mixing the dough, day two:
1¼ hours

Folding, proofing, and resting the dough:
4½ hours

Refrigerating the dough:
overnight

Proofing, day three:
2 to 2½ hours

Baking: **40 minutes**

Ingredients	Metric
WHOLE WHEAT STARTER	
whole wheat flour	15 g
water (70° to 78°F / 21° to 25.5°C)	10 g
Sourdough Starter (page 98)	10 g
DOUGH	
bread flour	175 g
whole wheat flour	175 g, plus more for dusting
spelt flour	100 g
buckwheat flour	25 g
einkorn flour	25 g
water (70° to 78°F / 21° to 25.5°C)	375 g
fine sea salt	10 g

1. **PREPARE THE WHOLE WHEAT STARTER:** In a small bowl, weigh the whole wheat flour, water, and sourdough starter. Stir together until well incorporated. Cover the bowl tightly, preferably with beeswax wrap. Let sit at room temperature overnight.

2. **FOR THE AUTOLYSE:** In the bowl of a stand mixer or in a large bowl, weigh the bread flour, whole wheat flour, spelt flour, buckwheat flour, einkorn flour, and water. Fit the mixer with the paddle attachment and

RECIPE CONTINUES

mix on low speed (or with a spatula if in a large bowl) until a dough forms. Cover and let stand for 1 hour.

3. Very lightly brush the inside of a rectangular plastic storage container with a lid or a large bowl with water.

4. **MAKE THE FINAL DOUGH:** Add the whole wheat starter to the dough. With the dough hook, mix on low to medium-low speed until a smooth, slightly sticky dough forms, 4 to 5 minutes. Alternatively, the dough can be mixed by folding by hand, 6 to 8 minutes. Add the salt and mix (or fold if using the spatula) until it is distributed, about 2 minutes.

5. Transfer the dough to the storage container or the bowl. Lightly drizzle the top of the dough with water. Cover the container with the lid or the bowl tightly with beeswax wrap. Let sit at room temperature for 1 hour.

6. If the dough is in a storage container, with slightly damp hands, pat the dough into a rectangle and fold from the top and then the bottom like a business letter. Slide both hands under the dough and fold from left then right like a letter.

If the dough is in a bowl, the dough can be folded like a letter as above in the bowl or turned out onto a damp work surface for folding.

Add a little water to the bowl and dough as needed to keep the dough from sticking. Cover and let rest at room temperature for 1 hour.

7. Fold from top to bottom and then left to right and let rest at room temperature for 1 hour.

8. Repeat the folds one more time and let rest at room temperature for 1 hour more. Cover and refrigerate overnight.

9. Turn the dough out onto a lightly floured countertop and gently preshape into a round. Cover and let stand for 30 minutes. Press into a loose rectangle, about 7 by 9 inches (18 by 23 cm). Lightly press and pull the rounded corners as needed to create a straighter-sided rectangle. Transfer to a floured baking cloth or piece of parchment paper. Lift and gather the cloth or the parchment, using rolling pins or even rolled towels to support the sides. Cover so the beeswax wrap is

not pressed directly against the dough but is secure around the edges. Let stand at room temperature until pillowy, 1½ to 2 hours.

10. About 1 hour before baking, position one oven rack on the lowest rung and set a cast-iron skillet on it. Position the other oven rack in the center and set a large baking stone or steel on it.

Preheat the oven to 450°F (230°C).

11. Close to baking time, fill a medium bowl with about 1 cup of ice cubes to have ready to add to the skillet to create steam.

Remove the supports from the sides of the loaf. If it is on a baking cloth, gently transfer it to a parchment-covered peel, right side up. If it is already on parchment, slide it, still on the parchment, onto a peel. Dust the top with some whole wheat flour, and with a lame, a single-edged razor blade, or a serrated knife, score with 4 to 5 cuts on the diagonal in each direction to make diamonds.

Slide the loaf, still on the parchment paper, onto the stone or steel, pour the ice cubes into the skillet to produce steam, and close the door.

Bake until the loaf is a darker brown with light caramelization on the cuts, about 40 minutes.

12. Transfer to a wire rack and let cool completely.

Polenta Bread

When we rebuilt our original Boiceville bakery and refurbished the brick ovens, we updated our specialty bread menu to highlight locally grown grains. Although it's Italian in origin, polenta bread is a natural fit for our Catskills location, since local cornmeal is abundant and excellent. Be sure to buy whole stone-ground cornmeal (*polenta* is simply the Italian word for "cornmeal"), not sifted commercial meal. In addition, we use 100 percent New York State flour in the bread to give it a truly local flavor and pedigree (see page 356 for local flour options nearest you).

When making this bread, you'll see how easy it is to turn a little liquid wheat sourdough into a powerful rye starter, which will offset the sweetness of the cornmeal. My wife Julie and I slice this loaf, toast it, brush it with a little olive oil, and top with slices of prosciutto. It makes a good breakfast, lunch, or snack. One of the beauties of this bread is its long shelf life. The abundant oil in the cornmeal, combined with some olive oil, keeps it fresh for days. This is a large loaf. If you'd prefer to bake two smaller breads, just divide the dough in half equally before shaping and proceed as directed.

Makes 1 rectangular loaf, about 1.1 kilograms

Start to finish: **3 days**

Gathering ingredients, preparing the starter, and making the polenta, day one: **40 minutes**

Proofing the starter: **6 to 8 hours or up to overnight**

Gathering ingredients, autolyse, and mixing the dough, day two: **1 hour**

Folding, proofing, and resting the dough: **4½ hours**

Refrigerating the dough: **overnight**

Proofing, day three: **1½ hours**

Baking: **40 minutes**

Ingredients	Metric
RYE STARTER	
dark rye flour	50 g
water (70° to 78°F / 21° to 25.5°C)	65 g
Sourdough Starter (page 98)	10 g
POLENTA	
water	120 g
extra-virgin olive oil	10 g
fine sea salt	2 g
stone-ground cornmeal	50 g, plus more for dusting (optional)
DOUGH	
bread flour	500 g
water (70° to 78°F / 21° to 25.5°C)	300 g
fine sea salt	12 g
instant dry yeast	0.5 g
millet, whole corn flour, or stone-ground cornmeal, for sprinkling (optional)	50 g

RECIPE CONTINUES

1. **PREPARE THE RYE STARTER:** In the bowl of a stand mixer or in a large bowl, weigh the rye flour, water, and sourdough starter. Fit the mixer with the paddle attachment and mix on the Stir setting (or with a spatula if in a large bowl) until well incorporated. Cover the bowl tightly, preferably with beeswax wrap. Let sit at room temperature for 6 to 8 hours or up to overnight.

2. **PREPARE THE POLENTA:** In a medium saucepan over low heat, combine the water, olive oil, and salt and bring to a simmer. Slowly stream in the cornmeal while whisking. Lower the heat to keep at a simmer. Switch to a wooden spoon or spatula and continue to cook, stirring often, until the polenta is smooth and no longer has a raw taste, about 20 minutes (or the cook time indicated on the package instructions).

   Remove from the heat and let cool completely. To cool more quickly, transfer to a plate, spreading in an even layer. (If you'd like, you can prepare the polenta up to a day in advance, cover, and refrigerate. Let it come to room temperature before proceeding.)

3. **FOR THE AUTOLYSE:** Add the bread flour and water to the bowl with the rye starter. Add the cooled polenta and mix with the dough hook on low speed or with the spatula until combined, 3 to 5 minutes. Cover and let stand for 30 minutes.

4. Very lightly brush the inside of a rectangular plastic storage container with a lid or a large bowl with water. (Since this is a fairly soft dough, add water only as needed to keep from sticking throughout the folding process.)

5. **MAKE THE FINAL DOUGH:** Add the salt and the yeast to the bowl and mix on low speed (or fold if using a spatula) until distributed and the dough is more cohesive, about 5 minutes. The dough will be a bit soft.

6. Transfer the dough to the storage container or the bowl. Lightly drizzle the top of the dough with water. Cover the container with the lid or the bowl tightly with beeswax wrap.

   Let sit at room temperature for 1 hour.

7. If the dough is in a storage container, with slightly damp hands, pat the dough into a rectangle and fold from the top and then the bottom like a business letter. Slide both hands under the dough and fold from left then right like a letter.

If the dough is in a bowl, the dough can be folded like a letter as above or turned out onto a damp work surface for folding.

Add a little water to the bowl and dough as needed to keep the dough from sticking. Cover and let rest at room temperature for 1 hour.

8. Fold from top to bottom and then left to right and let rest at room temperature for 1 hour.

9. Repeat the folds one more time and let rest at room temperature for 1 hour more.

10. If using millet to coat the bread, line a rimmed baking sheet with parchment paper.

11. Sprinkle about one-third of the millet onto the center of the parchment in an even layer where the dough will be turned out (a rectangle about 6 by 10 inches, or 15 by 25 cm). Turn the dough out onto the work surface and let it expand naturally into a rectangle, about 7 by 9 inches (18 by 23 cm). Lightly press and pull the rounded corners as needed to create a straighter-sided rectangle. Sprinkle the remaining millet on the top and sides.

Lift and gather the parchment on all sides, using rolling pins or even rolled kitchen towels to support the sides. Cover so the beeswax wrap is not pressed directly against the dough but is secure around the edges. Refrigerate overnight. (If not using millet, simply shape the dough as directed above, using cornmeal to dust the work surface.)

12. Remove the loaf from the refrigerator. Cover with an inverted box or plastic tub and let sit at room temperature to warm up and proof until pillowy, about 1½ hours.

RECIPE CONTINUES

13. Meanwhile, set up the oven: Position one oven rack on the lowest rung and set a cast-iron skillet on it. Position the other oven rack in the center and set a large baking stone or steel on it.

Preheat the oven to 450°F (230°C).

14. Close to baking time, fill a medium bowl with about 1 cup of ice cubes to have ready to add to the skillet to create steam.

Remove the supports from the sides of the loaf. This loaf will not be scored.

Slide the loaf, still on the parchment paper, onto the stone, pour the ice cubes into the skillet to produce steam, and close the door.

Bake until the loaf is a rich golden brown, about 40 minutes.

15. Transfer to a wire rack and let cool completely.

Lefort Levain

I learned to make my first pain au levain in an André Lefort oven at the original Moulin de la Vierge, the bakery owned by my friend and mentor Basil Kamir. I can't overstate how thrilling it was to bake a naturally fermented bread in a wood-fired oven built by the master mason. I knew right away I had to have ovens like these at Bread Alone, and was determined to get André, a fourth-generation craftsman, to come to the US for the first time to build them. Even today, these ovens, which have just been refurbished for use in our carbon-neutral Boiceville bakery, are my calling card when I introduce myself to European bakers. "Oh, you're the American guy with the Lefort ovens," they'll say. It gives me instant credibility.

Basil's original recipe was just sifted wheat flour, water, levain, and salt. Over the years I've tweaked the formula to include whole wheat, whole rye, and whole einkorn. The result is still a lighter style of country bread but with some satisfying whole-grain flavor. This is a large loaf. If you'd prefer to bake two smaller bâtards, just divide the dough in half equally before shaping and proceed as directed.

Makes 1 bâtard, about 1 kilogram

Start to finish: **3 days**

Gathering ingredients and preparing the starter, day one:
10 minutes

Proofing the starter:
overnight

Gathering ingredients, autolyse, and mixing the dough, day two:
1¼ hours

Folding, proofing, and resting the dough:
8½ hours

Refrigerating the dough:
overnight

Proofing, day three:
1½ hours

Baking:
40 to 45 minutes

Ingredients	Metric
EINKORN AND RYE STARTER	
einkorn flour	25 g
dark rye flour	25 g
water (70° to 78°F / 21° to 25.5°C)	50 g
Sourdough Starter (page 98)	10 g
DOUGH	
bread flour	300 g, plus more for dusting
whole wheat flour	200 g
water (70° to 78°F / 21° to 25.5°C)	390 to 400 g
fine sea salt	12 g

1. **PREPARE THE EINKORN AND RYE STARTER:** In a small bowl, weigh the einkorn flour, rye flour, water, and sourdough starter. Stir together until well incorporated. Cover the bowl tightly, preferably with beeswax wrap. Let sit at room temperature for 6 to 8 hours or up to overnight.

2. **FOR THE AUTOLYSE:** In the bowl of a stand mixer or in a large bowl, weigh the bread flour, whole wheat flour, and 375 g of the water. Fit

RECIPE CONTINUES

the mixer with the paddle attachment and mix on low speed (or with a spatula if in a large bowl) until a rough dough forms. Cover and let stand for 1 hour.

3. Very lightly brush the inside of a rectangular plastic storage container with a lid or a large bowl with water. (This will be a slightly soft and sticky dough, but up to 25 g of water may be added during the folding process as needed.)

4. **MAKE THE FINAL DOUGH:** Add the einkorn and rye starter to the dough. Switch to the dough hook and mix on low to medium-low speed until incorporated, about 4 minutes. Alternatively, the dough can be mixed by folding by hand.

Add the salt and mix (or fold if using the spatula) until it is distributed and the dough is well-developed, another 4 minutes.

5. Transfer the dough to the storage container or the bowl. Lightly drizzle the top of the dough with 10 g of the water. Cover the container with the lid or the bowl tightly with beeswax wrap.

Let sit at room temperature for 1 hour.

6. If the dough is in a storage container, drizzle the dough with 3 to 5 g of water, pat the dough into a rectangle, and fold from the top and then the bottom like a business letter. Slide both hands under the dough and fold from left then right like a letter.

If the dough is in a bowl, the dough can be folded like a letter as above in the bowl or turned out onto a damp work surface for folding.

Add 3 to 5 g of water to the bowl and dough as needed to keep the dough from sticking. Cover and let rest at room temperature for 1 hour.

7. Drizzle with 3 to 5 g of water for additional hydration only as needed. Fold from top to bottom and then left to right and let rest at room temperature for 1 hour.

8. Repeat the folds (with a 1-hour rest in between) two more times, drizzling with 3 to 5 g of water only as needed. If the dough is too soft, add only enough water to make the folds. The water is to add additional hydration, if possible, but not make the dough too soft.

RECIPE CONTINUES

After the final fold (a total of five folds), let the dough rest at room temperature for 3 hours.

9. Dust the work surface with bread flour. Set a flour-dusted linen or large kitchen towel on a baking sheet (for ease of moving it into the refrigerator to rest overnight).

To preshape the dough, gather the edges and bring them together to make a round bundle. Turn the dough seam side down. Cup your hands over the round, making tight circles as you bring the round toward you, bringing any rough pieces of dough underneath. Continue until the round is smooth and the top is taut. Dust the top with flour and cover with a clean kitchen towel. Let sit for 10 minutes.

10. To shape into a bâtard, turn the round seam side up and gently press out any air bubbles, while pressing and stretching the dough into a rectangular shape. Fold the bottom half of the dough up and over about two-thirds of the dough, then fold the top down to cover the first fold completely. Press along the bottom edge of the dough to seal.

Turn the dough, now in a log shape, seam side down. Place your hands together, palms down, in the middle of the log. Using light, even pressure, roll the log back and forth as you spread your hands apart. Repeat two or three times until the bâtard is the desired length, tapering the ends by increasing downward pressure at the tips.

Set the bâtard on the flour-dusted linen. Gather the linen gently against the sides of the bâtard, using rolling pins or even kitchen towels to support the sides. Cover so the beeswax wrap is not pressed directly against the dough but is secure around the edges. Refrigerate overnight.

11. Remove the bâtard from the refrigerator. Cover with an inverted box or plastic tub and let sit at room temperature to warm up and proof until slightly pillowy, about 1½ hours.

12. Meanwhile, set up the oven: Position one oven rack on the lowest rung and the other in the center.

If using a cast-iron baking pan with a lid, set it on the center rack.

If using a stone or steel, set it on the center rack and set a cast-iron skillet on the lower rack.

Preheat the oven to 450°F (230°C).

13. If using a stone or steel, close to baking time, fill a medium bowl with about 1 cup of ice cubes to have ready to add to the skillet to create steam.

Carefully turn the bâtard onto a transfer peel and then a baking peel. With a lame, a single-edged razor blade, or a serrated knife, score the loaf with one straight cut down the center.

Slide the bâtard onto the stone or steel, pour the ice cubes into the skillet to produce steam, and close the door.

If using a cast-iron baking pan with a lid, use heavy-duty oven mitts or potholders to remove the pan from the oven. Place it on a heatproof surface and remove the lid.

Carefully turn the rectangular loaf onto a transfer peel and then a baking peel. With a lame, a single-edged razor blade, or a serrated knife, score the loaf with one straight cut down the center. Slide the loaf into the pan.

Return the lid to the pan and the pan to the center rack.

14. If baking on the stone or steel, bake until the loaf is a rich golden brown, slightly darker where scored, 40 to 45 minutes.

If baking in the cast-iron pan, bake with the lid on for 20 minutes. Remove the lid and bake until the loaf is golden brown with caramel and dark caramel tones on the cut edges, 20 to 25 minutes more.

15. Transfer to a wire rack and let cool completely.

Buckwheat Triangle

French bakers are using buckwheat flour more and more, partly because of its health properties (it contains all the essential amino acids) and partly because of its unique flavor. I love the French name of the grain, *blé noir*, which means "black wheat," although when ground, the flour is a rich gray. These triangular loaves taste like the earth, in the best way. I like them with a really sharp, well-aged cheese, like a pungent Roquefort, to balance the pronounced and distinctive flavor of the grain. In France, bakers will add a tiny amount of yeast to naturally leavened doughs for insurance. I occasionally do it as well, especially when using alternative flours and whole grains. It's entirely optional. The sourdough starter will raise this bread. But a little yeast will speed and stabilize the process slightly. This is a large loaf. If you'd prefer to bake two smaller triangles, just divide the dough in half equally before shaping and proceed as directed.

Makes 1 triangular loaf, about 1 kilogram

Start to finish: **2 days**

Preparing the starter, day one: **10 minutes**

Proofing the starter: **6 hours or up to overnight**

Gathering ingredients, autolyse, and mixing the dough, day two: **1¼ hours**

Folding, proofing, and resting the dough: **3 to 5 hours**

Resting, shaping, and proofing: **1½ to 2 hours**

Baking: **40 minutes**

Ingredients	Metric
RYE STARTER	
dark rye flour	75 g
water (70° to 78°F / 21° to 25.5°C)	75 g
Sourdough Starter (page 98)	20 g
DOUGH	
bread flour	400 g, plus more for dusting
buckwheat flour	100 g
water (70° to 78°F / 21° to 25.5°C)	375 g
honey	10 g
fine sea salt	10 g
instant dry yeast (optional)	1 g

1. **PREPARE THE RYE STARTER:** In a small bowl, weigh the rye flour, water, and sourdough starter. Stir together until well incorporated. Cover and let sit at room temperature for 6 hours or up to overnight.

2. **FOR THE AUTOLYSE:** In the bowl of a stand mixer or in a large bowl, weigh the bread and buckwheat flours, 325 g of the water, and the honey. Fit the mixer with the dough hook and mix together on low

RECIPE CONTINUES

speed (or with a spatula if in a large bowl) until a rough dough forms. Cover and let rest for 1 hour.

3. Very lightly brush the inside of a rectangular plastic storage container with a lid or a large bowl with water.

4. **MAKE THE FINAL DOUGH:** Add the rye starter to the dough and mix on low speed for about 4 minutes. Add the salt and yeast, if using, and mix on low speed for about 3 minutes.

With the mixer running on low speed, gradually drizzle in the remaining water, a teaspoon at a time, about every 45 seconds. Depending on your flour, the amount of additional water added will vary. Alternatively, the dough can be mixed by folding by hand.

5. Transfer the dough to the storage container or the bowl. Cover the container with the lid or the bowl tightly with beeswax wrap.

Let sit at room temperature for 1 hour.

6. If the dough is in a storage container, with slightly damp hands, pat the dough into a rectangle and fold from the top and then the bottom like a business letter. Slide both hands under the dough and fold from left then right like a letter.

If the dough is in a bowl, the dough can be folded like a letter as above in the bowl or turned out onto a damp work surface for folding.

Add some water to the bowl and dough as needed to keep the dough from sticking. Cover and let rest at room temperature for 1 hour.

7. Fold from top to bottom and then left to right and let rest at room temperature for 1 hour.

8. Repeat the folds one more time. If at this point the dough still feels soft and slack, another 2-hour rest and fold cycle can be added in.

9. Dust the work surface with bread flour. Line a peel or rimless baking sheet with parchment paper and dust with flour as well.

To preshape the dough into a round, gather the edges and bring them together to make a round bundle. Turn the dough seam side down. Cup your hands over the round, making tight circles as you bring the round toward you, bringing any rough pieces of dough underneath.

Continue until the round is smooth and the top is taut. Dust the top with flour and cover with a clean kitchen towel. Let sit for 10 minutes.

10. To shape into a round, repeat the steps taken for the preshaping, cupping your hands over the ball and then moving them in tight circles to create a tight ball with a taut skin. Dust the top with flour and cover with a clean kitchen towel. Let sit for 10 minutes.

11. Press the round to flatten slightly. Fold the left side in at a forty-five degree angle, followed by the right side at a forty-five degree angle, and then the top down to make a triangle. Pinch the seams together, flip the loaf over, and set on the prepared parchment paper.

Lift and gather the parchment on the three sides, using rolling pins or even rolled towels to support the sides. Cover with an inverted box or plastic tub and let sit at room temperature to proof until pillowy and slightly risen, 1 to 1½ hours.

12. Meanwhile, set up the oven: Position one oven rack on the lowest rung and set a cast-iron skillet on it. Position the other oven rack in the center and set a large baking stone or steel on it.

Preheat the oven to 500°F (260°C).

13. Close to baking time, fill a medium bowl with about 1 cup of ice cubes to have ready to add to the skillet to create steam.

Remove the supports from the sides of the loaf and with a lame, a single-edged razor blade, or a serrated knife, score the loaf with a Y shape.

Slide the loaf, still on the parchment paper, onto the stone or steel, pour the ice cubes into the skillet to produce steam, and close the door.

14. Bake for 20 minutes.

15. Without opening the oven, lower the oven temperature to 450°F (230°C) and bake until the triangle is a rich golden brown, about 20 minutes more.

16. Transfer to a wire rack and let cool completely.

Baltic Dark Rye

Years ago when I was writing my book *Local Breads*, I traveled to Riga, Latvia, to visit Lāči Bakery, renowned for its Baltic rye breads. I was fascinated by the claylike dough fermenting in large troughs, which bakers hand-shaped onto peels and slid directly into ovens with little or no final proof. But even more fascinating to me was a three-stage fermentation system that owner and head baker Normunds Skauģis showed me, designed specifically to give whole rye breads structure and lift.

Because rye has very little gluten, which in white breads provides the scaffolding for a high-rising loaf, rye breads require a very powerful starter as leavener. The Lāči breads are thus built in three stages. During the first stage, the sourdough is combined with rye flour, water, rye malt, and salt. After fermentation, more flour and water are added in the second stage, to give the yeast another feeding. And then during a third fermentation, this "feeding" is repeated, but instead of giving the dough another proof, it is immediately shaped and baked. The idea is to stimulate as much yeast activity as possible in the final dough, for a burst of yeast activity when it hits the oven.

When I'm at home, I find that building a similar bread in two stages rather than three confers the benefits of the Lāči method in less time. Not only does this method encourage yeast activity, but it also gives the bread its characteristically robust flavor. Also contributing to its distinctive flavor is rye malt, available online. Dark molasses can be substituted. At Lāči, black bread is made both with and without anise and fennel seed, to accommodate customers' personal preferences.

RECIPE CONTINUES

Start to finish:
about 18 hours

Gathering ingredients
and preparing the
starter, day one:
10 minutes

Proofing the starter:
**8 hours or
up to overnight**

Gathering ingredients
and preparing the
first dough, day two:
15 minutes

Resting the first dough:
4 to 6 hours

Gathering ingredients
and preparing the
second dough:
15 minutes

Resting the second
dough: **3 hours**

Baking: **about 1 hour**

Ingredients	Metric
RYE STARTER	
dark rye flour	100 g
water (70° to 78°F / 21° to 25.5°C)	125 g
Sourdough Starter (page 98)	10 g
FIRST DOUGH	
dark rye flour	210 g
water (70° to 78°F / 21° to 25.5°C)	140 g
rye malt or dark molasses	20 g
anise seed, freshly ground (optional)	1 to 1.5 g
fennel seed, freshly ground (optional)	1 to 1.5 g
SECOND DOUGH	
dark rye flour	300 g
fine sea salt	14 g
honey	10 g
water (70° to 78°F / 21° to 25.5°C)	180 g

1. **PREPARE THE RYE STARTER:** In the bowl of a stand mixer or in a large bowl, weigh the rye flour, water, and sourdough starter. Stir together until well incorporated. Cover the bowl tightly, preferably with beeswax wrap. Let sit at room temperature for 8 hours or up to overnight.

2. **PREPARE THE FIRST DOUGH:** Weigh the first dough ingredients in the bowl with the starter: the rye flour, water, rye malt, and the anise and fennel seeds, if using. Fit the mixer with the paddle attachment and mix on the Stir setting for a few seconds (or with a spatula if in a large bowl) to keep the flour from coming out of the bowl. Increase the speed to low to medium-low and mix until combined, about 2 minutes. It will be quite stiff.

    Cover and let sit at room temperature for 4 to 6 hours. The dough will be slightly porous with small holes on the surface.

3. **PREPARE THE SECOND DOUGH:** Weigh the second dough ingredients in the bowl with the first dough: the rye flour, salt, honey, and water. Mix on the Stir setting for a few seconds (or with a spatula if in a large bowl) to keep the flour from coming out of the bowl. Increase the speed to low to medium-low and mix until combined, about 2 minutes. The dough should be thick and spongy with some resistance, and not soft

enough to squish through your fingers. (Think of the consistency of a thick buttercream frosting.) Add additional water as needed to reach this consistency, but do not add so much that it is too loose, like pancake batter.

Cover and let sit at room temperature for 3 hours. The dough will soften a bit and the surface will be porous with small holes.

4. Meanwhile, set up the oven: Position one oven rack on the lowest rung and the other in the center.

If using a cast-iron baking pan with a lid, set it on the center rack.

If using a stone or steel, set it on the center rack and set a cast-iron skillet on the lower rack.

Preheat the oven to 450°F (230°C).

5. Line a rimless baking sheet or baking peel with parchment paper.

Dampen the work surface with a little bit of water. Using a bowl scraper, turn the dough out onto the work surface and mold it into an 8-inch (20 cm) log with rounded ends. Add more water as needed to smooth the surface of the log, removing any fissures. Carefully lift onto the parchment paper. If the dough does not release easily, use a large spatula to transfer it to the parchment paper.

Using your fingertips, make channels along the top and sides of the dough, four to five in total. (Depending on the dough that particular day, the channels may be more or less distinctive in the final bake.) Let rest for 10 minutes.

6. If using a stone or steel, close to baking time, fill a medium bowl with about 1 cup of ice cubes to have ready to add to the skillet to create steam. Slide the loaf, still on the parchment, onto the stone or steel, pour the ice cubes into the skillet to produce steam, and close the door.

If using a cast-iron baking pan with a lid, use heavy-duty oven mitts or potholders to remove the pan from the oven. Place it on a heatproof surface and remove the lid. Carefully lift the loaf, still on the parchment, and place it in the pan. Return the lid to the pan and the pan to the center rack.

For both methods, bake at 450°F (230°C) for 20 minutes. If using a stone or steel, lower the oven temperature to 375°F (190°C) and bake until deep caramel, about 30 minutes more. If using a cast-iron baking pan, remove the lid, lower the oven temperature to 375°F (190°C), and continue to bake for 30 minutes more, until deep caramel in color with a firm crust. Transfer to a wire rack and let cool completely.

Black Bread with Raisins

I developed this recipe as a tribute to the almost-black pumpernickel loaves my grandfather and I used to buy at Kaufman's Bakery in Buffalo when I was a kid. In addition to dark rye, I use other dark ingredients, including cocoa powder, espresso, and raisins, to give it real depth of flavor. Key to the bread's allure is blackstrap molasses, which has a slightly bitter edge and gives this bread a unique but not at all cloying sweetness. For the richest color, choose a dark cocoa powder. If you are a pumpernickel fan, give this one a try. You won't be disappointed.

I like to make this bread as a boule, but it also works well as a bâtard. This is a large loaf. If you'd prefer to bake two smaller breads, just divide the dough in half equally before shaping and proceed as directed.

Makes 1 boule, about 1.1 kilograms

Start to finish: **3 days**

Gathering ingredients and preparing the starter, day one: **10 minutes**

Proofing the starter: **6 to 8 hours or up to overnight**

Gathering ingredients, autolyse, and mixing the dough, day two: **1 hour**

Folding, proofing, and resting the dough: **3 to 5 hours**

Refrigerating the dough: **overnight**

Proofing, day three: **3 hours**

Baking: **40 minutes**

Ingredients	Metric
RYE STARTER	
dark rye flour	50 g
water (70° to 78°F / 21° to 25.5°C)	50 g
Firm Sourdough Starter (page 100)	10 g
DOUGH	
espresso, warm to hot	70 g
blackstrap molasses	30 g
bread flour	320 g, plus more for dusting
dark rye flour	80 g
buckwheat flour	20 g
cocoa powder	10 g
fine sea salt	8 g
instant dry yeast (optional)	0.5 g
water (70° to 78°F / 21° to 25.5°C)	260 g
raisins	125 g
sesame seeds, for rolling (optional)	50 g

1. **PREPARE THE RYE STARTER:** In the bowl of a stand mixer or in a large bowl, weigh the rye flour, water, and sourdough starter. Stir together

RECIPE CONTINUES

until well incorporated. Cover the bowl tightly, preferably with beeswax wrap. Let sit at room temperature for 6 to 8 hours or up to overnight.

2. **FOR THE AUTOLYSE:** Weigh the warm espresso in the bowl with the starter. Stir in the molasses to dissolve and incorporate. Weigh the bread flour, rye flour, buckwheat flour, cocoa powder, salt, and yeast, if using, in the bowl. Fit the mixer with the dough hook and mix on medium-low speed (or with a spatula if in a large bowl), stopping to scrape the sides as needed, until combined, about 10 minutes. The molasses weighs this dough down, so it needs to mix until it is all incorporated and the dough lightens in both color and texture. If needed, mix a bit longer. Cover and let stand for 30 minutes.

3. Very lightly brush the inside of a rectangular plastic storage container with a lid or a large bowl with some of the water. (Since this is a fairly soft dough, add water only as needed to keep from sticking throughout the folding process.)

4. **MAKE THE FINAL DOUGH:** Add the raisins and mix on medium-low speed until evenly distributed, about 2 minutes more.

5. Transfer the dough to the storage container or the bowl. Lightly drizzle the top of the dough with more of the water. Cover the container with the lid or the bowl tightly with beeswax wrap.
   Let sit at room temperature for 1 hour.

6. If the dough is in a storage container, with slightly damp hands, pat the dough into a rectangle and fold from the top and then the bottom like a business letter. Slide both hands under the dough and fold from left then right like a letter.
   If the dough is in a bowl, the dough can be folded like a letter as above in the bowl or turned out onto a damp work surface for folding.
   Add a little of the water to the bowl and dough as needed to keep the dough from sticking. Cover and let rest at room temperature for 1 hour.

7. Fold from top to bottom and then left to right. Let rest at room temperature for 5 to 6 hours. (If you used yeast, the rise will be more like 3 hours.)

RECIPE CONTINUES

8. Lightly dust the work surface with bread flour.

To preshape the dough into a round, gather the edges and bring them together to make a round bundle. Turn the dough seam side down. Cup your hands over the round, making tight circles as you bring the round toward you, bringing any rough pieces of dough underneath. Continue until the round is smooth and the top is taut. Dust the top with flour and cover with a clean kitchen towel. Let sit for 10 minutes.

To shape the boule, repeat the steps taken for the preshaping, cupping your hands over the ball and then moving them in tight circles to create a tight ball with a taut skin around it. Roll the boule in the sesame seeds, if using. Transfer seam side up to a banneton dusted with flour or to a medium bowl lined with a kitchen towel generously dusted with flour. Alternatively, line the basket or bowl with parchment paper (or even a hairnet) and transfer the boule seam side down.

Cover so the beeswax wrap is not pressed directly against the dough but is secure around the edges. Refrigerate overnight.

9. Remove the boule from the refrigerator. Cover with an inverted box or plastic tub and let sit at room temperature to warm up and proof until slightly pillowy, about 1½ hours.

10. Meanwhile, set up the oven: Position one oven rack on the lowest rung and the other in the center.

If using a Dutch oven, set it on the center rack.

If using a stone or steel, set it on the center rack and set a cast-iron skillet on the lower rack.

Preheat the oven to 400°F (205°C).

11. If using a stone or steel, close to baking time, fill a medium bowl with about 1 cup of ice cubes to have ready to add to the skillet to create steam.

Carefully turn the boule onto a peel (or lift the boule still on the parchment onto the peel). Dust with flour and then with a lame, a single-edged razor blade, or a serrated knife, score the loaf with two cuts in an X pattern.

Slide the boule onto the stone or steel, pour the ice cubes into the skillet to produce steam, and close the door.

If using a Dutch oven, use heavy-duty oven mitts or potholders to remove the Dutch oven from the oven. Place it on a heatproof surface and remove the lid.

Carefully turn the boule onto a peel (or lift the boule still on the parchment onto the peel). Dust with flour and then with a lame, a single-edged razor blade, or a serrated knife, score the loaf with two cuts in an X pattern. Set the boule in the Dutch oven.

Return the lid to the Dutch oven and the Dutch oven to the center rack.

If baking on a stone or steel, bake until the loaf is a rich golden brown, about 40 minutes.

If baking in a Dutch oven, bake with the lid on for 35 minutes. Remove the lid and bake for 5 minutes more.

12. Transfer to a wire rack and let cool completely.

24-Hour Slow-Baked Pumpernickel

Before I went to Germany, my idea of pumpernickel rye was the brown bread served at Jewish delis in Buffalo. The color in that bread comes from molasses or cocoa powder and food coloring. At a bakery called Prünte, in Münsterland, that was known for traditional pumpernickel bread, the sixth-generation baker showed me his special ovens designed to bake pumpernickel breads at low temperatures for 24 hours. It's the full day in the oven that precipitates a Maillard reaction, giving the bread its distinctive brown color and caramelized flavor. The key to success at home is wrapping the pan tightly with oiled aluminum foil, allowing the bread to steam and not dry out. Before placing the loaf in the oven, check to make sure that your oven is no higher than 250°F (120°C). A higher temperature will result in a dry bread.

Makes 1 loaf, about 1.2 kilograms

Start to finish: about 37 hours

Gathering ingredients and preparing the soaker and starter, day one: 20 minutes

Proofing the starter: 8 hours or up to overnight

Gathering ingredients and mixing the dough, day two: 1½ hours

Resting the dough: 3 hours

Baking: 24 hours

Cooling: At least 8 hours

Ingredients	Metric
CRACKED RYE SOAKER	
cracked rye	75 g
boiling water	125 g
CRACKED RYE STARTER	
cracked rye	160 g
boiling water	200 g
Firm Sourdough Starter (page 100)	8 g
COOKED RYE BERRIES	
rye berries	120 g
water	175 g
FINAL DOUGH	
cracked rye	265 g
water (70° to 78°F / 21° to 25.5°C)	200 g, plus more as needed
fine sea salt	10 g
vegetable oil, for brushing the loaf pan	

RECIPE CONTINUES

1. **PREPARE THE CRACKED RYE SOAKER:** In a small bowl, weigh the cracked rye and the boiling water. Stir to combine. Cover the bowl tightly, preferably with beeswax wrap. Let sit at room temperature for 8 hours.

2. **PREPARE THE CRACKED RYE STARTER:** Meanwhile, in the bowl of a stand mixer or in a large bowl, weigh the cracked rye and the boiling water. Stir to combine and let cool slightly. Add the sourdough starter and mix until well incorporated. Cover the bowl tightly, preferably with beeswax wrap. Let sit at room temperature for 8 hours or up to overnight.

3. **COOK THE RYE BERRIES:** Weigh the rye berries and the water in an Instant Pot and cook on High for 35 minutes, followed by a natural release. Alternatively, combine the rye berries and water in a saucepan, cover, and bring to a simmer. Cook, adding water as needed to keep the berries covered until very tender, about 1 hour 15 minutes. Drain and let cool completely.

4. Very lightly brush the inside of a rectangular plastic storage container with a lid or a large bowl with water.

5. **MAKE THE FINAL DOUGH:** In the stand mixer bowl or large bowl with the cracked rye starter, add the cracked rye, 100 g of the water, and the salt. Add the cracked rye soaker and the cooked rye berries. Fit the mixer with the paddle attachment and mix on medium-low speed (or with a spatula if in a large bowl), adding the remaining 100 g water as needed (you may not need the entire 100 g) until well blended, 3 to 4 minutes. The mixture will be grainy and should have the consistency of a thick porridge.

    Transfer the dough to the storage container or the bowl. Lightly drizzle the top of the dough with water. Cover the container with the lid or the bowl tightly with beeswax wrap. Let sit at room temperature for 1½ hours. The dough will soften a bit and the surface will be porous with small holes.

6. Brush a traditional loaf pan, 8½ by 4½ by 2½ inches (21.5 by 10 by 6 cm), lightly with oil.

7. Add the dough to the prepared pan, spreading it until it is smooth with no gaps. Cover the top tightly with a lightly oiled piece of aluminum foil, the oiled side facing the loaf. Tightly wrap the entire pan with a second piece of foil.

   Let sit at room temperature for 1½ hours.

8. Preheat the oven to 250°F (120°C).

9. Bake the bread for 24 hours. It will be a darkly caramelized brownish-red color.

10. Transfer the pan to a wire rack for about 15 minutes. Carefully turn out and then let cool completely on the rack for at least 8 hours and up to 24 hours. Remove the foil before serving.

6.

GREAT GRAINS AND LOCAL LOAVES

100% Whole Wheat Sourdough, PAGE 147

I 'VE ALWAYS CONSIDERED MYSELF A LOCAL baker. My home in the rustic Catskills influenced the kinds of rustic breads we baked; we often adjusted our menu to the changing tastes and needs of our local customer base. Bread Alone shops and cafes became community hangouts. We cultivated relationships with local farmers and bought their pumpkins, corn, and herbs for our pies, muffins, and focaccia. But until recently I couldn't claim that our flour came from wheat grown in our home state.

When Bread Alone opened in 1983, my focus was solely on purchasing organic flour that baked flavorful, distinctive breads. Like many others of my generation, I had been greatly influenced by *Diet for a Small Planet* by Frances Moore Lappé and wanted to help people make healthy, plant-based eating choices that would also be healthy for the environment and our society. At that time, there were so few organic suppliers that when you found a reliable one, you were thrilled. For the first few years, we bought our flour from Little Bear Trading, an organic foods company with a mill in western Wisconsin that had exclusive contracts with a handful of organic farmers and sent a truck loaded with flour to the East Coast every two weeks. I connected with the company's independent organics certifier (at that time, there was no government agency that did this work; the USDA began its organic certi-

fication program in 2002) and met a few of those farmers, all of them located in cold and faraway places like Wyoming, Montana, and North Dakota. Wheat for bread in the US seemed limited to a few hard red spring varieties grown in the northern plains. No one—not farmers, not millers, not bakers—spoke about wheat with any more specificity than this.

As the interest in organic foods began to grow in the early '90s, so too did our options. Several premium mills, including Heartland Mills in Kansas, Central Milling in Utah, Natural Way Mills in Minnesota, and Lindley Mills in North Carolina, began milling and marketing organic grain. Instead of struggling just to find suppliers, we began to have choices. It seemed like a small miracle.

Farmers and millers were also responding to a small but growing wave of interest in artisan baking. The Bread Bakers Guild of

America was founded in 1993. Master French baker Didier Rosada was hired by Bay State Milling and then as the guild's first baking instructor, and nearly single-handedly trained a new generation of American bakers in French baking techniques and recipes. I remember attending a class with maybe twenty baby bakers like myself at Steve Sullivan's Acme Bread Company in San Francisco, with Raymond Calvel, the legendary baking teacher, who discussed with us the importance of protein *quality* over *quantity* in flour when fermenting sourdough breads for a long stretch of time. Bakers zealously began talking about the differences between European and American flours, spring wheat versus winter wheat, and what kind of extraction rates and ash contents were better for baking authentic baguettes and Poilâne-style miches. Millers like Nicky Giusto at Central Milling began offering European-style flours ground from hard winter wheat, like their Type 85, an almost whole wheat flour with just 15 percent of the bran sifted out. Even General Mills got into the game, advertising their Harvest King flour as a hard winter wheat flour with the strength, tolerance, and extensibility necessary for making slow-fermented breads.

Local Wheat

As time went by, we gradually transitioned to buying some grain grown a little closer to home. In 2000, I was visiting a bunch of French bakers who had immigrated to Montreal when I discovered, through some of them, La Milanaise, a flour mill in the Quebec province. Its founder, Robert Beauchemin, had responded to local demand by stone-grinding organic Canadian-grown wheat in the French style. Robert became one of our primary millers, custom milling wheat to our specifications. Around the same time, we started sourcing organic Pennsylvania spelt flour from Small Valley Milling, outside Lancaster.

It wasn't until relatively recently that we baked with New York State grain. In the late 1990s, a few local farmers began sowing wheat with names like Red Fife and Redeemer, varieties that had had some success in the area before wheat farming moved West in the early twentieth century. One of these farmers, Thor Oechsner, got his start growing feed grain for the organic dairy industry, with four hundred acres in production in Newfield, New York. Gradually expanding his acreage, he transitioned around 2008 to growing heritage grain for craft bakers and brewers. Realizing that he'd have to mill his own grain in order to sell it locally, he partnered with novice millers Greg Russo, Erick Smith, and Neal Johnston to construct a small stone-milling operation called Farmer Ground Flour. In 2010, in support of farmers like Thor and to build demand for New York State grains, the Greenmarket began requiring participating bakers to use a minimum of 15 percent local grain in our breads. The Greenmarket was a long-standing Bread Alone partner, we love selling bread on the streets of New York, and we were game to provide them with the "local" bread they wanted.

The back-to-the-lander in me was intrigued by the idea of using the same varieties of wheat that had been grown in the Hudson Valley in the eighteenth and nineteenth centuries, but I have to admit I was initially skeptical that a tiny upstart could mill flour to the same standard as an experienced operation like La Milanaise. To determine Farmer Ground flour's quality, we baked test loaves of our signature whole wheat sourdough bread with the flour we had been using, and with the local flour, side by side every day over the course of several weeks. It was clear that the product was world class. By modern artisan milling standards, Farmer Ground was and is at present a very small mill with limited output. We bought what we could from them to meet the Greenmarket's minimum requirement for local grain in baked goods, which increased to 25 percent in 2019. Today we buy 100 percent of our spelt from local sources and keep increasing our use of locally grown wheat and rye from La Milanaise, Farmer Ground, and Small Valley Farms at our new climate-neutral bakery in Boiceville (which accounts for an increasing quantity of Bread Alone's total bread output).

June Russell, who spearheaded the GrowNYC Grains initiative when she was at the Greenmarket, is thrilled with what she calls the initiative's "proof of concept." New York State farms are growing good wheat varieties, bakers are making beautiful breads, and Greenmarket customers are buying them at the price point that bakers need. But there's still much to be done. "Through the early years, it was a luxury to prime the market. Today it's a necessity. We now understand we need to decentralize our food system for greater resilience and to increase opportunities for farmers to diversify their crops," says June.

Local wheat is still a decidedly boutique and limited option for professional bakers. In 2021, there were 125,000 acres of wheat planted in New York, accounting for about 2 percent of the farmland in the state. Compare that to the tens of millions of acres of wheat fields in North Dakota, Kansas, and Montana that supply most of the US with wheat. While small bakeries that produce a couple hundred loaves a day, like Backdoor Bread in Charlotte, Vermont, or Wide Awake Bakery in Trumansburg, New York, might be able to bake exclusively with local heritage flours, there is simply not enough of it to supply a larger craft bakery like Bread Alone. The infrastructure—which would consist of a community of farmers, adequate grain storage, a research facility with grain scientists and lab equipment for wheat testing, a large local mill with trained staff, and government and private incentives and support—doesn't yet exist. But June, who is now the director of regional food programs at the Glynwood Center for Regional Food and Farming, in the Hudson Valley, is optimistic. With strong advocacy and technical support of organizations like Glynwood, obvious opportunities for entrepreneurs and corporate partners in milling and farming, and consumers' growing desire to participate in a local food system that provides environmental resilience and regional economic prosperity, a vibrant local wheat-mill-bake system is around the corner.

The Northeast Grainshed and Beyond

When you start looking for them, you can find regional grain initiatives all over the US focused on expanding local wheat production. I recently joined the Northeast Grainshed steering committee to help assist them in their own mission to get local farmers to grow more wheat. The difficulty is in making local wheat farming a robust and economically significant movement. That's where local research organizations come in. Farmers who have grown corn or other animal feed in the past have to be convinced that wheat and other grains for human consumption can be grown successfully and profitably. With little or no experience growing wheat for bread, they need advice from agronomists on the types of wheat that might grow best on their land, the support of a local lab for testing the baking properties of their wheat, and guidance from experienced entrepreneurs in marketing this new product. There needs to be a place where people interested in the opportunity to mill these grains can learn how to do so. And bakers need advice on both how to bake with local flour and how to build healthy bakery businesses in their communities.

Hartwick College in Oneonta, New York,

has already had great success in providing similar resources to the brewing and distilling community here on the East Coast. In 2014, taking advantage of grants from the Appalachian Regional Commission, and an incentive from the Empire State Development Corporation, the college hired Aaron MacLeod, a food science researcher who had been working with the Canadian Grain Commission in western Canada, and Harmonie Bettenhausen, a grain scientist from Colorado State University, to head its newly established Center for Craft Food & Beverage. The governor at the time had authorized incentives for farm brewers using local New York grains and hops, but MacLeod and Bettenhausen recognized that small farmers who had never grown grain for beer needed guidance and information to deliver a product that would meet craft brewers' and distillers' standards. Prior to the opening of the center, there was no fee-for-service testing available for malting barley in the Northeast. Now, farmers can go to Hartwick for such technical support and more. The labs at the center offer testing services for barley, malt, and hops as well as locally brewed beer. A staff of scientists provides advice to farmers and brewers. Leading researchers and brewing industry members regularly convene for conferences on barley improvement and professional development events like the Microbiology of Brewing Symposium. Currently, the center has about six hundred clients: three hundred farmers, one hundred malt houses, and two hundred breweries and distilleries. The center has been instrumental in helping the New York State craft brewing community grow from 95 breweries in 2012 to 504 in 2021.

As I write, Hartwick is organizing the launch of its brand-new Grain Innovation Center (I have been serving as the center's interim director while a search for a permanent director is undertaken). The mission is similar to that of the Center for Craft Food & Beverage—to provide farmers with an assessment of the quality of wheat cultivars for whole-grain milling and baking and also to support the growth of small milling and baking businesses across the state. "It all starts with getting good wheat grown," says Aaron. "Quality is key. There's not a lot of access to local wheat right now. Farmers need to be made aware of the value add for local grain, and the potential demand for it locally." Millers and bakers need a place where they can connect with farmers as well as educational resources for working with local grain and help in starting and running profitable shops.

With a local research facility taking the lead not only in testing grain but in helping farmers, millers, and bakers develop their businesses, the regional grain economy can only gain steam. It is our hope that as demand increases, public and private partners will step in to fund larger storage and milling facilities to provide local flour on a larger scale. As has manifested with farm and craft brewing and distilling, it is possible to imagine microbakeries popping up in small towns and cities around the state, contributing to the revitalization of New York's small business economy. And there's no reason why similar engines for local grain economies couldn't be established all over the country.

Noncommodity Wheat for Everybody

I have seen a lot of changes in the way Americans bake bread over the course of my career. But I think the most significant advance in recent years is the increasing availability of what I call noncommodity flour to anyone who wants it.

Consumers had few choices in the early 1980s when I first started baking. There was supermarket flour, milled by large companies like General Mills from wheat purchased on the commodity market from farms across the Midwest. And there was whole wheat flour from the health-food store, which was sold from bins and whose provenance was murky but was most likely also a commodity product. "Sometime about one hundred years ago," says Greg Russo of Farmer Ground Flour, "we decided to concentrate the grain economy elsewhere, and told ourselves that wheat couldn't be grown outside the Great Plains." But that was never really true, and especially not today. "We have the sophistication and technology," says Greg, to make wheat farming entirely manageable in most parts of the country.

As interest in the healthfulness and flavor of flour grew, along with an appreciation for organics and sustainability, small farmers and partner millers from Maine to California began to work together to provide an alternative—noncommodity wheat grown for a specific mill, milled and sold directly from that mill to both professional bakers and individual consumers. Operating outside the conventional food system, these small farmers were able to grow and test wheat varieties specifically chosen for their baking qualities, using organic and sustainable methods, knowing that there was a nearby mill that would buy their crop and bakers who would want this flour. In general, noncommodity white flour is less refined and more rustic. These flours taste different because they are generally stone-ground and have been milled relatively recently. Using this flour will not only be good for your bread, it will also support your local food system, which is good for the local environment and the local economy.

A little bit of research turns up at least one small mill in almost every state of the union. For freshly milled flour near you, consult the list on page 356 and the internet—because after a century of decline, small milling is a growing and thriving industry. Many of these mills are also good sources for whole grains for home milling.

Commodity flour is a blend of a variety of wheats, chosen to produce a consistent product from bag to bag, year after year. Noncommodity local flour lacks this consistency. Don't be taken aback if your trusty bread recipe doesn't give you the same results that you've gotten when you've used commercial flour, even if it's a high-quality organic bag from King Arthur or Bob's Red

Mill. Likewise, don't be surprised when you get different results with each bag of local flour that you buy, since the contents are milled from different harvests, from different farms, and at different times. Still, there are techniques you can use and signs you can look out for to produce good bread with every batch of local flour that you buy.

During stone milling, larger particles of bran can be sifted away, but smaller particles will remain. This type of sifted flour, often called "high-extraction" flour, is a sandy-brown color rather than the snowy-white product available from big flour companies. (A higher extraction rate actually means that less bran is removed from the flour during milling.) Fragments of bran and germ in the flour will disrupt gluten development to a certain extent, giving you a tighter, less-open crumb than you'd get with commodity flour, but generally these flours will absorb more water, which helps create moist, delicious, and flavorful breads. When using local stone-ground flour, you'll want to pay special attention to the steps that will encourage gluten to form: folding the dough periodically, preshaping it before final shaping. But it's also important to adjust your expectations. What you might lose in lightness, you will gain in fresh and distinctive flavor and memorable texture.

While your freshly milled flour (your local noncommodity flour will most certainly be relatively fresh) will generally absorb more water than commodity flour, it might take longer to do so. Your dough might feel sticky and slack initially, but after an autolyse of at least 30 minutes, it will have absorbed what at first seemed like too much liquid. This is where your developing soft skills (see page 38) and knowledge of techniques like bassinage (see page 188) will help you out. It will take some experience to know if and when to add more water to your dough so that it is properly but not overly hydrated.

You also might notice that your bread ferments more quickly when it contains local flour, which is rich in nutrients and enzymes. Keep a careful eye on the dough as it rises, and think about letting it ferment slowly in the refrigerator rather than on the countertop for a few hours, which will also encourage gluten development and proper hydration without the risk of the dough breaking down and losing its strength.

If you are new to local flour, it's okay to start gradually, using 10 to 20 percent noncommodity flour along with your regular bread flour. A small amount will give your bread a flavor boost without affecting the way the dough behaves. With subsequent bakes, experiment with adding greater percentages, while keeping in mind previous results.

Finally, keep your noncommodity flour in the freezer, to prevent the healthy oils in the germ from going rancid.

100% Whole Wheat Sourdough

I have been drawn to 100 percent whole wheat breads since I began baking. Their pure wheat flavor, combined with their healthfulness, has always lured me in. The challenge has been baking a loaf that has a lightness to it and a broad appeal. Whole wheat breads are never going to have the big, bubbly texture of breads made with white flour. But with some extra care, it is possible to make a very well-risen loaf with a beautiful honeycomb interior.

As local stone mills have proliferated, offering stone-ground whole wheat flour to a larger public, I was determined to develop a local whole wheat loaf with superb flavor and enviable structure for this book. It would have been easier if I'd chosen flour from a big mill like King Arthur, which would have been stronger and more finely milled, guaranteeing my bread good volume. But I was up for the challenge of working with less-predictable local noncommodity flour, ready to use my "soft skills" to evaluate my dough at every stage and learn from each bake what my dough required.

As I had anticipated, it took me four tries to achieve the result I wanted. Right off the bat, I knew I'd need a higher-protein flour to get the gluten development that I wanted, so I chose a whole wheat flour from Maine Grains with 12 percent protein. Anything less would have given me a dough too fragile to rise sufficiently. My first try, with 80 percent hydration, had respectable wheat flavor, but landed a bit heavy. Although the dough, which I had slowly kneaded in the mixer for 10 minutes, seemed soft, I was determined to get more water into it to produce more bubbles and thus more lift.

After autolyse, I mixed the starter and then the salt into the dough and kneaded on low until the salt was distributed, about 5 minutes. Then with the mixer on low, I slowly drizzled another 20 grams of water into the bowl, a few drops at a time, until it was completely absorbed, about 8 minutes total. Finally, I turned the mixer to medium and kneaded for another 2 minutes, to smooth out the dough. I was surprised at how much extra water I was able to add when I did it this way. The texture of the dough was velvety and extensible.

Not only was the flavor of the bread enhanced, but the rise and structure were impressive for a whole wheat loaf. As an added benefit, the bread made with more water stayed fresh an additional few days.

If you are making this recipe with flour from your own local mill, keep in mind those soft skills that I discussed starting on page 38. Your flour will undoubtedly behave slightly, or even vastly, differently from mine, so adjust your response to it accordingly. And keep trying. The rewards of learning how to make bread with noncommodity flour make the process worthwhile.

RECIPE CONTINUES

Start to finish: **3 days**

Gathering ingredients
and preparing the
starter, day one:
10 minutes

Proofing the starter:
overnight

Gathering ingredients,
autolyse, and mixing
the dough, day two:
2 hours 40 minutes

Folding, proofing, and
resting the dough:
7 hours

Refrigerating the dough:
overnight

Proofing, day three:
1½ hours

Baking: **40 minutes**

Ingredients	Metric
WHOLE WHEAT STARTER, DAY ONE	
whole wheat flour	100 g
water (70° to 78°F / 21° to 25.5°C)	70 g
Firm Sourdough Starter (page 100)	20 g
DOUGH, DAY TWO	
whole wheat flour	500 g, plus more for dusting
water (70° to 78°F / 21° to 25.5°C)	420 g
fine sea salt	10 g

1. **PREPARE THE WHOLE WHEAT STARTER:** In the bowl of a stand mixer, weigh the whole wheat flour, water, and sourdough starter. Fit the mixer with the paddle attachment and mix on medium-low speed until well incorporated. Remove the bowl from the mixer and knead, while still in the bowl, a few times by hand. This is a stiff starter. Transfer to a small bowl and cover tightly, preferably with beeswax wrap. Let sit at room temperature overnight.

2. **FOR THE AUTOLYSE:** In the bowl of a stand mixer, weigh the whole wheat flour and 400 g of the water and mix with the paddle attachment until a dough forms. Cover and let stand for 2 hours.

3. Very lightly brush the inside of a rectangular plastic storage container with a lid or a large bowl with water.

4. **MAKE THE FINAL DOUGH:** Add the whole wheat starter to the dough. Switch to the dough hook and mix on low to medium-low speed until incorporated, about 4 minutes.

   Add the salt to the bowl and mix on low to medium-low speed until the salt is distributed and the dough isn't as soft, about 5 minutes. Check the dough carefully to see how developed the gluten is. It should feel elastic but still with a degree of firmness and strength to it. With the mixer on low speed, slowly drizzle the remaining 20 g water into the bowl, a few drops at a time, until it is completely absorbed, about 8 minutes total. Increase the speed to medium and mix for 2 minutes, allowing the dough to develop a velvety texture. At this point, the dough will be soft and delicate.

5. Transfer the dough to the storage container or the bowl. Cover the container with the lid or the bowl tightly with beeswax wrap. Let sit at room temperature for 1 hour.

6. If the dough is in a storage container, with slightly damp hands, pat the dough into a rectangle and fold from the top and then the bottom like a business letter. Slide both hands under the dough and fold from left then right like a letter.

   If the dough is in a bowl, the dough can be folded like a letter as above in the bowl or turned out onto a damp work surface for folding.

   Add a little water only as needed to keep the dough from sticking. Cover and let rest at room temperature for 1 hour.

7. Fold from top to bottom and then left to right and let rest at room temperature for 1 hour.

8. Fold from top to bottom and then left to right a second time and let rest at room temperature for 1 hour.

9. Repeat the folds for a fourth time and let rest at room temperature for 3 hours.

10. To preshape the dough, gather the edges and bring them together to make a round bundle. Turn the dough seam side down. Cup your hands over the round, making tight circles as you bring the round toward you, bringing any rough pieces of dough underneath. Continue until the round is smooth and the top is taut. Dust the top with flour and cover with a clean kitchen towel. Let sit for 10 minutes.

11. To shape into a bâtard, turn the round seam side up and gently press out any air bubbles, while pressing and stretching the dough into a rectangular shape. Fold the bottom half of the dough up and over about two-thirds of the dough, then fold the top down to cover the first fold completely. Press along the bottom edge of the dough to seal.

    Turn the dough, now in a log shape, seam side down. Place your hands together, palms down, in the middle of the log. Using light, even pressure, roll the log back and forth as you spread your hands apart.

RECIPE CONTINUES

Repeat two or three times until the bâtard is the desired length, tapering the ends by increasing downward pressure at the tips.

Dust a linen or large kitchen towel with flour and place it on top of a baking sheet. Set the bâtard on the baking sheet (for ease of moving it into the refrigerator to rest overnight). Gather the linen gently against the sides of the bâtard, using rolling pins or even rolled kitchen towels to support the sides.

Cover so the beeswax wrap is not pressed directly against the dough but is secure around the edges. Refrigerate overnight.

12. Remove the bâtard from the refrigerator. Cover with an inverted box or plastic tub and let sit at room temperature to warm up and proof until slightly pillowy, about 1½ hours.

13. Meanwhile, set up the oven: Position one oven rack on the lowest rung and the other in the center.

If using a cast-iron baking pan with a lid, set it on the center rack.

If using a stone or steel, set it on the center rack and set a cast-iron skillet on the lower rack.

Preheat the oven to 500°F (260°C).

14. If using a stone or steel, close to baking time, fill a medium bowl with about 1 cup of ice cubes to have ready to add to the skillet to create steam.

Carefully turn the bâtard onto a transfer peel and then a baking peel. Dust generously with whole wheat flour. With a lame, a single-edged razor blade, or a serrated knife, score the loaf: Position the lame at the top of the loaf, about 1 inch (2.5 cm) off center. Make one long, straight slash to the bottom.

Slide the bâtard onto the stone or steel, pour the ice cubes into the skillet to produce steam, and close the door.

If using a cast-iron baking pan with a lid, use heavy-duty oven mitts or potholders to remove the pan from the oven. Place it on a heatproof surface and remove the lid.

Carefully turn the bâtard onto a transfer peel and then a baking peel. Dust generously with whole wheat flour. With a lame, a single-edged razor blade, or a serrated knife, score the loaf: Position the lame at the top of the loaf, about 1 inch (2.5 cm) off center. Make one long, straight slash to the bottom. Slide the bâtard into the pan.

Return the lid to the pan and the pan to the center rack.

15. For both baking methods, bake at 500°F (260°C) for 20 minutes.

If baking on the stone or steel, after 20 minutes, without opening the oven, lower the oven temperature to 450°F (230°C) and bake until the loaf is a rich golden brown, slightly darker where scored, about 20 minutes more.

If baking in the cast-iron pan, after 20 minutes, lower the oven temperature to 450°F (230°C), remove the lid, and bake until the loaf is a rich golden brown, slightly darker where scored, about 20 minutes more.

16. Transfer to a wire rack and let cool completely.

7.

BEYOND WHEAT AND RYE

SOURDOUGH BREADS MADE WITH FERMENTED GRAINS, SEEDS, AND LEGUMES

Chickpea and
Wheat Bran–Fermented Boule

———

Seeded Bread from Local Fields

———

Hearty Seeded Sandwich Loaf

———

Fermented Wheat Bran
and Barley Épis with Beet

Chickpea and Wheat Bran–Fermented Boule, PAGE 160

WHEN I FIRST BEGAN TO BAKE BREAD, even before we opened Bread Alone, I chose organic whole-grain flours specifically for the health benefits they conferred. Rich in fiber, B vitamins, minerals, and essential fatty acids, and free of any traces of herbicides and pesticides, organic whole-grain bread as part of a healthy diet has been proven to lower the risk of many diseases, including diabetes, heart disease, stroke, and cancer.

As years and decades passed, and organic whole grains became our bakery's baseline, we turned our focus to getting the most out of them by using European artisan techniques. Sourdough starters, long fermentation times, and higher levels of hydration have all contributed to the great texture and flavor of our products. Many of these techniques were borrowed from bakers who had been selected as Meilleurs Ouvriers de France, a government designation identifying master craftspeople at the highest level. When I visited Amandio Pimenta in the Auvergne region of France, he explained how long fermentation is what gives his traditional white *couronne* great character and complexity. From Pierre Nury, also a master baker in the Auvergne, I saw how a dough so wet that it was almost pourable could be quickly stretched and baked to produce a re-

markably bubbly rye bread. In Alsace, I tasted the late Roland Herzog's green garlic bread, a light rye made with a sourdough starter that was midway in texture between liquid and stiff.

I had long considered these bakers to be upholders of tradition, and they certainly did that, baking authentic regional breads with local stone-ground flour. But I recently learned that they had joined forces with other Meilleurs Ouvriers to form a cutting-edge organization called Les Ambassadeurs du Pain. Les Ambassadeurs promotes a new kind of sourdough technique, formulated specifically to unlock the nutritional potential in bread dough. Christian Rémésy, a former director of research at the National Institute of Agricultural Research in Paris and also a member of Les Ambassadeurs, has become the voice of the group on this technique, explaining the reasons for using fermented seeds and pulses, rather than fermented wheat flour, to raise bread:

It is clear that wheat has become hegemonic in breadmaking because its particularly effective gluten does a great job in helping dough rise and because it has an excellent agronomic yield. However, pulses and small seeds of very diverse botanical origins have much higher levels of proteins, vitamins and essential fatty acids than those of wheat, not to mention their greater wealth of antioxidants or various micronutrients. The fact that the great biodiversity of seeds available has been so little used in modern food comes simply from a lack of know-how and an insufficient awareness of the great nutritional value of the group as a whole.

In addition to nutritional value, this starter adds as many new flavors as your imagination and pantry will allow. The recipe is simple: coarsely grind 200 grams of mixed seeds (sunflower, flax, pumpkin, sesame, hemp, poppy), grains (rye, barley, oats, corn), pseudograins (buckwheat, quinoa, rice), and pulses (chickpeas, fava beans, lentils) in your home mill; stir the mixture together with 250 grams of nearly boiling water and 3 grams of active sourdough culture; cover; and let it sit for 24 hours. The amount of culture added to the seed and grain mixture is deliberately tiny, requiring an extra-long fermentation time that allows for enzymes to improve the bioavailability of all the micronutrients contained in the selection of seeds, grains, and pulses. The mixture won't rise, because it doesn't contain much wheat gluten. But it will ferment, producing multiplying colonies of yeast and lactobacilli that will be able to raise bread.

To make bread dough, combine the supplement with 800 grams of high-extraction wheat flour (see page 145), 350 to 400 grams of water, and 5 grams of salt (an unusually small amount for this weight of dough, but all that is necessary, because the nutritional supplement adds so much flavor), and let ferment for 5 hours before shaping, proofing, and baking.

Extra-long fermentation is nothing new, but using fermented seeds and pulses as a leavener was something I had never seen and had to try. The science is compellingly explained in Les Ambassadeurs' books, which are available in French and English. Simply adding seeds to bread dough will give bread a higher fiber content but won't necessarily make it more nutritious, since the nutrients in those seeds are difficult for the body to access. During long fermentation, though, the phytases in sourdough break down component phytic acids in what Les Ambassadeurs have named *fermented nutritional supplements*, making the vitamins and minerals contained in these ingredients entirely bioavailable. The calcium, magnesium, and potassium in chickpeas; the manganese in flax; the folate in millet: all of these can be absorbed after they are fermented. Each of Les Ambassadeurs' experimental breads has been analyzed in the lab to make sure that this is the case.

The breads are not light in style like many popular sourdough loaves we see now. They have a dense, rich texture and are deeply satisfying to eat. And then there is the very attractive environmental component to this practice: varying the grains and seeds we use in bread can contribute to maintaining the agricultural biodiversity that is essential to the ecological health of our planet.

I was so intrigued by this idea that I flew to the group's baking center in Les Herbiers, not far from Nantes, to participate in a three-day workshop—held monthly and taught by a rotating roster of master bakers—on fermented nutritional supplements. The nondescript warehouse contained a simple but incredibly well-organized bakeshop, where I met my teacher, Thomas Planchot, and just two other students: one a longtime baker getting ready to take his Meilleurs Ouvriers de France qualifying exam, and the other a younger Parisian pastry chef who wanted to add healthier breads to her shop menu.

The morning of day one was spent learning about the history and core values of Les Ambassadeurs. In general, French people are eating less bread than they used to, and the bread that they do eat is less nutritious than it used to be, containing fewer whole grains and frequently raised with commercial yeast rather than sourdough. As the providers of a fundamental food, one that has a profound importance in French culture, these bakers considered it their responsi-

bility, in the face of an increasingly industrialized bread business, to promote and provide healthful loaves to the population. In conversations with grain scientists and nutritionists, they began to understand that even if they continued to make wonderful handmade breads from sifted wheat flour, those breads would always have a limited nutritional value. Even high-extraction wheat flour has had some of its nutritional components stripped away during sifting. Wheat flour would never have the essential amino acids found in chickpea flour, nor would it be as rich in lignans and omega-3 fatty acids as flaxseed. To create a protein- and nutrient-rich bread, they came up with the idea of the fermented nutritional supplement, partnered with nutritionists who tested their formulas, and a new style of baking was born. I've often said that when it comes to bread, there is nothing new under the sun, but that week in June I was proven wrong.

Thomas was serious about showing us the variety of breads that might be made with different fermented nutritional supplements. That afternoon, we made the supplements, twelve in total, using an astounding variety of ingredients. As skilled as any baker in the world, Thomas was a whirlwind of activity, demonstrating how to make these starters. We used rice bran, barley, quinoa, spelt bran, pine nuts, corn flour, chia, teff, ground chickpeas, mung beans, goji berries, and even banana flour in our starters. Some of them contained a proportion of whole seeds to give the finished breads some texture. Others were ground in a countertop mill so they were uniformly but still only roughly pulverized. To each supplement we added a minute amount—I'm talking 3 grams—of ripe sourdough. And then we covered them and allowed them to ferment until the next day.

First thing on day two, we inspected our supplements. They didn't double in volume like sourdough starters made with wheat flour. But they had the distinctive aroma that comes from the development of yeast and lactic acids. In the afternoon we combined them with dough ingredients and let the doughs ferment overnight. On day three we baked, producing some of the most distinctively flavored breads I've ever had. One of the loaves, raised with a ground lentil starter, had the mildly sour flavor of an Indian dosa. Another, a baguette that included barley and bran in its starter, had a subtly nutty flavor. These were remarkably and uniquely grain-, seed-, and legume-forward breads. I've eaten German rye breads packed with seeds, but the seeds in these breads were softer and better incorporated into the doughs. Because these breads were raised with such a tiny amount of sourdough, they had a much milder sourdough flavor, allowing the flavors of the grains and seeds to really shine.

Just as striking was the attitude of our instructor, which was far different from the usual authoritarianism of the typical French artisan. Rather than giving us exact formulas and instructions for these breads and expecting us to follow them to the letter, Thomas encouraged us to look at the huge palette of colors and textures and shapes that we might work with to create our own custom whole-grain breads outside his classroom. He suggested that we formulate our breads with our personal histories, health concerns, and local grain situations in mind.

The following recipes were inspired by the breads I baked in class with Thomas, and ones I read about in the three volumes published by Les Ambassadeurs so far.

The Mockmill Messenger

Ten years ago, when I first started hearing about bakers milling their own flour, I was pretty skeptical. I had visited many artisan mills in the US, Canada, France, and Italy over the years, and had seen firsthand how much care, experience, and nuance went into producing top-quality flour for consistently great bread. At Bread Alone, we figured we'd leave milling to the experts and stick with what we knew: baking.

Yet when I retired and dove back into amateur baking, I was immediately struck by how many passionate home bakers were milling their own grain and rhapsodizing about the breads they were making. I promptly bought a home mill to see what all the fuss was about. The instant I turned it on to process some recently harvested and cleaned wheat berries from Maine Grains, I was hit with the intense and lovely fragrance of wheat. I immediately understood the appeal of freshly milled grain.

Home milling seemed to me to have come out of nowhere in a matter of a couple of years. I got in touch with the people at Mockmill, the German company that has had so much success popularizing the practice, to understand its rapid rise and the diverse uses of the mill. I learned it had been thirty-five years in the making! I spoke with Paul Lebeau, described on the Mockmill website as a Mockmill missionary. The description is accurate. Paul is more than a salesman. He is a true believer in the importance of eating a variety of healthy, noncommodity grains. He described his journey from selling medical diagnostic technologies to selling home mills.

"I got into this seven years ago, after a thirty-year career introducing novel technologies to medical communities," Paul says. "It was my job to convince medical professionals to do things differently for the health of their patients." His friend

Wolfgang Mock, inventor of the mill that bears his name, had been trying for decades to convince people to mill their own flour, for their health as well as for the quality of their bread. Seeing that Paul had had so much success in convincing doctors to try innovative new tests for tuberculosis and cervical cancer, Wolfgang thought he might be able to convince bakers to try the Mockmill.

"I brought the mill to artisan baking experts all over the country, including people at the Bread Bakers Guild of America, and asked, 'What do you think? Can you bake with this flour?'" From the outset, professional bakers liked that the mill gave them full control over how much—or how little—they wanted to process their grain. The countertop mill could help bakers bake whole-grain breads. "We've come a long way from the way we used to make bread, using a variety of seeds and grains, ground whole," Paul explains. "Today, for the most part, we eat just a highly processed portion of one seed. The plurality of what we used to put in bread has gotten lost. Plant-based carbohydrates are best consumed together with the fibrous material that nature has always packaged them in."

Another advantage that pros identified was the ease with which a countertop mill allowed them to add a spectrum of grains, beans, and seeds to their breads, for the sake of both health and the environment. In addition to wheat, there was buckwheat, which has all nine essential amino acids. Grains like quinoa and amaranth, which grow well in hotter and drier conditions that are the result of climate change, mill beautifully. Beans, peas, lentils, and chickpeas can all be ground into flour and used in breads when wheat is in short supply. As long as you are baking with 75 percent wheat flour, you can add any other type of flour you can grind yourself—other cereal grains, beans, seeds—to make bread. "The home mill is a great tool if you are a creative baker," claims Paul. "Just let your imagination run wild." Milling at home is a way that consumers can take back the power to determine what they are eating, instead of remaining dependent on the commodity-based food industry.

As for myself, I've found my mill to be incredibly helpful in making multigrain and seed breads. I can easily get freshly milled noncommodity flour where I live in Maine. But what I can't easily get are small quantities of quinoa flour, corn flour, chickpea flour, and so many other grains that I have been especially eager to experiment with since I took a class with Les Ambassadeurs du Pain at their school in France.

Chickpea and
Wheat Bran–Fermented Boule

The idea of using ground chickpeas in a bread recipe initially sounded weird to me when I read about it in Les Ambassadeurs' first book. But then I remembered the dosas I ate in India, made with fermented lentil flour, which is rich in zinc and iron, and the idea of using legumes in bread suddenly intrigued me. And I love the flavor of chickpeas in traditional socca, the chickpea flour flatbread served in Provence. I was suddenly curious to find out what flavors fermented ground chickpeas would lend to bread. It turns out that the starter itself has an assertively nutty flavor that is tempered but definitely recognizable when added to the wheat flour in the dough. If you like the flavor of traditional socca, you will love this bread. This is a large loaf. If you'd prefer to bake two smaller rounds, just divide the dough in half equally before shaping and proceed as directed.

Makes 1 boule, about 1 kilogram

Start to finish: **2 days**

Gathering ingredients and preparing the starter, day one: **20 minutes**

Proofing the starter: **24 hours**

Gathering ingredients, autolyse, and mixing the dough, day two: **2 hours 20 minutes**

Folding, proofing, and shaping the dough: **6 hours**

Baking: **40 minutes**

Ingredients	Metric
FERMENTED CHICKPEA AND WHEAT BRAN STARTER	
freshly milled chickpeas	75 g
freshly milled wheat bran	15 g
warm water (120°F/50°C)	125 g
Sourdough Starter (page 98)	3 g
DOUGH	
whole wheat flour	350 g, plus more for dusting
bread flour	150 g
water (70° to 78°F / 21° to 25.5°C)	325 g
instant dry yeast (optional)	1 g
fine sea salt	5 g

1. PREPARE THE FERMENTED CHICKPEA AND WHEAT BRAN STARTER: In a small bowl, weigh the milled chickpeas, milled wheat bran, and warm water. Stir with a spatula to combine. Let cool slightly. Add the sourdough starter and mix until well incorporated. Cover the bowl tightly, preferably with beeswax wrap. Let sit at room temperature for 24 hours.

RECIPE CONTINUES

2. **FOR THE AUTOLYSE:** In the bowl of a stand mixer or in a large bowl, weigh the whole wheat flour, bread flour, and water. Mix with the paddle attachment (or with a spatula if in a large bowl) until a rough dough forms. Cover and let stand for 2 hours.

3. Very lightly brush the inside of a rectangular plastic storage container with a lid or a large bowl with water.

4. **MAKE THE FINAL DOUGH:** Add the fermented chickpea and wheat bran starter and the yeast, if using, to the bowl of the stand mixer or to the large bowl. Switch to the whisk attachment and mix on low speed or by hand with a spatula until incorporated, 3 to 4 minutes.

   Add the salt to the dough and mix (or fold if using the spatula) until it is distributed, about 3 minutes.

5. Transfer the dough to the storage container or the bowl. Lightly drizzle the top of the dough with water. Cover the container with the lid or the bowl tightly with beeswax wrap.

   Let sit at room temperature for 2 hours.

6. If the dough is in a storage container, with slightly damp hands, pat the dough into a rectangle and fold from the top and then the bottom like a business letter. Slide both hands under the dough and fold from left then right like a letter.

   If the dough is in a bowl, the dough can be folded like a letter as above in the bowl or turned out onto a damp work surface for folding.

   Add a little water to the bowl and dough as needed to keep the dough from sticking. Cover and let rest at room temperature for 2 hours.

7. Fold from top to bottom and then left to right. If at this point the dough still seems soft, cover and let rest for 1 hour more and repeat the folds.

   After the final fold, cover and let the dough rest for 30 minutes.

8. To preshape the dough into a round, gather the edges and bring them together to make a round bundle. Turn the dough seam side down. Cup your hands over the round, making tight circles as you bring the round toward you, bringing any rough pieces of dough underneath.

Continue until the round is smooth and the top is taut. Dust the top with flour and cover with a clean kitchen towel. Let sit for 10 minutes.

9. To shape the boule, repeat the steps taken for the preshaping, cupping your hands over the ball and then moving them in tight circles to create a tight ball with a taut skin around it. Transfer seam side up to a banneton generously dusted with whole wheat flour or to a medium bowl lined with a kitchen towel generously dusted with flour. Alternatively, line the basket or bowl with parchment paper (or even a hairnet) and transfer the boule seam side down.

Cover with an inverted box or plastic tub and let proof at room temperature until pillowy, about 1 hour.

10. Meanwhile, set up the oven: Position one oven rack on the lowest rung and the other in the center.

If using a Dutch oven, set it on the center rack.

If using a stone or steel, set it on the center rack and set a cast-iron skillet on the lower rack.

Preheat the oven to 500°F (260°C).

11. If using a stone or steel, close to baking time, fill a medium bowl with about 1 cup of ice cubes to have ready to add to the skillet to create steam.

Carefully turn the boule onto a peel (or lift the boule still on the parchment onto the peel). Dust with whole wheat flour and then with a lame, a single-edged razor blade, or a serrated knife, score the loaf with an X.

Slide the boule onto the stone or steel, pour the ice cubes into the skillet to produce steam, and close the door.

If using a Dutch oven, use heavy-duty oven mitts or potholders to remove the Dutch oven from the oven. Place it on a heatproof surface and remove the lid.

Carefully turn the boule onto a peel (or lift the boule still on the parchment onto the peel). Dust with whole wheat flour and then with a lame, a single-edged razor blade, or a serrated knife, score the loaf with an X. Set the boule in the Dutch oven.

Return the lid to the Dutch oven and the Dutch oven to the center rack.

RECIPE CONTINUES

12. For both baking methods, bake at 500°F (260°C) for 20 minutes.

   If baking on a stone or steel, after 20 minutes, lower the oven temperature to 450°F (230°C) and bake until the loaf is a rich golden brown, about 20 minutes more.

   If baking in a Dutch oven, after 20 minutes, lower the oven temperature to 450°F (230°C), remove the lid, and bake until the loaf is a rich golden brown, about 20 minutes more.

13. Transfer the loaf to a wire rack and let cool completely.

Seeded Bread from Local Fields

Farms all over the country are growing not only wheat but flax, buckwheat, and other small grains and seeds that are great for bread. I like to include corn flour, sunflower seeds, and whole millet from some of my favorite Maine farms in this loaf's starter. Use this recipe as a template, and substitute your own mixture of whole grains and seeds for a loaf with local flavor. This is a large loaf. If you'd prefer to bake two smaller bâtards, just divide the dough in half equally before shaping and proceed as directed.

Makes 1 bâtard, about 1.3 kilograms

Start to finish: **2 days**

Gathering ingredients and preparing the starter. day one: **20 minutes**

Proofing the starter: **overnight**

Gathering ingredients and mixing the dough, day two: **20 minutes**

Folding, proofing, and shaping the dough: **5½ to 6 hours**

Baking: **40 minutes**

Ingredients	Metric
FERMENTED MIXED GRAIN AND SEED STARTER	
freshly milled chickpeas	80 g
corn flour (masa harina)	50 g
buckwheat groats	40 g
sunflower seeds, lightly toasted	20 g
flaxseeds	20 g
pumpkin seeds	20 g
millet	20 g
warm water (120°F/50°C)	255 g
Sourdough Starter (page 98)	3 g
DOUGH	
bread flour	500 g, plus more for dusting
water (70° to 78°F / 21° to 25.5°C)	300 g
Sourdough Starter (page 98)	5 g
fine sea salt	10 g
mixed seeds, for rolling the dough	50 g

1. PREPARE THE FERMENTED MIXED GRAIN AND SEED STARTER: In a small bowl, weigh the milled chickpeas, corn flour, buckwheat groats, sunflower seeds, flaxseeds, pumpkin seeds, millet, and warm water. Stir with a spatula to combine. Let cool slightly. Add the sourdough starter and mix until well incorporated. Cover the bowl tightly, preferably with beeswax wrap. Let sit at room temperature overnight.

RECIPE CONTINUES

2. Very lightly brush the inside of a rectangular plastic storage container with a lid or a large bowl with water. (Since this is a soft dough, only add water as needed to keep from sticking throughout the folding process.)

3. **MAKE THE FINAL DOUGH:** Weigh the bread flour, water, additional sourdough starter, and salt into the bowl of the stand mixer or the large bowl. Switch to the whisk attachment and mix on low speed or by hand with a spatula until incorporated, 3 to 4 minutes. The dough will be soft.

4. Transfer the dough to the storage container or the bowl. Lightly drizzle the top of the dough with water. Cover the container with the lid or the bowl tightly with beeswax wrap.
    Let sit at room temperature for 1 hour.

5. If the dough is in a storage container, with slightly damp hands, pat the dough into a rectangle and fold from the top and then the bottom like a business letter. Slide both hands under the dough and fold from left then right like a letter.
    If the dough is in a bowl, the dough can be folded like a letter as above in the bowl or turned out onto a damp work surface for folding.
    Add a little water to the bowl and dough as needed to keep the dough from sticking. Cover and let rest at room temperature for 1 hour.

6. Fold from top to bottom and then left to right and let rest at room temperature for 1 hour.

7. Repeat the folds one more time and let rest at room temperature for 30 minutes.

8. Dust the work surface with flour.
    To preshape the dough, gather the edges and bring them together to make a round bundle. Turn the dough seam side down. Cup your hands over the round, making tight circles as you bring the round toward you, bringing any rough pieces of dough underneath. Continue until the round is smooth and the top is taut. Dust the top with flour and cover with a clean kitchen towel. Let sit for 10 minutes.

RECIPE CONTINUES

9. To shape into a bâtard, turn the round seam side up and gently press out any air bubbles, while pressing and stretching the dough into a rectangular shape. Fold the bottom half of the dough up and over about two-thirds of the dough, then fold the top down to cover the first fold completely. Press along the bottom edge of the dough to seal.

Turn the dough, now in a log shape, seam side down. Place your hands together, palms down, in the middle of the log. Using light, even pressure, roll the log back and forth as you spread your hands apart. Repeat two or three times until the bâtard is the desired length with slightly rounded, snub ends.

Spread the mixed seeds on a plate. Roll the bâtard in the seeds.

Set the bâtard on a flour-dusted linen or large kitchen towel. Gather the linen gently against the sides of the bâtard, using rolling pins or even rolled kitchen towels to support the sides.

Cover with an inverted box or plastic tub and let proof at room temperature until slightly pillowy, 1½ to 2 hours.

10. Meanwhile, set up the oven: Position one oven rack on the lowest rung and the other in the center.

If using a cast-iron baking pan with a lid, set it on the center rack.

If using a stone or steel, set it on the center rack and set a cast-iron skillet on the lower rack.

Preheat the oven to 500°F (260°C).

11. If using a stone or steel, close to baking time, fill a medium bowl with about 1 cup of ice cubes to have ready to add to the skillet to create steam.

Carefully turn the bâtard onto a transfer peel and then a baking peel. With a lame, a single-edged razor blade, or a serrated knife, score with one straight cut slightly off-center.

Slide the bâtard onto the stone or steel, pour the ice cubes into the skillet to produce steam, and close the door.

If using a cast-iron baking pan with a lid, use heavy-duty oven mitts or potholders to remove the pan from the oven. Place it on a heatproof surface and remove the lid.

Carefully turn the bâtard onto a transfer peel and then a baking peel. With a lame, a single-edged razor blade, or a serrated knife, score with one straight cut slightly off-center. Slide the bâtard into the pan.

Return the lid to the pan and the pan to the center rack.

12. Immediately for both methods, lower the oven temperature to 450°F (230°C).

If baking on the stone or steel, bake until the loaf is a rich golden brown, slightly darker where scored, about 40 minutes.

If baking in the cast-iron pan, bake for 20 minutes. Remove the lid and bake until the loaf is golden brown with caramel and dark caramel tones on the cut edges, about 20 minutes more.

13. Transfer to a wire rack and let cool completely.

Hearty Seeded Sandwich Loaf

I've been baking multigrain and seed loaves for many years. In this variation, the seeds exceed the flour in volume and are fermented before being added to the dough, to make available omega-3 fatty acids, antioxidants, and iron. Seven-grain mix is available from many specialty mills. I like the one from Maine Grains. This is a dough that requires patience and perseverance. In the early stages, it will test your confidence because it is so wet. Blending the soupy grain mixture with the autolyse flour takes some careful folding. The dough won't begin to feel cohesive until around the third fold but then will magically transform. Your effort will be rewarded with a remarkably flavorful and beautifully textured loaf.

Makes 1 loaf, about 900 grams

Start to finish: **2 days**

Gathering ingredients and preparing the starter, day one:
20 minutes

Proofing the starter:
24 hours

Gathering ingredients, autolyse, and mixing the dough, day two:
1½ hours

Folding, proofing, and shaping the dough:
8½ to 9 hours

Baking: **40 minutes**

Ingredients	Metric
FERMENTED MIXED GRAIN AND SEED STARTER	
7-grain mix	125 g
boiling water	150 g
Sourdough Starter (page 98)	3 g
DOUGH	
whole wheat flour	150 g
spelt flour	150 g
water (70° to 78°F / 21° to 25.5°C)	162 g
honey	40 g
additional Sourdough Starter (page 98)	50 g
instant dry yeast	0.5 g
fine sea salt	6 g
vegetable oil, for brushing the loaf pan	
pumpkin seeds, for pressing (optional)	50 g

1. **PREPARE THE FERMENTED MIXED GRAIN AND SEED STARTER:** In a small bowl, weigh the 7-grain mix and boiling water. Stir with a spatula to combine. Let cool slightly. Add the sourdough starter and mix until well incorporated. Cover the bowl tightly, preferably with beeswax wrap. Let sit for 24 hours.

RECIPE CONTINUES

2. **FOR THE AUTOLYSE:** In the bowl of a stand mixer or in a large bowl, weigh the whole wheat flour, spelt flour, and water. With the paddle attachment, mix on low speed or by hand with a spatula until incorporated, about 2 minutes. Cover and let stand for 1 hour.

3. Very lightly brush the inside of a rectangular plastic storage container with a lid or a large bowl with water. (Since this is a soft dough, add water only as needed to keep from sticking throughout the folding process.)

4. **MAKE THE FINAL DOUGH:** Break the dough into about 8 pieces in the bowl. Add the fermented mixed grain and seed starter, the honey, additional sourdough starter, yeast, and salt. Switch to the dough hook and mix (or fold if using the spatula) until distributed, stopping to scrape down the sides and bottom as needed, 6 to 8 minutes. In the beginning, it may seem like the grains will not incorporate. It will have a consistency between a batter and a dough. Continue to mix on low speed until the dough is soft and sticky, about 10 minutes.

5. Transfer the dough to the storage container or the bowl. Lightly drizzle the top of the dough with water. Cover the container with the lid or the bowl tightly with beeswax wrap.
    Let sit at room temperature for 1 hour.

6. If the dough is in a storage container, with slightly damp hands, pat the dough into a rectangle and fold from the top and then the bottom like a business letter. Slide both hands under the dough and fold from left then right like a letter. Repeat this letter fold in each direction three or four times.
    If the dough is in a bowl, the dough can be folded like a letter as above in the bowl.
    Add a little water to the bowl and dough as needed to keep the dough from sticking. Cover and let rest at room temperature for 1 hour.

7. Fold from top to bottom and then left to right. Repeat the folds in both directions three or four times. Let rest at room temperature for 1 hour.

8. Repeat the multiple folds in both directions and 1 hour rest two more times with a 1-hour rest in between for a total of four series of folds. After the final series of folds, let the dough rest for 2 hours.

9. Brush a traditional loaf pan, 8½ by 4½ by 2½ inches (21.5 by 10 by 6 cm), lightly with oil. For easier removal of the bread, make handles to lift the bread out of the pan after baking and cooling: cut a piece of parchment paper 8½ inches (21.5 cm) by about 12 inches (30 cm), line the pan, and brush the paper lightly with oil.

10. Have the pumpkin seeds, if using, near the dough. The dough will have more structure at this point but will still be soft. Fold the dough from top to bottom and then left to right, then roll the dough from the top toward the bottom into a log-like shape. Press the pumpkin seeds into the top of the log and transfer seed side up to the prepared loaf pan.
    Cover the pan with an inverted box or plastic tub and let sit at room temperature to proof until risen to the top of the pan, about 2 hours.

11. Meanwhile, set up the oven: Position one oven rack on the lowest rung and the other in the center. Set a cast-iron skillet on the lower rack.
    Preheat the oven to 450°F (230°C).

12. Fill a medium bowl with about 1 cup of ice cubes to have ready to add to the skillet to create steam.
    Slide the pan onto the center rack, pour the ice cubes into the skillet to produce steam, and close the door.
    Bake for 20 minutes.
    Without opening the oven, lower the oven temperature to 400°F (205°C) and continue to bake until the loaf is golden brown and well risen, about 20 minutes more.

13. Transfer to a wire rack and let cool for 10 minutes. Carefully remove the loaf from the pan and let cool completely on the rack.

Fermented Wheat Bran and Barley Épis with Beet

I love the épi shape, which reminds me of Provence. (You could also shape the dough into simple ovals, as shown on page 179.) Adding beets and their liquid to the dough gives these épis a subtle sweetness and lovely color. I had always thought of bran as a source of fiber, but according to Les Ambassadeurs, the fermentation of bran increases the bioavailability of its many nutrients, including B vitamins, iron, copper, zinc, magnesium, antioxidants, and phytochemicals. This is definitely a recipe for health-minded bakers who want a delicious baguette that packs a nutritional punch.

Makes 3 épis, about 400 grams each

Start to finish: **3 days**

Preparing the starter, day one: **20 minutes**

Proofing the starter: **18 to 24 hours**

Gathering ingredients, autolyse, and mixing the dough, day two: **3½ hours**

Folding, proofing, and resting the dough: **3½ hours**

Refrigerating the dough: **overnight**

Resting, shaping, and proofing, day three: **3 hours**

Baking: **23 to 27 minutes**

Ingredients	Metric
FERMENTED WHEAT BRAN AND BARLEY STARTER	
wheat bran	40 g
freshly milled barley or barley flakes	20 g
warm water (120°F/50°C)	85 g
Sourdough Starter (page 98)	1.5 g
COOKED BEETS	
2 medium beets, washed well	about 453 g
extra-virgin olive oil	1 tablespoon
fine sea salt, to taste	
freshly ground black pepper, to taste	
DOUGH	
bread flour	360 g, plus more for dusting
beet cooking liquid	220 g
instant dry yeast (optional)	0.3 g
fine sea salt	8 g
additional water (70° to 78°F / 21° to 25.5°C)	10 g

1. **PREPARE THE FERMENTED WHEAT BRAN AND BARLEY STARTER:** In a small bowl, weigh the wheat bran, milled barley, and warm water. Stir to combine and let cool slightly. Add the sourdough starter and mix until

RECIPE CONTINUES

well incorporated. Cover the bowl tightly, preferably with beeswax wrap. Let sit at room temperature for 18 to 24 hours.

2. To cook the beets, put the beets in a medium saucepan with water to cover by 1 inch (2.5 cm). Bring the water to a boil and then simmer until the beets are just tender when pierced with a paring knife, about 40 minutes.

Remove the beets from the water. Strain and reserve 220 g of the beet cooking liquid. Cool to room temperature.

Preheat the oven to 425°F (230°C).

Once the beets are cool enough to handle, peel them and cut them into ½-inch (1 cm) chunks. Toss in olive oil and season with salt and pepper. Transfer to a foil-lined baking sheet. Roast until the edges begin to caramelize, about 30 minutes.

3. **FOR THE AUTOLYSE:** In the bowl of a stand mixer or a large bowl, weigh the bread flour and the beet cooking liquid. With the paddle attachment (or with a spatula if in a large bowl), mix until a rough dough forms. Cover and let stand for 2 hours.

4. Very lightly brush the inside of a rectangular plastic storage container with a lid or a large bowl with water.

5. **MAKE THE FINAL DOUGH:** Add the fermented wheat bran and barley starter and yeast, if using, to the bowl of the stand mixer or the large bowl. Mix on low speed or by hand with a spatula until incorporated, 3 to 4 minutes.

Add the salt to the dough and mix (or fold if using the spatula) until it is distributed, about 3 minutes.

6. Spread the beets in the storage container or put in the bowl. Transfer the dough to the storage container or the bowl. Weigh the additional water in a small measuring cup or bowl. Drizzle some on top of the dough. (The beets will continue to incorporate and distribute evenly with the folds. Also, the goal is to add all of the additional 10 g of water to the container during this step and the subsequent folds.) Cover the container with the lid or the bowl tightly with beeswax wrap.

Let sit at room temperature for 1 hour.

7. If the dough is in a storage container, with slightly damp hands, pat the dough into a rectangle and fold from the top and then the bottom like a business letter. Slide both hands under the dough and fold from left then right like a letter.

If the dough is in a bowl, the dough can be folded like a letter as above in the bowl or turned out onto a damp work surface for folding.

Add some of the additional water to the bowl and dough as needed to keep the dough from sticking. Cover and let rest at room temperature for 1 hour.

8. Fold from top to bottom and then left to right and let rest at room temperature for 1 hour.

9. Repeat the folds one more time. Refrigerate the dough overnight.

10. Remove the dough from the refrigerator and let sit at room temperature for 30 to 45 minutes.

11. Dust the work surface with flour. Divide the dough into three equal pieces. Gently press them into small rectangles, about 3 by 5 inches (7.5 by 12 cm). Let rest for about 5 minutes.

12. Line a rimless baking sheet with parchment paper and dust with flour. (Alternatively, a linen can be used, and the baguettes can be moved to a transfer peel to transfer to the oven when time to bake.)

Working with one rectangle at a time, position it with a long side facing you. Fold the top of the dough down about one-third of the way toward the center and use the heel of your hand to seal it firmly, then fold up the bottom of the dough toward the center and seal firmly.

Fold the thin rectangle in half, bringing the top edge down to meet the bottom. Firmly seal with the heel of your hand.

Position your hands together, palms down, on the center of the log. Using light, even pressure, roll the log back and forth as you spread your hands apart, moving toward the ends. Repeat a few times until the baguette reaches the desired length of 14 to 16 inches (35 to 40 cm).

Lay the baguettes on the parchment paper, leaving about 3 inches (7.5 cm) between them. Dust the top with flour.

RECIPE CONTINUES

Cover with an inverted box or plastic tub and let sit at room temperature to proof until risen, 1 to 1½ hours.

13. Meanwhile, set up the oven: Position one oven rack on the lowest rung and set a cast-iron skillet on it. Position the other oven rack in the center and set a large baking stone or steel on it.
Preheat the oven to 500°F (260°C).

14. Close to baking time, fill a medium bowl with about 1 cup of ice cubes to have ready to add to the skillet to create steam.
Uncover the baguettes. Using scissors, make a cut about 3 inches (7.5 cm) up from the bottom at a 45-degree angle, cutting about three-quarters of the way through. Lay the cut piece to one side. Continue up the baguette, alternating the cut pieces to the opposite side. (Alternate the positions for each baguette so that they are not touching each other.)
Slide the épis, still on the parchment paper, onto the stone or steel, pour the ice cubes into the skillet to create steam, and close the door. Lower the oven temperature to 450°F (230°C) and bake until the loaves are a rich golden brown and well risen, 23 to 27 minutes.

15. Transfer to a wire rack and let cool completely.

8.

THAT TIME I WENT TO
PARIS TO COMPETE IN

THE GRAND

PRIX DE LA

BAGUETTE

Yeasted Baguettes

———

Sourdough Baguettes

O N THE FIRST MORNING OF MY FIRST TRIP to Paris, the first food I ate was a baguette, purchased at a boulangerie just a few meters from the Gare du Nord. I felt its warmth through the paper that was wrapped and twirled around its crisp crust. I tore *le quignon* (the heel) from the end of the loaf, inhaled the bread's scent, admired its open crumb, and devoured *le quignon* and most of the rest of the baguette as I walked toward my hotel on the Rue Monsieur le Prince. To this day, the sight, smell, and flavor of this iconic bread fill me with the memories and the intense emotions of that trip, and many others.

I was surprised to learn that the baguette is not a particularly ancient bread and did not even originate in France. Invented in Vienna at the end of the nineteenth century along with the first steam ovens, this lighter style of crusty bread with a cream-colored and bubbly interior became popular in France thanks to a law, passed in the 1920s, prohibiting bakers from firing up their ovens before 4 a.m. Unlike classic country boules, which take many hours to ferment and bake, long and thin baguettes could be produced in time to sell to the morning's customers at 8 a.m., and then continuously throughout the day. Unlike the large sourdough rounds that might stay fresh for a week, these breads were best eaten within a couple of hours of baking. Despite their short shelf life, they quickly became a staple, and even an addiction, as well as a symbol of French food and culture. Plenty of Parisians visit their local boulangerie twice a day, once in the morning and once on the way home from work. It is almost unimaginable to have a meal without bread (and wine) in France.

I've never stopped sampling Parisian baguettes, comparing them to one another, and asking bakers for their tips and techniques. It wasn't always easy. In the 1980s and early '90s, my French counterparts would often lament the degradation of the craft in general and of baguette production in particular. Traditional neighborhood bakeries were closing at an alarming rate. Industrial baking plants started distributing breads made with overly refined flours,

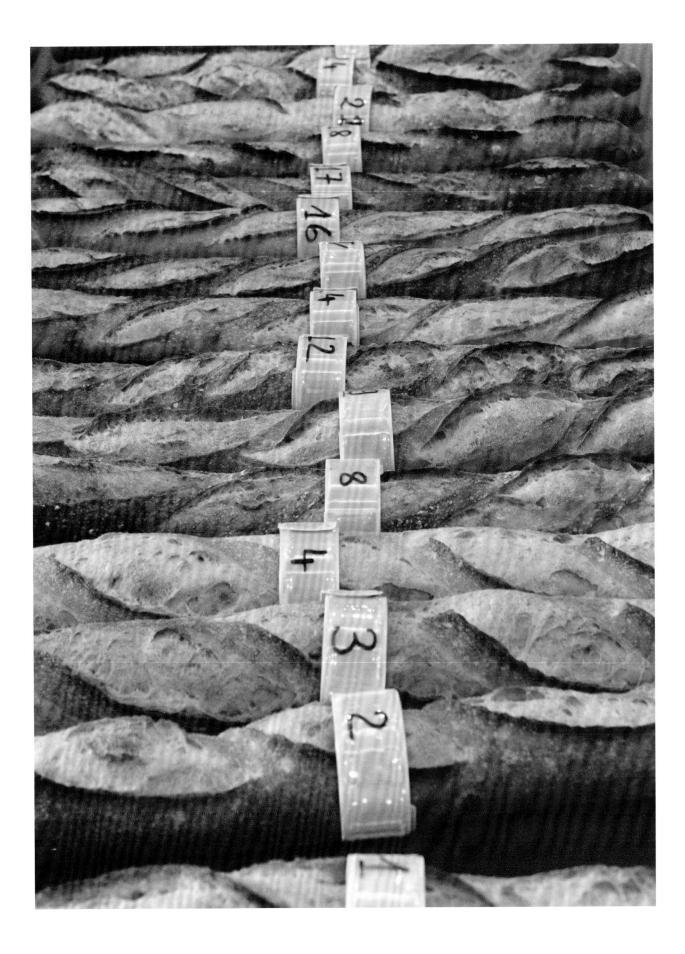

preservatives, and other additives and par-baked loaves that could be passed off as house made. The soul and spirit of boulangeries and baking life in general were evaporating along with the traditional French way of life represented by the baguette. In 1993, the government stepped in, passing the Décret Pain. This law requires a bakery to make its bread from start to finish on the premises in order to call itself a boulangerie. Boulangeries must display a small blue-and-yellow sign that reads, *"Votre boulanger. Un artisan authentique. Ici, on fait notre pain à la main,"* to let customers know they are the real thing. The Décret also codified the characteristics of the traditional baguette, to preserve and protect this national treasure and to ensure its integrity.

By law, a real baguette, or *baguette de tradition*, can contain only four ingredients: flour, water, salt, and yeast. It must weigh between 250 and 300 grams and measure between 55 and 70 centimeters in length. It must be made where it is sold and cannot be frozen at any stage in the process. While these specifications may seem restrictive, there is actually a lot of variability in how bakers make their baguettes. To raise their baguettes, they might use pâte fermentée, liquid levain, or even some dough left over from a previous batch. They are free to choose among a large variety of specialty flours offered by French millers and millers across the continent. They can play with timing, extending autolyse for up to twenty-four hours. With the advent of retarder proofers, bakers have gained more control over the fermentation process, easily customizing fermentation time by adjusting the temperature inside the proofer.

In 1997, then president Jacques Chirac inaugurated a contest, the Grand Prix de la Baguette, to focus attention on the baguette and to further protect and promote this quintessential French product. Since then, thousands of bakers have vied for the title, which comes with a prize of €4,000 and the honor of supplying baguettes to the Élysée Palace for a year. The Décret and the Grand Prix boosted the prestige of baking as a profession and helped give birth to a whole new generation of artisan bakers. For many years it seemed that many of my favorite bakeries were closing or being sold. These days, it seems that every time I visit Paris, a boulangerie has popped up where there wasn't one before. New shops like Mamiche, Boulangerie Utopie, Maison Landemaine, Liberté, and Joseph proudly sell *baguettes de tradition Française* alongside more innovative and creative breads. "Around the world, the baguette symbolizes the centrality of handmade products in French culture," says Olivia Polski, the deputy mayor of Paris in charge of trade, crafts, and liberal professions, who oversees the competition. When she visits Peru or China, she inevitably meets bakers who are trying to reproduce this quintessentially French bread. She is filled with national pride and is also happy that France has given the baguette to the world to enjoy.

In spring 2022, I fulfilled a decades-long dream of experiencing the Grand Prix in person. My friend Mickael Benichou at Boulangerie Liberté invited me to work alongside his crew as they competed against 133 other bakeries for the prize of Best Baguette in Paris. His original boulangerie (he now owns four shops, with many more in the works) is just a few meters from the Canal Saint-Martin on the Rue des Vinaigriers, in an old working-class quartier with a newly hip, young, vibrant vibe. In 2013, Mickael bought the old bakery, leaving it mostly as he found it. Vintage hexagonal tiles cover the floors. The walls are rough concrete. A large remnant of a cornice leans against a pillar, reminding customers of the building's history. The spot quickly became beloved by the neighborhood, both for its traditional breads and unique pastries. Baguettes, along with boules and rustic rye loaves, are displayed on metal racks. Mickael replaced the old counters with a large, slick, angular slab of marble that has become the focal point of the bakery. Customers sit at marble-topped bistro tables on teal-and-white bistro chairs enjoying superb brioche rolls and croissants.

I arrived on Tuesday morning, and head baker Eric Verthy was waiting for me in the basement bread area, which is reached by walking carefully down a winding stone staircase. *"Attention ne te conges pas la tête!"* he shouted, as the top of my head grazed a low stone ceiling that could easily have knocked me out cold. I quickly changed my clothes, and within minutes Eric had me scaling flour into the giant bowl of a vintage Mahot mixer, almost exactly like the one I

had purchased for Bread Alone in 1984. These enamel-coated, cream-colored machines are so solid that it's not unusual to find decades-old examples like this one (Mickael inherited it when he purchased the shop) at bakeries across France.

The process was very familiar to me, with nuances at each step that would ultimately make the Liberté baguettes unique. First, Eric and his bakers mixed together Type 65 flour from Moulins Bourgeois (seven of the ten finalists in this year's competition used flour from this mill) and water in the Mahot's mixing bowl. After a thirty-minute autolyse, they added a tiny amount—two grams for each kilogram of flour—of commercial yeast (Eric prefers yeast to liquid levain for his *baguette de tradition*) and stirred the dough to combine. With the mixer on low speed, the dough was kneaded for four minutes. The particular hum and vibration of the Mahot mixer made me feel right at home. Very slowly, water was drizzled into the bowl while kneading. This technique, called *bassinage*, is a subtle approach to hydrating the dough to the max. It takes experience and sensitivity to add just the right amount of water, waiting for the dough to fully absorb the water before adding more. Patience is key here, as is knowing when to stop. Midway through bassinage, salt was stirred in, and then the kneading and bassinage continued for five more minutes on low, and just one minute on medium, before Eric checked the dough's development. I watched as he grabbed a bit from the top of the bowl and stretched it a foot or so, performing a quick windowpane test. Determining that it was properly hydrated and kneaded, he covered the bowl to let the dough rest for forty-five minutes. At that point, he turned the mixer on briefly to fold the dough, and then let it rest for another forty-five minutes. Then he and his bakers divided the dough into five-kilogram pieces, placed them in plastic tubs, and immediately put them in the refrigerator, to slowly ferment overnight and to develop a stabilizing structure and a mild, sweet flavor.

Next, we got yesterday's dough from the refrigerator, cut it into 350-gram pieces, gently preshaped them, and let them rest for twenty minutes to warm up and relax. Then we shaped them into skinny baguettes on a soft white baker's felt and let them proof in linen couches for thirty to forty-five minutes. When they were properly risen, we slid them onto the URM spring-loaded oven loader, scored them with five quick cuts, and put them straight into the oven to bake for twenty-two minutes at 230°C (450°F). When Eric pulled the baguettes from the oven, every one of them was a little different. But it was obvious which ones were mine. Let's just say they lacked the perfect proportions and gentle tapering from center to ends that Eric's displayed.

Thursday was the day of the competition. After mixing some dough for Friday, the team shaped and baked the batch of baguettes from which Eric would choose just two for the Grand Prix. As they cooled on racks, he examined them carefully. Eric doesn't like his baguettes too dark. He eval-

uated each loaf's scoring, checking that the breads had bloomed sufficiently and beautifully where they were cut, with properly caramelized edges. He wanted loaves that tapered evenly and elegantly from the center to sharp points on each end.

Eric made his choice, and we packed up the bread and called an Uber. By the time our car had crossed the bridge over the Seine and rolled down the cobblestone street toward our destination, I was already floating on air. As we arrived at the Syndicat des Boulangers du Grand Paris on the Quai d'Anjou, so did dozens of other bakers, on foot, by bicycle and scooter, in bakery vans, and even a few in chauffeured black Mercedes sedans. There were skinny teenagers, old Frenchmen with big bellies, young women with stylish earrings and scarves, artisans with roots in Tunisia, China, and Japan. These bakers would light up when stopped by the TV crews lining the streets to cover the event as if waiting for celebrities to walk the red carpet. The arriving bakers joyfully discussed the primacy of the baguette in the world of breads. But it was a celebration of more than the baguette: it was a celebration of artisan French food, values, sensibilities, and culture. The winner would get bragging rights, but the vibe was definitely "vive la France."

There couldn't have been a more spectacular location for celebrating France than this ancient building, four stories tall and in a prime spot on the Île Saint-Louis. At the building's entrance, bakers were leaning against a stone wall, hugging, laughing, tell-ing stories about past contests, discussing their baguettes. It's not every day that hardworking members of a distinguished but backbreaking trade have the chance to congratulate each other and to bask in the admiration of the entire city and the world. Mickael filled out an entry form to obtain a number for Liberté. He was then given a yellow and an orange rubber band marked with this number to stretch around each of his baguettes. The breads were weighed and measured before we were allowed to bring them to the top floor, where the judging was to take place. We ascended the stairs to the sixth floor, and as I took in the north-facing views of the city from the competition room, I thought, "How appropriate is it that the baking office is in the best spot in France?"

The breads were lined up on two long tables, and three tables were set up as judging stations. I don't know whether it was an aesthetic decision or just a sublime coincidence, but the tables sat by windows that opened onto Juliet balconies with wrought-iron railings. Sunlight reflecting off the Seine landed on the breads and gave them a golden glow. This year's jury included Ms. Polski, along with last year's winner, Makram Akrout; the president of the Baker's Union of Greater Paris; journalists; a handful of French food celebrities; and a few lucky volunteers chosen randomly online. Jurors were given scorecards and asked to evaluate, on a scale of 1 to 4, the appearance, baking technique, aroma, crumb, and flavor of each bread. They began to pick up loaves, looking at them from every angle, before cutting into them to judge their interiors, their scent, and finally their taste. As the first dozen baguettes were sliced, the room was suddenly filled with the powerful and enticing fragrance of bread. It was almost overwhelming, even for someone who has spent a lifetime in a bakery. After two rounds of judging, the ten high scorers entered the final round before a winner was determined.

At the end of the day, the announcement was made: Damien Dedun of Boulangerie Frédéric Comyn was declared the baker of the best baguette in Paris for 2022. His "secrets": "Very good raw materials, long fermentation, and lots of love." Our team hardly needed consoling, but just in case, Eric reminded us of a first-prize winner from the early days of the Grand Prix who was unable to be notified of his victory because instead of writing his name on the entry form, he wrote, "I bake for my customers, not the judges." I felt like a winner myself, for being able to participate in such a fabulous celebration of good bread.

Note for all baguettes: Although baguette dough can be made in the mixer, it is a dough that comes together nicely by hand.

Yeasted Baguettes

This recipe is based on my experience in Paris with the Liberté bakers. The bread has a wheaty, clean flavor. Because it is made with yeast rather than sourdough, it is wonderfully mild, with a gentle sweetness from the grain. I tend to break into these baguettes about 20 minutes after they are out of the oven, so they are just warm but baked through. That's my favorite moment to have a baguette. With Morbier cheese, with butter and strawberry jam, with lentil soup—I can't count the ways that I've enjoyed this versatile loaf.

Makes 3 baguettes, about 220 g each

Start to finish:
about 31 hours

Gathering ingredients, autolyse, and mixing the dough, day one: **1 hour**

Folding, proofing, and resting the dough:
3½ hours

Refrigerating the dough:
24 hours

Resting, shaping, and proofing, day two:
2 hours

Baking:
23 to 27 minutes

Ingredients	Metric
bread flour	400 g, plus more for dusting
water (70° to 78°F / 21° to 25.5°C)	280 g
instant dry yeast	0.5 g
fine sea salt	8 g

1. **FOR THE AUTOLYSE:** In the bowl of a stand mixer or in a large bowl, weigh the flour and 260 g of the water. Fit the mixer with the paddle attachment and mix on medium-low speed (or with a spatula if in a large bowl) until a rough dough forms. Cover and let stand for 45 minutes.

2. Very lightly brush the inside of a rectangular plastic storage container with a lid or a large bowl with water.

3. **MAKE THE FINAL DOUGH:** Add the yeast and fold in with a spatula to mix by hand, about 4 minutes. Alternatively, fit the mixer with the dough hook and mix on low speed for about 4 minutes.

   Add the salt to the dough and fold in by hand or mix with the dough hook on low until it is distributed, about 3 minutes.

4. Transfer the dough to the storage container or the bowl. Weigh the remaining 20 g water in a small measuring cup or bowl. Drizzle some on top of the dough. (The goal is to add all the additional water to the

RECIPE CONTINUES

container during this step and the subsequent folds.) Cover the container with the lid or the bowl tightly with beeswax wrap.

Let sit at room temperature for 45 minutes to 1 hour.

5. If the dough is in a storage container, with slightly damp hands, pat the dough into a rectangle and fold from the top and then the bottom like a business letter. Slide both hands under the dough and fold from left then right like a letter.

If the dough is in a bowl, the dough can be folded like a letter as above in the bowl or turned out onto a damp work surface for folding.

Add some of the water to the bowl and dough as needed to keep the dough from sticking. Cover and let rest at room temperature for 1 hour.

6. Fold from top to bottom and then left to right and let rest at room temperature for 1 hour.

7. Repeat the folds one more time. Refrigerate the dough for 24 hours.

8. Remove the dough from the refrigerator and let sit at room temperature for 45 minutes.

9. Dust the work surface with flour. Divide the dough into three equal pieces. Gently press them into small rectangles, about 3 by 5 inches (7.5 by 12 cm). Let rest for about 5 minutes.

10. Line a rimless baking sheet with parchment paper and dust with flour. (Alternatively, a linen can be used, and the baguettes can be moved to a transfer peel to transfer to the oven when time to bake.)

Shape each rectangle into a baguette 14 to 16 inches (35 to 40 cm) long, or the length of your baking stone, if slightly shorter or longer.

Working with one baguette at a time, position it with a long side facing you. Fold the top of the dough down about one-third of the way toward the center and use the heel of your hand to seal it firmly, then fold up the bottom of the dough toward the center and seal firmly.

Fold the thin rectangle in half, bringing the top edge down to meet the bottom. Firmly seal with the heel of your hand.

Position your hands together, palms down, on the center of the log. Using light, even pressure, roll the log back and forth as you spread your hands apart, moving toward the ends. Repeat a few times until the baguette reaches the desired length of about 14 to 16 inches (35 to 40 cm).

Lay the baguettes on the parchment paper, leaving about 3 inches (7.5 cm) between them. Gently lift the parchment between the baguettes to make a pleat. This will also bring the baguettes closer together. Roll up two kitchen towels and slip them under the outside edges to support the baguettes. Dust the top of the baguettes with flour.

Cover with an inverted box or plastic tub and let sit at room temperature to proof until risen slightly, about 45 minutes.

11. Meanwhile, set up the oven: Position one oven rack on the lowest rung and set a cast-iron skillet on it. Position the other oven rack in the center and set a large baking stone or steel on it.

Preheat the oven to 500°F (260°C).

12. Close to baking time, fill a medium bowl with about 1 cup of ice cubes to have ready to add to the skillet to create steam.

Uncover the baguettes, remove the towels, and gently stretch the parchment paper so that it is flat and the loaves are separated. With a lame, a single-edged razor blade, or a serrated knife, score the loaves with five or six angled slashes, about ½ inch (1.25 cm) deep and about 2 inches (5 cm) long.

Slide the loaves, still on the parchment paper, onto the stone or steel, pour the ice cubes into the skillet to create steam, and close the door. Lower the oven temperature to 450°F (230°C) and bake until the loaves are a rich golden brown and well risen, 23 to 27 minutes.

13. Transfer to a wire rack and let cool completely.

Sourdough Baguettes

We have made many different styles of sourdough baguette at Bread Alone, and this one has been consistently popular. Depending on your sourdough, and depending on how long you refrigerate the dough, it will develop a real tang. Its texture is chewier than that of the yeasted baguette.

Makes 3 baguettes, about 220 g each

Start to finish:
3 days

Preparing the starter, day one: **10 minutes**

Proofing the starter:
**6 hours or
up to overnight**

Gathering ingredients, autolyse, and mixing the dough, day two: **1 hour**

Folding, proofing, and resting the dough:
3½ hours

Refrigerating the dough:
overnight

Resting, shaping, and proofing, day three:
4 hours

Baking:
23 to 27 minutes

Ingredients	Metric
STARTER	
bread flour	40 g
water (70° to 78°F / 21° to 25.5°C)	40 g
Sourdough Starter (page 98)	8 g
DOUGH	
bread flour	360 g, plus more for dusting
water	236 g
instant dry yeast (optional)	0.3 g
fine sea salt	8 g

1. **PREPARE THE STARTER:** In a small bowl, weigh the flour, water, and sourdough starter. Stir together until well incorporated. Cover the bowl tightly, preferably with beeswax wrap. Let sit at room temperature for 6 hours or up to overnight.

2. **FOR THE AUTOLYSE:** In the bowl of a stand mixer or in a large bowl, weigh the flour and 220 g of the water. Fit the mixer with the paddle attachment and mix on medium-low speed (or with a spatula if in a large bowl) until a rough dough forms. Cover and let stand for 45 minutes.

3. Very lightly brush the inside of a rectangular plastic storage container with a lid or a large bowl with water.

4. **MAKE THE FINAL DOUGH:** Add the starter and the yeast, if using, and fold in with a spatula to mix by hand, 2 to 3 minutes. Alternatively,

RECIPE CONTINUES

fit the mixer with the dough hook and mix on low speed for 2 to 3 minutes.

Add the salt to the dough and fold in by hand or mix with the dough hook on low until it is distributed, 2 to 3 minutes.

5. Transfer the dough to the storage container or the bowl. Weigh the remaining 16 g water in a small measuring cup or bowl. Drizzle some on top of the dough. (The goal is to add all the additional water to the container during this step and the subsequent folds.) Cover the container with the lid or the bowl tightly with beeswax wrap.

Let sit at room temperature for 1 hour.

6. If the dough is in a storage container, with slightly damp hands, pat the dough into a rectangle and fold from the top and then the bottom like a business letter. Slide both hands under the dough and fold from left then right like a letter.

If the dough is in a bowl, the dough can be folded like a letter as above in the bowl or turned out onto a damp work surface for folding.

Add some of the water to the bowl and dough as needed to keep the dough from sticking. Cover and let rest at room temperature for 1 hour.

7. Fold from top to bottom and then left to right and let rest at room temperature for 1 hour.

8. Repeat the folds one more time. Refrigerate the dough overnight.

9. Remove the dough from the refrigerator and let sit at room temperature for 45 minutes to 1 hour.

10. Dust the work surface with flour. Divide the dough into three equal pieces. Gently press them into small rectangles, about 3 by 5 inches (7.5 by 12 cm). Let rest for about 5 minutes.

11. Line a rimless baking sheet with parchment paper and dust with flour. (Alternatively a linen can be used, and the baguettes can be moved to a transfer peel to transfer to the oven when time to bake.)

Shape each rectangle into a baguette 14 to 16 inches (35 to 40 cm) long, or the length of your baking stone, if slightly shorter or longer.

Working with one baguette at a time, position it with a long side facing you. Fold the top of the dough down about one-third of the way toward the center and use the heel of your hand to seal it firmly, then fold up the bottom of the dough toward the center and seal firmly.

Fold the thin rectangle in half, bringing the top edge down to meet the bottom. Firmly seal with the heel of your hand.

Position your hands together, palms down, on the center of the log. Using light, even pressure, roll the log back and forth as you spread your hands apart, moving toward the ends. Repeat a few times until the baguette reaches the desired length of about 14 to 16 inches (35 to 40 cm).

Lay the baguettes on the parchment paper, leaving about 3 inches (7.5 cm) between them. Gently lift the parchment between the baguettes to make a pleat. This will also bring the baguettes closer together. Roll up two kitchen towels and slip them under the outside edges to support the baguettes. Dust the top of the baguettes with flour.

Cover with an inverted box or plastic tub and let sit at room temperature to proof until risen slightly, 1½ to 2 hours.

12. Meanwhile, set up the oven: Position one oven rack on the lowest rung and set a cast-iron skillet on it. Position the other oven rack in the center and set a large baking stone or steel on it.

Preheat the oven to 500°F (260°C).

13. Close to baking time, fill a medium bowl with about 1 cup of ice cubes to have ready to add to the skillet to create steam.

Uncover the baguettes, remove the towels, and gently stretch the parchment paper so that it is flat and the loaves are separated. With a lame, a single-edged razor blade, or a serrated knife, score the loaves. Position the lame at the top of the loaf, about 1 inch (2.5 cm) off center. Make one long, straight slash to the bottom.

Slide the loaves, still on the parchment paper, onto the stone or steel, pour the ice cubes into the skillet to create steam, and close the door. Lower the oven temperature to 450°F (230°C) and bake until the loaves are a rich golden brown and well risen, 23 to 27 minutes.

14. Transfer to a wire rack and let cool completely.

9.

CAFE
TREATS

Chilled Chocolate Tart PAGE 284

SCONES

Plain Scones

Roasted Red Pepper, Onion, and
Asparagus Scones

Lemon-Currant Einkorn Scones

MUFFINS

Corn Muffins

Buckwheat and
Mixed Berry Muffins

Morning Glory Muffins

COOKIES

Lemon Shortbread

Chocolate-Dipped
Hazelnut Shortbread

Pistachio–Brown Butter
Financiers

Canelés

PIES

Single-Crust Pie Dough

Apple-Raspberry Crumb Pie

Pumpkin Pie

Double-Crust Pie Dough

Strawberry-Rhubarb Pie

Peach-Apricot Pie

No-Churn Hint of Bourbon Ice
Cream

Blueberry Slab Pie

Swiss Chard–Leek Galette with
Ricotta

TARTS

Pâte Sucrée

Chocolate Pâte Sucrée

Cherry Tart

Nut Tart

Tarte à la Crème

Chilled Chocolate Tart

Blood Orange–Lemon Tart

BRIOCHE

Sweet Levain Brioche Dough

Brioche Loaf

Cinnamon-Raisin Loaf

Maple Sticky Buns

Mocha-Filled Brioche Buns

Red Pepper–Gruyère
Pull-Apart Rolls

Hamburger Rolls

Laminated Sweet Levain Brioche
Dough

Pull-Apart Laminated Brioche
Loaves

CROISSANTS

Sourdough Croissant Dough

Traditional Croissants

SNAILS

Pastry Cream for Snails

Pain aux Raisins

Apple Snails

Pesto Snails

MAKING PASTRY WAS NOT IN OUR INITIAL business plan. (As I've mentioned before, we didn't *have* an initial business plan.) But soon after opening our doors, we began to get daily requests from repeat customers for cookies, tarts, and other cafe treats. Not only did we want to make everyone happy, but we quickly realized that expanding our repertoire to include breakfast baked goods would strengthen our connection to the community and help our bottom line.

We dipped a flour-coated toe in with the easy stuff—muffins and scones to go with our freshly brewed coffee. These items—made without preservatives or hydrogenated oil— were our bid for dissatisfied convenience- store customers who knew they wanted something more wholesome than a day-old doughnut but didn't know exactly what they were looking for or where to find it. When devising recipes, we imagined what might have been produced in a farm country kitchen. We did the same when Thanksgiv- ing rolled around and our customers wanted pies. So we made our all-butter pie dough from scratch. Our fillings came not from cans but from nearby farms and orchards. On weekend mornings, people a half mile away could breathe in the buttery aroma coming from our little building hidden in the woods. Bread Alone became a Catskills destination.

I knew very little about French pastry. I had spent a few days at the CIA learning how to make laminated doughs, not enough to feel terribly comfortable with the tech- niques. When I graduated and moved to New York, there was a single shop in the city—Bonté Patisserie on Third Avenue and Seventy-Fifth Street—where authentic croissants were available. On my first trip to Paris in 1978, I was shocked to learn that there were hundreds of bakeries in the city that made laminated pastries of this quality.

Our customers were not clamoring for croissants, brioche, and puff pastry, because, aside from the giant napoleons sitting in lighted display cases in diners across New Jersey, these items so common in France were not part of the American bakery reper- toire. Many Americans were probably un- aware of the croissant's existence until Burger King debuted its Croissan'Wich in

1983. But I knew that if our customers could try the real thing, they would love French pastries just as much as they loved French bread.

In the late 1980s, we had the good fortune to hire a baker who had trained at Bonté and had been the head baker at the Plaza Hotel before retreating, as I had done a few years earlier, to the Catskills. His arrival was an opportunity to give people not only what they were asking for but what we knew they would love. When he came on board, he had enough practice and experience to produce brioche, croissants, and more in bulk. These products gave Bread Alone an air of sophistication and intrigue, since they were a bit unknown to many. On subsequent trips to Paris, I discovered canelés and financiers, which made their debut in Boiceville soon after.

Recently, my younger son, Noah, remarked on his atypical diet as a kid. He didn't taste Coca-Cola until he was a teenager. But by that time, he had probably eaten a thousand handmade muffins, scones, and croissants.

Neither of us would have had it any other way. When I look around at the hundreds of small bakeries across the country where you can now get a wholesome corn muffin made with stone-ground cornmeal, a richly spiced fresh pumpkin pie, or a flaky all-butter croissant, I take pleasure and a little bit of pride in knowing that Bread Alone has been a part of the movement toward quality baking, and may even have inspired others to follow this path.

Good baking has a ripple effect. As Nels likes to say, "We aspire to set an example, to reach more people with our actions than we can feed with our foods." Nels, too, grew up not on bread alone but on apple pies, nut tarts, and shortbread cookies. And now look at him: he's brainstormed the country's first carbon-neutral bakery and delivers well-priced, wholesome pastry and organic bread to corner stores and supermarkets for miles around. In other words, feed your children a thousand all-butter croissants and they might in turn help feed the world.

A Note on Flour for Your Cafe Treats

The following recipes provide a great opportunity to bake with local flour from smaller mills like Maine Grains, Janie's Mill, and Farmer Ground Flour. While noncommodity flour, which often isn't as strong and protein heavy as commercial flour, can present a challenge to the bread baker, it will likely perform beautifully in pastry recipes, where tenderness is prized. At the same time, it will lend its unique flavor to whatever you are baking. Flours from different mills will give you different results, which is part of the fun.

SCONES

When we first opened Bread Alone, we sold six types of bread, period. But when our earliest customers asked right off the bat if we had any coffee or tea, we pretty quickly set up a hot beverage station to accommodate them and make a little extra cash. And as soon as we started offering hot beverages, people asked for sweets and snacks.

Scones were the first nonbread item that we made at Bread Alone. The choice was deliberate. They were simple to make, endlessly adaptable depending on what mix-ins we had on hand, easy to store in the freezer for quick baking, and instantly popular. We quickly sold hundreds every day.

From a production point of view, they are perfect. The dough comes together in minutes—we are careful not to overwork it, to avoid toughness. When we roll it into precisely measured rectangles, we can easily cut those rectangles into triangles with absolutely no waste. The unbaked dough triangles freeze beautifully and can be baked almost directly from the freezer. In fact, by the time you put them on parchment-lined baking sheets, brush them with egg or cream, and sprinkle with sugar or sea salt, they will probably be thawed.

Bread Alone scones have a rugged crust with a little resistance in the break. Their interiors are dense and moist but never heavy. The core recipe can be modified to produce both sweet and savory variations. I've suggested a few that have been customer favorites over the years, but feel free to try combinations of your own.

Plain Scones

There is nothing plain about a plain scone, but this dough is also a solid and delicious foundation for additional ingredients like dried fruit, lightly toasted nuts, or a combination.

Makes 6 or 12 scones, about 75 grams (2½ ounces) each

Start to finish:
about 3 hours

Gathering ingredients and preparing the dough: **30 minutes**

Shaping, refrigerating, and/or freezing:
at least 2 hours but up to 3 weeks

Baking:
20 to 30 minutes

VARIATION(S):

If you prefer the addition of nuts and fruit, use 40 to 50 g (⅓ to ½ cup) for 6 scones or 80 to 100 g (⅔ to 1 cup) for 12 scones. Pistachios and cherries are delicious. Toasted, skinned, and coarsely chopped hazelnuts together with chopped bittersweet chocolate (we use Valrhona at the bakery) is another great combination.

Ingredients	Metric	Imperial	Metric	Imperial
	6 scones		**12 scones**	
unsalted butter, cold	93 g	3¼ ounces / 6½ tablespoons	186 g	6½ ounces / 13 tablespoons
egg yolk	9 g	2 teaspoons	18 g	1 large yolk
whole egg	15 g	1 tablespoon	30 g	2 tablespoons
heavy cream	117 g	½ cup	234 g	1 cup
pure vanilla extract or paste	3 g	¾ teaspoon	6 g	1½ teaspoons
all-purpose flour	198 g	1½ cups plus 2½ tablespoons, plus more for dusting	397 g	3¼ cups plus 1 tablespoon, plus more for dusting
granulated sugar	23 g	1 tablespoon plus 2¾ teaspoons	46 g	3 tablespoons plus 2½ teaspoons
baking powder	9 g	1¾ teaspoons	18 g	1 tablespoon plus ½ teaspoon
fine sea salt	3 g	½ teaspoon	6 g	1 teaspoon
EGG WASH				
whole egg	55 g	1 large egg	55 g	1 large egg
egg yolk	17 g	1 large yolk	17 g	1 large yolk
heavy cream	30 g	2 tablespoons	30 g	2 tablespoons

sanding sugar, for sprinkling (optional)

1. Sprinkle a large sheet of parchment paper lightly with flour.

   Cut the butter into ¼-inch (6 mm) cubes and return to the refrigerator. In a large spouted measuring cup, whisk together the egg yolk, egg, cream, and vanilla.

RECIPE CONTINUES

2. In the bowl of a stand mixer fitted with the paddle attachment, add the flour, granulated sugar, baking powder, and salt. Toss together or mix on the lowest setting for 1 minute. Add the cubed butter. Pulse on the lowest speed to begin to incorporate the butter and keep the flour in the bowl. Increase the speed to low, then increase to medium-low to continue to mix and break the butter into smaller pieces until the mixture resembles a coarse meal, about 3 minutes total.

3. With the mixer running on low speed, stream in the cream mixture and mix until combined and beginning to come together around the paddle, 1 to 2 minutes.

4. Transfer the dough to the prepared parchment paper and press evenly into a 7-inch (18 cm) round for six scones or a 10 by 6-inch (25 by 15 cm) rectangle for twelve scones. The dough should be ½ to ¾ inch (1.25 to 2 cm) thick. Wrap the parchment around the dough and refrigerate for 2 to 3 hours, until firm.

5. For the round, cut the round in half and then cut each half into three equal triangles, for a total of six triangular scones. For the rectangle, cut the block in half lengthwise and then cut each half into six equal pieces, for a total of twelve rectangular scones. Alternatively, for round scones, cut with a round cookie cutter. Any trimmings can be pushed together one time and used.

The scones can be baked at this point, refrigerated for a day, or frozen for up to 3 weeks.

6. Preheat the oven to 400°F (200°C). Line a rimmed baking sheet with parchment paper.

Set the scones on the prepared baking sheet, leaving about an inch (2.5 cm) between them.

MAKE THE EGG WASH: Whisk together the egg, yolk, and cream in a small bowl. Brush the scones with the egg wash and sprinkle with sanding sugar, if using. Bake until the scones are a rich golden brown, 20 to 30 minutes, depending on whether baking from cold or frozen.

7. Transfer the scones to a wire rack. Serve warm or at room temperature.

Roasted Red Pepper, Onion, and Asparagus Scones

These roasted vegetable scones, studded with a mixture of red pepper, onion, asparagus, and crumbled goat cheese, are wonderfully savory, with just a hint of sweetness. A little bit of rye flour contributes some earthy flavor, but you can use 100 percent all-purpose flour if you'd like. We sometimes offer these savory scones with soup, for a light but warming meal at our cafes.

Makes 6 or 12 scones, about 90 grams (3.2 ounces) each

Start to finish: about 4½ hours

Preparing and cooling the roasted vegetables: 1½ hours

Gathering ingredients and preparing the dough: 30 minutes

Shaping, refrigerating and/or freezing: at least 2 hours but up to 3 weeks

Baking: 20 to 30 minutes

Roasted Vegetables

Depending on the size of the vegetables, the weight may vary slightly. It is okay if there is slightly more or less for this recipe.

When roasting the vegetables, it is best to keep the asparagus whole. Depending on its thickness, it may finish roasting before the other vegetables and should be removed from the oven once tender. It will be easiest to peel the bell pepper if it is left in one large piece with any seeds and stem removed.

If you'd like, use jarred roasted red peppers, rinsed, patted dry, and roughly chopped, to save a little time.

Ingredients	Metric	Imperial	Metric	Imperial
	6 scones		12 scones	
onion, cut into 1-inch (2.5 cm) chunks	40 g	1½ ounces	80 g	3 ounces
asparagus, peeled	40 g	1½ ounces	80 g	3 ounces
red bell pepper, stemmed and seeded but whole	35 g	1¼ ounces	70 g	2½ ounces
extra-virgin olive oil, for tossing				
fine sea salt, for sprinkling				

1. Preheat the oven to 400°F (200°C).

2. Toss the vegetables in enough oil to coat, sprinkle with salt, and spread on a baking sheet. Roast until the vegetables are tender and the skin from the pepper is charred, 30 to 35 minutes.

RECIPE CONTINUES

Seasonally, substitute cubed butternut squash or sweet potato for the asparagus, or use all peppers and onion. In the summertime, we like to add chopped fresh basil and cherry tomatoes. Cut 1 pound (453 g) of cherry tomatoes in half and dry in a 200°F (95°C) oven until they are a little bit moist but not crisp, about 4 hours. Mix into the scone dough along with 2 tablespoons (3 g) of chopped basil. Depending on the moistness of the tomatoes, the dough will be a little sticky. Refrigerate as needed before cutting into individual scones, then refrigerate or freeze again before baking.

3. Remove from the oven. Once cool enough to handle, peel the skin from the pepper and discard. Let the vegetables cool completely. Roughly chop and then refrigerate until cold.

Scones

Ingredients	Metric	Imperial	Metric	Imperial
	6 scones		**12 scones**	
unsalted butter, cold	84 g	3 ounces / 6 tablespoons	167 g	6 ounces/ 12 tablespoons
egg yolk	9 g	2 teaspoons	18 g	1 large yolk
whole egg	14 g	2½ teaspoons	27 g	1 tablespoon plus 2 teaspoons
heavy cream	105 g	¼ cup plus 3 tablespoons	210 g	¾ cup plus 2 tablespoons
goat cheese, preferably chèvre	40 g	1½ ounces	80 g	3 ounces
Roasted Vegetables (page 208)	80 to 90 g	about 3 ounces	160 to 180 g	about 6 ounces
all-purpose flour	133 g	1 cup plus 1½ tablespoons, plus more for dusting	266 g	2 cups plus 3 tablespoons, plus more for dusting
whole rye flour	45 g	⅓ cup	90 g	⅔ cup
sugar	20 g	1 tablespoon plus 2 teaspoons	41 g	3 tablespoons plus 1 teaspoon
baking powder	8 g	1½ teaspoons	16 g	1 tablespoon
fine sea salt	3 g	½ teaspoon	6 g	1 teaspoon
EGG WASH				
whole egg	55 g	1 large egg	55 g	1 large egg
egg yolk	17 g	1 large yolk	17 g	1 large yolk
heavy cream	30 g	2 tablespoons	30 g	2 tablespoons

flaky sea salt, for sprinkling (optional)

1. Sprinkle a large sheet of parchment paper lightly with flour.
   Cut the butter into ¼-inch (6 mm) cubes and return to the refrigerator. In a large spouted measuring cup, whisk together the egg yolk, egg, and cream. Gently combine the cheese and vegetables.

2. In the bowl of a stand mixer fitted with the paddle attachment, add the all-purpose flour, rye flour, sugar, baking powder, and salt. Toss together or mix on the lowest setting for 1 minute. Add the cubed butter. Pulse on the lowest speed to begin to incorporate the butter and keep the flour in the bowl. Increase the speed to low, then increase to medium-low to continue to mix and break the butter into smaller pieces until the mixture resembles a coarse meal, about 3 minutes total.

3. With the mixer running on low speed, stream in the cream mixture and mix until combined and beginning to come together around the paddle, 1 to 2 minutes. Stop the mixer, add the roasted vegetable and goat cheese mixture, pulse, and then mix on medium-low speed until combined and the roasted vegetables are distributed, about 1 minute more.

4. Transfer the dough to the prepared parchment paper and press evenly into a 7-inch (18 cm) round for six scones or a 10 by 6-inch (25 by 15 cm) rectangle for twelve scones. The dough should be ½ to ¾ inch (1.25 to 2 cm) thick. Refrigerate for 2 to 3 hours, until firm.

5. For the round, cut the round in half and then cut each half into three equal triangles, for a total of six triangular scones. For the rectangle, cut the block in half lengthwise and then cut each half into six equal pieces, for a total of twelve rectangular scones. Alternatively, for round scones, cut with a round cookie cutter. Any trimmings can be pushed together one time and used.

   The scones can be baked at this point, refrigerated for a day, or frozen for up to 3 weeks.

6. Preheat the oven to 400°F (200°C). Line a rimmed baking sheet with parchment paper.

   Set the scones on the baking sheet, leaving about an inch (2.5 cm) between each.

   MAKE THE EGG WASH: Whisk together the egg, yolk, and cream in a small bowl. Brush the scones with the egg wash and sprinkle with flaky sea salt, if using. Bake until the scones are a rich golden brown, 20 to 30 minutes, depending on whether baking from cold or frozen.

7. Transfer the scones to a wire rack. Serve warm.

Lemon-Currant Einkorn Scones

Einkorn flour has a gentle but distinct aroma, nutty and a little bit herbal. It gives this scone dough a very silky feel. Lemon zest and Zante currants add tartness and sweetness, along with some texture. This recipe will work with all-purpose flour if you don't have any einkorn flour in your pantry.

Makes 6 or 12 scones, about 85 grams (3 ounces) each

Start to finish: **about 3 hours**

Gathering ingredients and preparing the dough: **30 minutes**

Shaping, refrigerating, and/or freezing: **at least 2 hours but up to 3 weeks**

Baking: **20 to 30 minutes**

VARIATION(S):

Other dried fruits, nuts, or combinations can be added to either an orange or lemon zest-based dough.

Ingredients	Metric	Imperial	Metric	Imperial
	6 scones		**12 scones**	
unsalted butter, cold	93 g	3¼ ounces / 6½ tablespoons	186 g	6½ ounces / 13 tablespoons
egg yolk	9 g	2 teaspoons	18 g	1 large yolk
whole egg	15 g	1 tablespoon	30 g	2 tablespoons
heavy cream	117 g	½ cup	234 g	1 cup
granulated sugar	23 g	1 tablespoon plus 2¾ teaspoons	46 g	3 tablespoons plus 2½ teaspoons
lemon zest	5 g	1½ teaspoons	10 g	1 tablespoon
whole einkorn flour	198 g	1½ cups plus 2½ tablespoons, plus more for dusting	397 g	3¼ cups plus 1 tablespoon, plus more for dusting
baking powder	9 g	1¾ teaspoons	18 g	1 tablespoon plus ½ teaspoon
fine sea salt	3 g	½ teaspoon	6 g	1 teaspoon
Zante currants	50 g	¼ cup	100 g	½ cup
EGG WASH				
whole egg	55 g	1 large egg	55 g	1 large egg
egg yolk	17 g	1 large yolk	17 g	1 large yolk
heavy cream	30 g	2 tablespoons	30 g	2 tablespoons

coarse sugar, for sprinkling (optional)

1. Sprinkle a large sheet of parchment paper lightly with flour.
   Cut the butter into ¼ inch (6 mm) cubes and return to the refrigerator. In a large spouted measuring cup, whisk together the egg yolk, egg, and cream.

RECIPE CONTINUES

2. In the bowl of a stand mixer fitted with the paddle attachment, add the granulated sugar and lemon zest. stirring to incorporate until combined and fragrant. Add the flour, baking powder, and salt. Toss together or mix on the lowest setting for 1 minute. Add the cubed butter. Pulse on the lowest speed to begin to incorporate the butter and keep the flour in the bowl. Increase the speed to low, then increase to medium-low to continue to mix and break the butter into smaller pieces until the mixture resembles a coarse meal, about 3 minutes total.

3. With the mixer running on low speed, stream in the cream mixture and mix until combined and beginning to come together around the paddle, 1 to 2 minutes. Stop the mixer, add the currants, pulse and then mix on medium-low until combined, about 1 minute more.

4. Transfer the dough to the prepared parchment paper and press evenly into a 7-inch (18 cm) round for six scones or a 10 by 6-inch (25 by 15 cm) rectangle for twelve scones. The dough should be ½ to ¾ inch (1.25 to 2 cm) thick. Refrigerate for 2 to 3 hours, until firm.

5. For the round, cut the round in half and then cut each half into three equal triangles, for a total of six triangular scones. For the rectangle, cut the block in half lengthwise and then cut each half into six equal pieces, for a total of twelve rectangular scones. Alternatively, for round scones, cut with a round cookie cutter. Any trimmings can be pushed together one time and used.

The scones can be baked at this point, refrigerated for a day, or frozen for up to 3 weeks.

6. Preheat the oven to 400°F (200°C). Line a rimmed baking sheet with parchment paper.

Set the scones on the prepared baking sheet, leaving about an inch (2.5 cm) between them.

MAKE THE EGG WASH: Whisk together the egg, yolk, and cream in a small bowl. Brush the scones with the egg wash and sprinkle with coarse sugar, if using. Bake until the scones are a rich golden brown, 20 to 30 minutes, depending on whether baking from cold or frozen.

7. Transfer the scones to a wire rack. Serve warm or at room temperature.

MUFFINS

As with scones, we introduced muffins at Bread Alone because of customer demand. Muffins—first morning glory, then corn, then berry—complemented the simplicity and authenticity of the breads.

Developing the muffin menu, and in fact the entire pastry menu, was a haphazard, unpredictable, and undeniably fun process. Whoever was in the pastry department had the freedom to whip up muffins depending on the season and what they were in the mood for. Over the years, various bakers have made little changes—some fresh corn here, a little orange zest there, some oat topping. There are our core recipes, which we always bake, and also recipes that come and go at the whim of the staff. With our breads, it's all about science and consistency. On the pastry side, and especially with muffins, we get to experiment every day and have a little fun. But every Bread Alone muffin is easy to make, full of flavor, and not too sweet. Sometimes we'll add a little spelt, rye, or whole wheat flour to the formula, but all-purpose flour predominates, giving the muffins a light texture and a good rise.

Corn Muffins

Corn muffins are the muffins that bridge the gap between sweet and savory in both their taste and what they can be served with. A corn muffin is equally at home with morning coffee or a cup of soup. Likewise, it can be enjoyed with or without maple or herb butter (recipes follow). Frozen corn works well in this recipe, but there is nothing like stripping sweet and milky kernels from a fresh ear of corn and adding them to the batter.

Makes 6 large muffins (about 200 grams / 7 ounces each) or 12 traditional muffins (about 100 grams / 3½ ounces each)

Start to finish:
about 3 hours

Gathering ingredients and preparing the batter:
about 20 minutes

Refrigerating the batter:
at least 2 hours but up to 1 day

Baking:
22 to 25 minutes

Ingredients	Metric	Imperial
buttermilk (any fat content)	255 g	1 cup plus 2 teaspoons
canola oil	156 g	½ cup plus 3 tablespoons
eggs	110 g	2 large eggs
honey	9 g	1¼ teaspoons
orange zest (optional)	5 g	1 tablespoon
all-purpose flour	227 g	1¾ cups plus 2 tablespoons
cornmeal, medium-grind	138 g	¾ cup plus 2½ tablespoons
sugar	97 g	½ cup
baking powder	13 g	2¾ teaspoons
fine sea salt	3 g	½ teaspoon
corn kernels, fresh or frozen and thawed	150 g	1 cup plus 3 tablespoons

Maple Butter or Herb Butter, for serving (recipes follow; optional)

1. Set a 3-quart (3-liter) storage container on the work surface.

2. In a large spouted measuring cup, whisk together the buttermilk, oil, eggs, honey, and orange zest, if using.

3. In the bowl of a stand mixer fitted with the paddle attachment, add the flour, cornmeal, sugar, baking powder, and salt. Toss together or mix on the lowest setting for 1 minute. With the mixer running on low speed, stream half of the buttermilk mixture into the bowl. Stop the mixer and scrape the sides, bottom, and the paddle to begin to

RECIPE CONTINUES

incorporate any dry pockets. Return the mixer to low speed and stream in the remaining buttermilk mixture. Stop the mixer before the mixture is completely combined. The batter should still look lumpy, but there shouldn't be any visible dry areas at this point. Remove the bowl from the mixer, scraping any batter from the paddle into the bowl.

4. Fold in the corn until just distributed. Transfer the mixture to the storage container. Refrigerate for at least 2 hours but ideally overnight.

5. Preheat the oven to 425°F (230°C). Line the cups of a large 6-cup muffin pan or a traditional 12-cup muffin pan with paper liners. Divide the batter evenly among the cups.

6. Bake the muffins for 10 minutes. Then, without opening the door, lower the oven temperature to 350°F (175°C) and continue to bake until a skewer inserted in the center of the muffins comes out clean, about 15 minutes more for the large muffins and 12 to 13 for the traditional muffins.

7. Transfer to a wire rack. Let cool in the pan for about 10 minutes. Remove and serve warm or let cool completely on the rack. Serve with Maple Butter or Herb Butter, if desired.

Maple Butter

Makes 170 grams (about 6 ounces / ⅔ cup)

Ingredients	Metric	Imperial
unsalted butter, softened	115 g	4 ounces / 8 tablespoons
pure maple syrup	55 g	3½ tablespoons

In the bowl of a stand mixer fitted with the paddle attachment, mix the butter and maple syrup on medium-low to medium speed until combined and fluffy, 2 to 3 minutes.

Herb Butter

Makes 120 grams (about 4 ounces / ½ cup)

When making herb butter, there are some herbs that stand out when left alone, like chives, and others that are great combined with zest: flat-leaf parsley with lemon zest, cilantro with lime zest, or rosemary and thyme with orange zest.

Ingredients	Metric	Imperial
unsalted butter, softened	115 g	4 ounces / 8 tablespoons
finely chopped fresh herbs	2 to 4 g	1½ teaspoons to 1 tablespoon
lemon or lime zest (optional)	1.5 g	¾ teaspoon

In the bowl of a stand mixer fitted with the paddle attachment, mix the butter, herbs, and zest, if using, on medium-low to medium speed until combined and fluffy, 2 to 3 minutes.

Buckwheat and Mixed Berry Muffins

At the bakery, we like the combination of fresh blueberries and raspberries, but fresh blackberries could be included or substituted for one of the two here. When local berries are abundant in the summer, I'll throw bags of them into the freezer for winter baking. Toss frozen berries in a bit of the flour once thawed to keep them from "bleeding" into the muffin batter. Now that I'm living in Maine, I've become a fan of the small local blueberries, which have a deep, intense flavor. I like to support local farms by using frozen Maine blueberries out of season. Look for Blue Ox or Alexander blueberries, which are sold year-round at supermarkets across the country. Or go to Blue-Zee Farm (bluezeefarm.com), my local source in Penobscot, Maine, to order one-, three-, and five-pound boxes shipped to your door.

Makes 6 large muffins (about 160 grams / 5½ ounces each) or 12 traditional muffins (about 80 grams / 3 ounces each)

Start to finish:
about 3 hours

Gathering ingredients and preparing the batter: **about 20 minutes**

Refrigerating the batter: **at least 2 hours but up to 1 day**

Baking:
25 to 30 minutes

Ingredients	Metric	Imperial
buttermilk (any fat content)	191 g	¾ cup plus ½ tablespoon
canola oil	109 g	½ cup
whole eggs	110 g	2 large eggs
fresh lemon juice	14 g	2¾ teaspoons
pure vanilla extract or paste	6 g	1½ teaspoons
all-purpose flour	212 g	1¾ cups
buckwheat flour	60 g	½ cup
granulated sugar	136 g	½ cup plus 3 tablespoons
baking powder	13 g	2¾ teaspoons
fine sea salt	1 g	¼ teaspoon
blueberries	100 g	⅔ cup
raspberries	100 g	⅔ cup

Oat Topping or Lemon Sugar (recipes follow; optional) or coarse sugar, for sprinkling (optional)

1. Set a 3-quart (3-liter) storage container on the work surface.

2. In a large spouted measuring cup, whisk together the buttermilk, oil, eggs, lemon juice, and vanilla.

RECIPE CONTINUES

3. In the bowl of a stand mixer fitted with the paddle attachment, add the all-purpose flour, buckwheat flour, granulated sugar, baking powder, and salt. Toss together or mix on the lowest setting for 1 minute. With the mixer running on low speed, stream half of the buttermilk mixture into the bowl. Stop the mixer and scrape the sides, bottom, and the paddle to begin to incorporate any dry pockets. Return the mixer to low speed and stream in the remaining buttermilk mixture. Stop the mixer before the mixture is completely combined. The batter should still look lumpy, but there shouldn't be any visible dry areas at this point. Remove the bowl from the mixer, scraping any batter from the paddle into the bowl.

4. Fold in the berries until just distributed. Transfer the mixture to the storage container. Refrigerate for at least 2 hours but ideally overnight.

5. Preheat the oven to 425°F (230°C). Line the cups of a large 6-cup muffin pan or a traditional 12-cup muffin pan with paper liners. Divide the batter evenly among the cups. Sprinkle with the oat topping, lemon sugar, or coarse sugar, if using.

6. Bake the muffins for 10 minutes. Then, without opening the door, lower the oven temperature to 350°F (175°C) and continue to bake until a skewer inserted in the center of the muffins comes out clean, 18 to 20 minutes more for the large muffins and about 15 minutes more for the traditional muffins.

7. Transfer to a wire rack. Let cool in the pan for about 10 minutes. Remove and serve warm or let cool completely on the rack.

Oat Topping

Makes about 130 grams (4½ ounces / scant 1 cup)

Ingredients	Metric	Imperial
unsalted butter, cold	30 g	1 ounce / 2 tablespoons
all-purpose or buckwheat flour	30 g	¼ cup
light or dark brown sugar	30 g	2½ tablespoons
rolled oats	37 g	¼ cup plus 3 tablespoons
fine sea salt	0.6 g	⅛ teaspoon

1. Cut the butter into ¼-inch (6 mm) cubes and return to the refrigerator.

2. In the bowl of a stand mixer fitted with the paddle attachment, combine the flour, brown sugar, oats, and salt on the Stir setting until combined, about 30 seconds.

3. Add the butter and mix on medium speed until crumbly, 1 to 2 minutes. (The mixture should not come together into a single mass.)

Lemon Sugar

Makes 135 grams (about 4¾ ounces / ⅔ cup)

Ingredients	Metric	Imperial
1 lemon		
sugar	130 g	⅔ cup

With a vegetable peeler, peel the zest from the lemon in strips, then scrape as much of the white pith off the zest as possible. Roughly chop the zest and put in a food processor with the sugar. Pulse until the zest is finely ground and incorporated, about 2 minutes.

Morning Glory Muffins

Morning glory muffins have been around since the advent of "health food" in the late '70s, just a handful of years before Bread Alone opened. We've made countless variations, with pineapple, peaches, and pears. But I like to stick close to the original. No need to mess with a classic.

Makes 6 large muffins (about 170 grams / 6 ounces each) or 12 traditional muffins (about 85 grams / 3 ounces each)

Start to finish:
about 3 hours

Gathering ingredients and preparing the batter: about 30 minutes

Refrigerating the batter:
at least 2 hours but up to 1 day

Baking:
22 to 25 minutes

Ingredients	Metric	Imperial
buttermilk (any fat content)	104 g	¼ cup plus 3 tablespoons
canola oil	124 g	½ cup plus 1 tablespoon
eggs	165 g	3 large eggs
pure vanilla extract or paste	5 g	1 teaspoon
all-purpose flour	166 g	1¼ cups plus 2 tablespoons
sugar	124 g	½ cup plus 2 tablespoons
wheat bran	15 g	¼ cup plus 2 teaspoons
baking powder	8 g	1½ teaspoons plus ⅛ teaspoon
baking soda	8 g	1½ teaspoons plus ⅛ teaspoon
fine sea salt	1 g	¼ teaspoon
ground cinnamon	1 g	½ teaspoon
shredded carrot	104 g	1 cup plus 2½ tablespoons
shredded apple	104 g	1 cup
dried cranberries or Zante currants	52 g	¼ cup plus 1 tablespoon
pecans, lightly toasted at 350°F (175°C) for 8 to 10 minutes, coarsely chopped	27 g	¼ cup
shredded unsweetened coconut, lightly toasted at 350°F (175°C) for 8 to 10 minutes	25 g	¼ cup plus 1 tablespoon

1. Set a 3-quart (3-liter) storage container on the work surface.

2. In a large spouted measuring cup, whisk together the buttermilk, oil, eggs, and vanilla.

RECIPE CONTINUES

3. In the bowl of a stand mixer fitted with the paddle attachment, add the flour, sugar, wheat bran, baking powder, baking soda, salt, and cinnamon. Toss together or mix on the lowest setting for 1 minute. With the mixer running on low speed, stream half of the buttermilk mixture into the bowl. Stop the mixer and scrape the sides, bottom, and the paddle to begin to incorporate any dry pockets. Return the mixer to low speed and stream in the remaining buttermilk mixture. Stop the mixer before the mixture is completely combined. The batter should still look lumpy, but there shouldn't be any visible dry areas at this point. Remove the bowl from the mixer, scraping any batter from the paddle into the bowl.

4. Add the carrot, apple, cranberries, pecans, and coconut. Fold in just until distributed. Transfer the mixture to the storage container. Refrigerate for at least 2 hours but ideally overnight.

5. Preheat the oven to 425°F (230°C). Line the cups of a large 6-cup muffin pan or a traditional 12-cup muffin pan with paper liners. Divide the batter evenly among the cups.

6. Bake the muffins for 10 minutes. Then, without opening the door, lower the oven temperature to 350°F (175°C) and continue to bake until a skewer inserted in the center of the muffins comes out clean, about 15 minutes more for the large muffins and about 12 minutes more for the traditional muffins.

7. Transfer to a wire rack. Let cool in the pan for about 10 minutes. Remove and serve warm or let cool completely on the rack.

COOKIES

The secret to our cookie success is easy to understand. Once we perfected simple recipes for classics, we were able to create flavor variations depending on the season, availability of special ingredients, or the cravings of the bakers on a particular day. This way, we could provide customers with a comforting old favorite like shortbread but excite them with a lavender, pistachio, or lemon and dried blueberry example on any given day. You, too, can perfect a simple cookie recipe and then experiment with flavors so you are always serving an old favorite that is also new.

I'm also including two personal favorites, recipes for financiers and canelés. These small items fall somewhere between a cookie and a pastry, but no matter how you classify them, they are delectable treats that should be in every baker's repertoire.

Lemon Shortbread

If I have a go-to cookie, it's shortbread. I love its slightly grainy, melt-in-your-mouth texture. I love how simple it is to make. And I love how flexible it is. In addition to citrus and nut versions, we've made shortbread with lavender or rosemary; spices including cinnamon, cardamom, and ginger; dried chopped cranberries, cherries, or blueberries; and flavorings including espresso powder and vanilla bean. We use a little almond flour (or another nut flour) in our shortbread at Bread Alone. It is the secret to the soulfulness of French sablé cookies, and to the soulfulness of ours as well.

For a bit more lemon flavor and an additional decorative touch, add slices of dried lemon. Very thinly slice 1 to 2 lemons and carefully remove any seeds. Lay on a baking sheet lined with a silicone baking mat and then lay another baking mat on top (to keep the slices from curling). Dry in a very low oven (200°F/90°C) until completely dried, 6 to 8 hours. Alternatively, the slices can be dried in a dehydrator, but they should also be weighted slightly to keep from curling.

Makes twenty
2-inch (5 cm)
squares

Start to finish:
about 4 hours

Gathering ingredients
and preparing the
dough: 30 minutes

Shaping and
refrigerating:
at least 2 hours
but up to overnight

Baking:
about 25 minutes

Cooling and glazing:
1 hour

VARIATION(S):

Substitute another
citrus zest and juice,
such as lime, grapefruit,
or blood orange.

Ingredients	Metric	Imperial
SHORTBREAD		
unsalted butter, at room temperature	226 g	8 ounces / 16 tablespoons
fine sea salt	3 g	½ teaspoon
powdered sugar	75 g	½ cup plus 2½ tablespoons
lemon zest, finely grated	5 g	1 tablespoon
all-purpose flour	240 g	2 cups
almond flour	120 g	1 cup plus 1 tablespoon
fresh lemon juice	25 g	1 tablespoon plus 2 teaspoons
GLAZE		
powdered sugar	85 g	¾ cup
whole milk	20 g	1 tablespoon plus 1 teaspoon
lemon zest, finely grated	4 g	2 teaspoons
fresh lemon juice	3 g	½ teaspoon

dried lemon slices (see headnote; optional)

1. **MAKE THE SHORTBREAD:** In the bowl of a stand mixer fitted with the paddle attachment, add the butter, salt, powdered sugar, and lemon

RECIPE CONTINUES

zest. Mix on the Stir setting for about 15 seconds to begin to incorporate the sugar. Increase the speed to low and continue to mix, stopping to scrape the bottom and sides of the bowl once, just until the mixture comes together, about 1 minute more.

2. Add the all-purpose flour, almond flour, and lemon juice to the bowl. Mix on the Stir setting for about 15 seconds to begin to incorporate. Increase the speed to low and continue to mix, stopping to scrape the bottom and sides of the bowl once (particularly the bottom for any dry bits that may have settled there), until the mixture comes together, about 2 minutes more.

3. Line a baking sheet with parchment paper. Mound the dough on the work surface and with a bench scraper or the heel of your hand, push it together to form an 8 by 10-inch (20 by 25 cm) rectangle. Transfer to the lined baking sheet. Cover and refrigerate for at least 2 hours or up to overnight.

4. Position the oven racks in the upper and lower thirds of the oven. Preheat the oven to 325°F (160°C).

Line two baking sheets with parchment paper.

5. Using a chef's knife, cut the rectangle into twenty 2-inch (5 cm) squares (five across and four down if a long end of the dough is positioned in front of you). Arrange ten on each baking sheet and transfer to the oven. Bake, switching the shelf position of the pans and rotating once during baking, until the shortbread are golden brown, about 25 minutes.

6. Transfer the baking sheets to wire racks and let cool for 15 minutes. After that, the shortbread can be carefully moved to the racks to cool completely.

7. **MEANWHILE, PREPARE THE GLAZE:** Using a small whisk or a spatula, combine the powdered sugar, milk, lemon zest, and lemon juice in a small bowl.

8. Using a small spatula, spread the glaze on top of the shortbread, top with the lemon slices, if using, and return them to the wire rack for about 10 minutes for the glaze to set.

Chocolate-Dipped Hazelnut Shortbread

I may be primarily a bread baker by day, but I dream of hazelnut shortbread by night. The toasted flavor of hazelnuts combined with butter is classic. Dipping the cookies in chocolate makes them that much more irresistible.

Makes eighteen 1⅓ by 3-inch (3.3 by 7.5 cm) rectangles

Start to finish:
about 4 hours

Gathering ingredients and preparing the dough: **30 minutes**

Shaping and refrigerating:
at least 2 hours or up to overnight

Baking:
25 to 30 minutes

Cooling and dipping:
1 hour

VARIATION(S):

Substitute another nut flour, such as pistachio or almond, along with finely chopped pistachios or almonds.

Ingredients	Metric	Imperial
unsalted butter, at room temperature	226 g	8 ounces / 16 tablespoons
fine sea salt	3 g	½ teaspoon
powdered sugar	75 g	½ cup plus 2½ tablespoons
all-purpose flour	240 g	2 cups
hazelnut flour	120 g	1 cup plus 1 tablespoon
pure vanilla extract or paste	3 g	¾ teaspoon
milk or semisweet chocolate, coarsely chopped	250 g	9 ounces
toasted skinned hazelnuts, finely chopped (optional)	56 g	2 ounces

1. In the bowl of a stand mixer fitted with the paddle attachment, add the butter, salt, and powdered sugar. Mix on the Stir setting for about 15 seconds to begin to incorporate the sugar. Increase the speed to low and continue to mix, stopping to scrape the bottom and sides of the bowl once, just until the mixture comes together, about 1 minute more.

2. Add the all-purpose flour, hazelnut flour, and vanilla to the bowl. Mix on the Stir setting for about 15 seconds to begin to incorporate. Increase the speed to low and continue to mix, stopping to scrape the bottom and sides of the bowl once (particularly the bottom for any dry bits that may have settled there), until the mixture comes together, about 2 minutes more.

RECIPE CONTINUES

3. Line a baking sheet with parchment paper. Mound the dough on the work surface and with a bench scraper or the heel of your hand, push it together to form an 8 by 9-inch (20 by 23 cm) rectangle. Transfer to the lined baking sheet. Cover and refrigerate for at least 2 hours or up to overnight.

4. Position the oven racks in the upper and lower thirds of the oven. Preheat the oven to 325°F (160°C).
   Line two baking sheets with parchment paper.

5. Using a chef's knife, cut the rectangle into eighteen 1⅓ by 3-inch (3.3 by 7.5 cm) rectangles (three across and six down if a long end of the dough is positioned in front of you). Arrange nine on each baking sheet and transfer to the oven. Bake, switching the shelf position of the pans and rotating once during baking, until the shortbread are golden brown, 25 to 30 minutes.

6. Transfer the baking sheets to wire racks and let cool for 15 minutes. After that, the shortbread can be carefully moved to the racks to cool completely.

7. Meanwhile, melt the chocolate in a microwave or double boiler.

8. Line a baking sheet with wax paper or parchment paper.
   Dip one end of each rectangle in the chocolate and set on the wax paper. Sprinkle with the chopped nuts, if using, and let sit until the chocolate has firmed up, about 10 minutes.

Pistachio–Brown Butter Financiers

A delicious financier has a gentle crust that encases a pleasingly spongy interior that is never too sweet. It's a mainstay and classic that can also be varied in a dozen different ways. This version gets its wonderful flavor and fragrance from a little bit of brown butter and its pleasing texture by grinding your own pistachios for the flour and paste. (You can grind the almonds as well.) For the flour, put whole pistachios in a food processor and pulse until they reach the desired consistency: some small pieces, not too finely ground. For the paste, pulse as you would the flour until the mixture has more of a butter consistency.

We've made financiers flavored with lemon, hazelnut, chocolate, mocha, vanilla, and dried cranberries. Financiers, which can be devoured in three bites, are *the* snack with a cup of tea. For dessert, serve a financier on a small plate with a little scoop of ice cream and some cherry sauce. If you aren't using a nonstick financier pan or silicone baking mold, the molds should be lightly greased with room-temperature unsalted butter.

Makes eight 50-gram (1¾-ounce) financiers

Start to finish:
about 1¼ hours

Gathering ingredients and preparing the batter: **30 minutes**

Baking:
12 to 15 minutes

Cooling:
about 30 minutes

Ingredients	Metric	Imperial
sugar	100 g	½ cup plus 1 teaspoon
pistachio flour (see headnote)	50 g	¼ cup plus 1½ tablespoons
almond flour	40 g	¼ cup plus 3 tablespoons
all-purpose flour	30 g	¼ cup
egg whites	90 g	4 large whites
unsalted butter	90 g	3 ounces / 6 tablespoons
pistachio paste (see headnote)	18 g	1 tablespoon plus ½ teaspoon
pure vanilla extract or paste	2 g	½ teaspoon
matcha powder, for dusting (optional)		

1. Preheat the oven to 350°F (175°C). Set an 8-cavity financier pan on the work surface.

In a large bowl, add the sugar, pistachio flour, almond flour, and all-purpose flour. Whisk to combine and break up any lumps. Set a fine-mesh strainer over the bowl.

RECIPE CONTINUES

2. In the bowl of a stand mixer fitted with the whisk attachment, add the egg whites. Whip on medium speed until stiff peaks form, 2 to 3 minutes.

3. Melt the butter in a small saucepan over medium heat. As soon as it has melted, whisk it to keep it from separating. Continue to cook, whisking occasionally, to keep the solids from settling and burning on the bottom of the pan, until the butter is a medium golden brown, 3 to 5 minutes. Remove from the heat and pour through the strainer into the dry ingredients.

With a spatula, mix in the brown butter followed by the pistachio paste and vanilla until the batter is smooth. Add about one-third of the egg whites and mix in to incorporate and loosen the batter. Top with half of the remaining whites, folding them in gently, then add the remaining whites, folding them in as well.

4. Divide the batter among the cavities in the pan, gently spooning it in. The pan can be lightly tapped to level the tops.

Bake until a skewer inserted in the center of the cakes comes out clean, 12 to 15 minutes.

5. Transfer to a wire rack and let cool in the pan for 5 to 10 minutes. After that, the financiers can be carefully moved to the rack to cool completely.

6. Using a small fine-mesh strainer, dust the tops of the financiers with matcha powder, if you like.

Canelés

With their deeply caramelized exteriors and custard-like interiors, canelés are a delightful example of the beauty of contrasting textures. I will never forget the first canelé I bought at Gérard Mulot's bakery, Maison Mulot, next to the Marché Saint-Germain in Paris. I was enchanted, and figuring out how to make them became a passion.

They are baked in molds made from copper, which conducts heat rapidly and produces their characteristic caramelization. If you are making canelés with new molds, season them first by generously brushing the insides with vegetable oil, placing them right side up on a baking sheet, and heating them in a 350°F (175°C) oven for an hour, then flipping them upside down and heating for another 15 minutes. French bakers traditionally brush the insides of the seasoned molds with a mixture of beeswax and melted butter, but at Bread Alone we find that brushing high-quality molds with just butter is sufficient, and much less messy. The batter does need to rest in the refrigerator for 48 hours, but will be okay to use for up to 24 hours after that, so you can bake 12 canelés at once or spread out your baking over two days, to enjoy your canelés when they are fresh, since they are best eaten the day they are made.

Makes 12 canelés, about 70 grams (2½ ounces) each

Start to finish:
about 3 days

Gathering ingredients and preparing the batter, day one:
1½ hours

Refrigerating the batter:
48 hours

Baking, day three:
1 hour

Cooling:
about 30 minutes

Ingredients	Metric	Imperial
whole milk	525 g	2 cups plus 1 tablespoon
½ vanilla bean pod		
sugar	250 g	1¼ cups plus 1 tablespoon
egg yolks	54 g	3 large yolks
rum	50 g	¼ cup
all-purpose flour	100 g	¾ cup plus 1 tablespoon plus 1 teaspoon
corn flour, lightly toasted	20 g	2½ tablespoons
cornstarch	25 g	3 tablespoons
unsalted butter	5 g	⅛ ounce / ¾ teaspoon
unsalted butter, softened, for greasing		

1. In a medium saucepan, add the milk. Scrape the seeds of the vanilla bean pod half into the milk and add the half pod as well. Bring to a simmer over medium-high heat, whisking to distribute the seeds.

RECIPE CONTINUES

Remove from the heat and let steep for 1 hour to infuse the milk with the vanilla flavor.

2. In a large bowl, add the sugar, egg yolks, and rum. Stir until smooth. Sift together the all-purpose flour, corn flour, and cornstarch and stir into the sugar mixture.

3. Add the butter to the steeped milk, whisking it to melt. The milk should still be warm enough to melt the butter (if it's not, heat just enough to warm).

4. Whisk the butter and milk into the sugar mixture, removing the vanilla bean pod and breaking up any lumps. Pour through a fine-mesh strainer into a bowl.

5. Cover the bowl and refrigerate for 48 hours.

6. Preheat the oven to 500°F (260°C).
Brush the canelé molds with the softened butter. Set on a baking sheet, leaving a couple of inches between them.

7. Remove the batter from the refrigerator and whisk to recombine. Pour the batter into the molds, stopping about ¼ inch (6 mm) from the top. Canelé molds come in slightly different sizes, so you may get one or two more or fewer depending on the size of yours.

8. Bake for 15 minutes. Without opening the oven, lower the oven temperature to 350°F (175°C) and continue to bake until the canelés are a rich golden brown, 55 minutes to 1 hour.

9. Transfer to a wire rack. Immediately and carefully (because they will be hot), turn the molds over to release the canelés and let them cool completely, about 45 minutes.

PIES

In the early years at Bread Alone, a holiday would roll around and people would say, "Bread is great, but I also want to order a pie." So we started baking them. Whoever happened to be working in the pastry shop would decide on fillings. There were many farms and orchards in the area, so we focused on local fruit—apples, strawberries, rhubarb, peaches, blueberries, plums—when it was available.

Even today, the pie menu is never static. Sure, we have apple, pumpkin, and blueberry at certain times of the year, but we might top the apple with crumbs, use maple syrup to sweeten the pumpkin, or combine the blueberries with plums, depending on what we are craving and how the walk-in is stocked.

We don't oversweeten our pies. Even the tartest apples and berries will caramelize naturally in the oven, so to preserve our pies' fresh fruit flavor, we go easy on the sugar.

Single-Crust Pie Dough

We've done a lot of pie dough comparison tests—using all butter, some butter and some lard, and some butter and some vegetable shortening. Long ago, we decided on an all-butter crust, for its rich flavor. It's true that it's easier to get a tender and flaky result with some lard or shortening. But we believe that all-butter crusts just taste better. To ensure that our crusts are tender, we are extra careful to add just enough liquid so the dough holds together. We've also found that stone-ground all-purpose flour tends to absorb more liquid than commercially milled flour, so there's less chance of overhydrating the dough during mixing.

At the bakery, we use a pie press to form pie crusts, but at home I use a French rolling pin, without handles, which lets me really feel the dough as I gently roll it out in as few passes as possible, between sheets of wax paper. Too much rolling will toughen the dough.

This recipe can also be made with white spelt flour instead of all-purpose flour, though you might have to add an extra tablespoon or two of water to get the dough to come together.

Makes enough dough for one 9-inch (23 cm) single-crust traditional pie

Start to finish:
about 2¼ hours

Gathering ingredients and preparing the dough:
about 15 minutes

Refrigerating the dough:
at least 2 hours but up to 2 days

Ingredients	Metric	Imperial
unsalted butter, cold	95 g	3⅓ ounces / 6½ tablespoons
ice water	32 g	2 tablespoons
distilled white vinegar	2 g	½ teaspoon
all-purpose flour	157 g	1¼ cups plus 1 tablespoon
fine sea salt	3 g	½ teaspoon

1. Cut the butter into ¼-inch (6 mm) cubes and return to the refrigerator. Add the ice water and vinegar to a small spouted measuring cup.

2. In the bowl of a stand mixer fitted with the paddle attachment, add the flour and salt. Toss together or mix on the lowest setting for about 30 seconds. Add the cubed butter. Pulse on the lowest speed to begin to incorporate the butter and keep the flour in the bowl. Increase the speed to low, then increase to medium-low to continue to mix and break the butter into smaller pieces until the mixture resembles a coarse meal, about 3 minutes total.

RECIPE CONTINUES

3. With the mixer running on low speed, add the water and vinegar mixture and mix until combined and the dough comes together around the paddle, about 1 minute.

4. Lift the dough from the bowl and form into a disk. Wrap in beeswax wrap or plastic wrap. Refrigerate the dough for at least 2 hours or up to 2 days. At this point the dough can also be frozen for up to 1 month and thawed in the refrigerator when ready to use.

Apple-Raspberry Crumb Pie

I love apple pie as much as the next guy, but I love apple filling with a handful of raspberries even better. In this pie, the raspberries remain separate from the apples, providing bursts of raspberry flavor in every other bite. You can almost feel the color of the raspberries in your mouth, if that makes sense. We make this pie in September, when the last of the local raspberries are available and the first of the local apples have been picked.

Makes one 9-inch (23 cm) traditional pie

Start to finish: **about 5½ hours**

Gathering ingredients and making and refrigerating the pie dough: **about 2¼ hours**

Preparing the oat topping: **10 minutes**

Assembling and baking the pie: **about 2 hours**

Cooling: **1 hour**

Ingredients	Metric	Imperial
Single-Crust Pie Dough (page 241)		
OAT TOPPING		
unsalted butter, cold	30 g	1 ounce / 2 tablespoons
rolled oats	37 g	¼ cup plus 3 tablespoons
all-purpose flour	30 g	¼ cup, plus more for dusting
light or dark brown sugar	30 g	2½ tablespoons
fine sea salt	0.6 g	⅛ teaspoon
PIE FILLING		
apples, firm	1.1 kg	2½ pounds
sugar	30 g	2½ tablespoons
tapioca flour (also known as tapioca starch)	9 g	1 tablespoon plus ¾ teaspoon
all-purpose flour	6 g	2 teaspoons
ground cinnamon	2 g	1 teaspoon
raspberries	150 g	5 ounces

1. Remove the pie dough from the refrigerator and let it warm up at room temperature for about 30 minutes.

2. **MEANWHILE, PREPARE THE OAT TOPPING:** Cut the butter into ¼-inch (6 mm) cubes and return to the refrigerator.

3. In the bowl of a stand mixer fitted with the paddle attachment, add the oats, flour, brown sugar, and salt and mix on the Stir setting until combined, about 30 seconds.

RECIPE CONTINUES

4. Add the butter and mix on medium speed until crumbly, 1 to 2 minutes. (The mixture should not come together into a single mass.) Refrigerate until ready to use.

5. Set a 9-inch (23 cm) traditional pie plate or pan on the work surface. Unwrap the dough and put it between two large pieces of wax paper, parchment paper lightly dusted with all-purpose flour, or plastic wrap. To help keep the dough from cracking, pound a rolling pin across the dough to flatten it. Next, roll the dough from the center out to the edges, turning the dough until it is 11 to 12 inches (28 to 30 cm) across.

6. Remove the top piece of paper. Invert the dough, still on the other piece of paper, and lay it across the top of the plate. Using the paper, gently press the dough into the bottom and edges of the plate, smoothing and removing any air bubbles. Carefully peel off the paper, leaving the excess dough extending over the top edges of the plate.

   To crimp the top (optional), position the thumb and index finger of your right hand, as if ready to pinch, against the outside edge of the dough. Using the index finger of your left hand, push the inner edge out, while pinching the outer edge in around the left index finger with the right fingers. Repeat around the entire edge of the pie.

   If not crimping, run the rolling pin over the top of the pan to remove the excess dough and leave a smooth top. Use that excess dough to patch any thin spots and/or repair any cracks. Cover and refrigerate for at least 30 minutes or up to 4 hours.

7. Preheat the oven to 375°F (190°C).

8. **MAKE THE PIE FILLING:** Peel and core the apples, then cut them into ¼-inch (6 mm) slices.

   Combine the sugar, tapioca flour, all-purpose flour, and cinnamon in a medium bowl. Add the apple slices and toss to evenly coat.

9. Arrange the raspberries in the chilled dough. Top with the apples followed by the cold oat topping and a few more raspberries for decoration.

10. Bake until the apples are tender, about 1 hour 15 minutes.

11. Transfer to a wire rack. Once cooled, it is best to serve the pie the day it is made. Cut into slices to serve.

Pumpkin Pie

Years ago, when one of our farmer friends had a surplus of pumpkins, we took some off his hands, made pumpkin puree, and used it in our Thanksgiving pies. We never used canned pumpkin again. Canned pumpkin has been pureed to within an inch of its life. In contrast, fresh pumpkin, roasted and then pureed at the bakery or at home, maintains some resemblance to the fruit on the vine. There is more texture and flavor to enjoy. We've found that all kinds of pumpkins make great pie filling, and larger specimens are just as good for baking as smaller ones. Since making your own puree takes a little bit of work, it makes sense to make enough for two or more pies and freeze the extra for another day. We often freeze pumpkin puree so we can offer pumpkin pie at Bread Alone well past Thanksgiving and into the spring.

Makes one 9-inch (23 cm) traditional pie

Start to finish:
about 7½ hours

Gathering ingredients and making and refrigerating the pie dough: **about 2¼ hours**

Preparing the pumpkin puree: **1½ hours**

Assembling and baking the pie: **about 2½ hours**

Cooling: **1 hour**

Ingredients	Metric	Imperial
Single-Crust Pie Dough (page 241)		
heavy cream	178 g	¾ cup
whole milk	119 g	¼ cup plus 3½ tablespoons
whole egg	14 g	1 tablespoon
pure vanilla extract or paste	8 g	2 teaspoons
light or dark brown sugar	84 g	¼ cup plus 3 tablespoons
granulated sugar	71 g	¼ cup plus 2 tablespoons
all-purpose flour	8 g	1 tablespoon, plus more for dusting
ground cinnamon	2.5 g	1¼ teaspoons
ground nutmeg	pinch	pinch
ground allspice	pinch	pinch
fine sea salt	3 g	¼ teaspoon
Roasted Pumpkin Puree (recipe follows)	395 g	1⅔ cups
pumpkin seeds, toasted and salted (optional)		

1. Remove the pie dough from the refrigerator and let it warm up at room temperature for about 30 minutes.

RECIPE CONTINUES

2. Set a 9-inch (23 cm) traditional pie plate or pan on the work surface. Unwrap the dough and put it between two large pieces of wax paper, parchment paper lightly dusted with flour, or plastic wrap. To help keep the dough from cracking, pound a rolling pin across the dough to flatten it. Next, roll the dough from the center out to the edges, turning the dough until it is 11 to 12 inches (28 to 30 cm) across.

3. Remove the top piece of paper. Invert the dough, still on the other piece of paper, and lay it across the top of the pie plate. Using the paper, gently press the dough into the bottom and edges of the plate, smoothing and removing any air bubbles. Carefully peel off the paper, leaving the excess dough extending over the top edges of the plate. Small pieces can be trimmed to patch any thin spots and/or repair any cracks.

To crimp the top, position the thumb and index finger of your right hand, as if ready to pinch, against the outside edge of the dough. Using the index finger of your left hand, push the inner edge out, while pinching the outer edge in around the left index finger with the right fingers. Repeat around the entire edge of the pie.

Cover and refrigerate for at least 30 minutes or up to 4 hours.

4. Preheat the oven to 375°F (190°C).

Prick the bottom of the dough with a fork. Line the shell with parchment paper and fill with uncooked beans, rice, or pie weights.

5. Bake until the edges of the dough are a light golden brown, 15 to 20 minutes.

Remove the crust from the oven. Lower the oven temperature to 325°F (160°C). Carefully remove the beans and parchment and let sit while preparing the filling.

6. Add the cream, milk, egg, and vanilla to a spouted measuring cup or a bowl and whisk to combine.

7. In the bowl of a stand mixer fitted with the paddle attachment, add the brown sugar, granulated sugar, flour, cinnamon, nutmeg, allspice, and salt. Toss together or mix on the lowest setting for 1 minute. Add the pumpkin and mix on medium-low speed until smooth, about 1 minute. With the mixer running on low speed, stream in the liquid

ingredients and then continue to mix until smooth, 1 to 2 minutes more, stopping to scrape the bottom and sides to incorporate all the ingredients.

8. Pour the filling into the parbaked pie shell and bake until the filling is set but still wobbly like a trampoline, 1 hour to 1 hour 10 minutes.

9. Transfer to a wire rack and let cool completely. Sprinkle with pumpkin seeds, if using, and cut into slices to serve.

Roasted Pumpkin Puree

Makes about 800 grams (3¼ cups) pumpkin puree, enough for 2 pies

Ingredients	Metric	Imperial
baking pumpkin(s)	2.3 kg	5 pounds
extra-virgin olive oil	26 g	2 tablespoons
fine sea salt	6 g	1 teaspoon

1. Preheat the oven to 400°F (200°C).

2. Cut the pumpkin into quarters. Using a large spoon, scoop out the seeds. Set the pieces on a baking sheet. Drizzle with the olive oil and sprinkle with the salt. Roast until completely tender, about 1 hour.

3. Once cool enough to handle, spoon the pumpkin flesh into a food processor or high-powered blender and puree until smooth.

The puree can be used at this point or refrigerated for up to 2 days. It can also be frozen for up to 6 months and thawed in the refrigerator when ready to use.

Double-Crust Pie Dough

This recipe can also be made with white spelt flour instead of all-purpose flour, though you might have to add an extra tablespoon or two of water to get the dough to come together.

Makes enough dough for one 9-inch (23 cm) double-crust traditional pie

Start to finish:
about 2¼ hours

Gathering ingredients and preparing the dough:
about 15 minutes

Refrigerating the dough:
at least 2 hours but up to 2 days

Ingredients	Metric	Imperial
unsalted butter, cold	190 g	6½ ounces / 13 tablespoons
ice water	64 g	¼ cup plus 1 teaspoon
distilled white vinegar	4 g	¾ teaspoon
all-purpose flour	314 g	2½ cups plus 1 tablespoon plus 2 teaspoons
fine sea salt	6 g	1 teaspoon

1. Cut the butter into ¼-inch (6 mm) cubes and return to the refrigerator. Add the ice water and vinegar to a small spouted measuring cup.

2. In the bowl of a stand mixer fitted with the paddle attachment, add the flour and salt. Toss together or mix on the lowest setting for about 30 seconds. Add the cubed butter. Pulse on the lowest speed to begin to incorporate the butter and keep the flour in the bowl. Increase the speed to low, then increase to medium-low to continue to mix and break the butter into smaller pieces until the mixture resembles a coarse meal, about 3 minutes total.

3. With the mixer running on low speed, add the water and vinegar mixture and mix until combined and the dough comes together around the paddle, about 1 minute.

4. Lift the dough from the bowl, divide in half, and form into two disks. Wrap individually in beeswax wrap or plastic wrap. Refrigerate the dough for at least 2 hours or up to 2 days. At this point the dough can also be frozen for up to 1 month and thawed in the refrigerator when ready to use.

Strawberry–Rhubarb Pie

Seasonality is great, but there's also something to be said for tasting spring in the fall or even the winter. When we hear from a farmer who has an abundance of rhubarb or strawberries in May or June, we'll buy more than we know we'll need, chop the rhubarb, stem the strawberries, and freeze them in separate five-pound bags to use later on. You can do this at home too. Buy enough fruit for several strawberry-rhubarb pies, prep it, freeze it, and you will be able to enjoy spring's first fruit in August, October, or even January.

Don't skip the sauce, which is made with the flavorful liquid thrown off by the fruit as it macerates. It adds a yummy flavor layer and delicious richness to each slice of pie.

Makes one 9-inch (23 cm) traditional pie

Start to finish:
about 13½ hours

Preparing the pie filling, day one: **15 minutes**

Refrigerating the pie filling:
8 hours or up to overnight

Gathering ingredients and making and refrigerating the pie dough, day two: **about 2¼ hours**

Assembling and baking the pie: **about 2 hours**

Cooling: **1 hour**

Preparing the sauce: **20 minutes**

Cooling the sauce: **20 minutes**

Ingredients	Metric	Imperial
strawberries	450 g	1 pound
rhubarb	450 g	1 pound
granulated sugar	225 g	1 cup plus 3 tablespoons
Double-Crust Pie Dough (page 250)		
all-purpose flour, for dusting		
tapioca flour (also known as tapioca starch)	5 g	2 teaspoons
EGG WASH		
whole egg	55 g	1 large egg
egg yolk	18 g	1 large yolk
heavy cream	30 g	2 tablespoons

sanding sugar, for sprinkling

Strawberry Rhubarb Sauce, for serving (recipe follows; optional)

1. The night before making the pie, start the pie filling. Hull the strawberries and cut them into ½- to ¾-inch (1.25 to 2 cm) pieces. Trim the ends from the rhubarb and discard. Cut the stalks into ½-inch (1.25 cm) pieces. Put the strawberries and rhubarb in a medium bowl and toss with the sugar. Cover and refrigerate for 8 hours or up to overnight.

2. Remove the dough from the refrigerator and let it warm up for about 30 minutes.

RECIPE CONTINUES

3. Set a 9-inch (23 cm) traditional pie plate or pan on the work surface. Unwrap the first disk of dough and put it between two large pieces of wax paper, parchment paper lightly dusted with all-purpose flour, or plastic wrap. To help keep the dough from cracking, pound a rolling pin across the dough to flatten it. Next, roll the dough from the center out to the edges, turning the dough until it is 11 to 12 inches (28 to 30 cm) across.

4. Remove the top piece of paper. Invert the dough, still on the other piece of paper, and lay it across the top of the pie plate. Using the paper, gently press the dough into the bottom and edges of the plate, smoothing and removing any air bubbles. Carefully peel off the paper, leaving the excess dough extending over the top edges of the plate. Small pieces can be trimmed to patch any thin spots and/or repair any cracks. Cover the dough.

Unwrap the second disk of dough for the top crust and put it between two large pieces of wax paper, parchment paper lightly dusted with all-purpose flour, or plastic wrap. To help keep the dough from cracking, pound a rolling pin across the dough to flatten it. Next, roll the dough from the center out to the edges, turning the dough until it is 11 to 12 inches (28 to 30 cm) across. Slide onto a parchment-lined baking sheet.

Cover and refrigerate the dough for at least 30 minutes or up to 4 hours.

5. Remove the dough from the refrigerator.
Preheat the oven to 425°F (215°C).

6. Drain the strawberries and rhubarb, reserving the liquid. Return the strawberries and rhubarb to the bowl.

Combine 3 tablespoons (50 g) of the macerating liquid with the tapioca flour. Add to the bowl and toss to evenly coat. Spoon the filling into the pie plate. Reserve the remaining liquid for the sauce or another use. Lay the full dough round over the top.

7. Trim the edges of the dough so that it extends ¼ to ½ inch (6 to 12 mm) beyond the rim of the pie plate. Gently press the top and bottom pieces together.

RECIPE CONTINUES

To crimp the top, position the thumb and index finger of your right hand, as if ready to pinch, against the outside edge of the dough. Using the index finger of your left hand, push the inner edge out, while pinching the outer edge in around the left index finger with the right fingers. Repeat around the entire edge of the pie. With a sharp paring knife, cut ½-inch (1.25 cm) V shapes across the top for steam to escape during baking.

Any dough trimmings can be pressed together and rerolled. Cut into decorative shapes and add to the top, if desired.

8. **MAKE THE EGG WASH:** Whisk together the egg, yolk, and cream and brush the top of the pie.

Bake for 15 minutes. Lower the oven temperature to 350°F (175°C). Continue to bake until the filling is bubbling and the crust is a rich golden brown, 30 to 35 minutes more.

9. Transfer to a wire rack and let cool completely. Cut into slices to serve. Drizzle with the strawberry-rhubarb sauce.

Strawberry–Rhubarb Sauce

Makes about 200 grams (⅔ cup)

Ingredients	Metric	Imperial
reserved strawberry-rhubarb macerating liquid (page 252)	300 g	1 cup
heavy cream	60 g	¼ cup
unsalted butter	30 g	1 ounce / 2 tablespoons
fine sea salt	pinch	pinch

1. Heat the reserved macerating liquid in a small, high-sided saucepan fitted with a candy thermometer. Bring to a boil and cook until the mixture reaches 225° to 230°F (107° to 110°C).

2. Pour in the cream, being careful because it will bubble up. Stir to incorporate, then add the butter and stir until melted. Remove from the heat and stir in a generous pinch of salt.

3. Let the sauce cool to slightly warm or room temperature. The sauce can be made ahead and refrigerated; rewarm before using.

Peach–Apricot Pie

We're always trying new combinations at the bakery, and this is one of my favorites. When I first moved to the Hudson Valley, local orchards focused primarily on apples. But in response to demand, farmers soon planted stone fruit trees as well. In August, peaches and apricots are harvested nearby, and we combine them in a single pie. Local apricots are especially wonderful. When they're shipped from far away, they never get as sweet as when they are allowed to ripen on the trees. Which isn't to say that local peaches aren't a treat. Choose firm but not hard medium-size peaches. Larger fruit can be mealy.

Makes one 9-inch (23 cm) traditional pie

Start to finish: **about 6 hours**

Gathering ingredients and making and refrigerating the pie dough: **about 2¼ hours**

Assembling and baking the pie: **about 2½ hours**

Cooling: **1 hour**

Ingredients	Metric	Imperial
Double-Crust Pie Dough (page 250)		
4 peaches	680 g	1½ pounds
8 apricots	450 g	1 pound
granulated sugar	70 g	¼ cup plus 2 tablespoons
light or dark brown sugar	70 g	¼ cup plus 2 tablespoons
all-purpose flour	30 g	¼ cup, plus more for dusting
ground nutmeg	0.3 g	⅛ teaspoon
EGG WASH		
whole egg	55 g	1 large egg
egg yolk	18 g	1 large yolk
heavy cream	30 g	2 tablespoons

No-Churn Hint of Bourbon Ice Cream (page 259), for serving

1. Remove the pie dough from the refrigerator and let it warm up at room temperature for about 30 minutes.

2. Set a 9-inch (23 cm) traditional pie plate or pan on the work surface. Unwrap the first disk of dough and put it between two large pieces of wax paper, parchment paper lightly dusted with flour, or plastic wrap.

RECIPE CONTINUES

VARIATION: PEACH CRUMB PIE

For a peach (or peach-apricot) crumb pie, prepare and chill the dough for a single-crust pie instead (page 241). Prepare the oat topping for the Apple-Raspberry Pie (page 243) and add ⅓ cup (30 g) lightly toasted and chopped almonds. Sprinkle the filling with the topping. Bake at 375°F (190°C) until the peaches are tender and the top is golden brown, 45 to 50 minutes.

To help keep the dough from cracking, pound a rolling pin across the dough to flatten it. Next, roll the dough from the center out to the edges, turning the dough until it is 11 to 12 inches (28 to 30 cm) across.

3. Remove the top piece of paper. Invert the dough, still on the other piece of paper, and lay it across the top of the plate. Using the paper, gently press the dough into the bottom and edges of the plate, smoothing and removing any air bubbles. Carefully peel off the paper, leaving the excess dough extending over the top edges of the plate. Small pieces can be trimmed to patch any thin spots and/or repair any cracks. Cover the dough.

Unwrap the second disk of dough for the top crust and put it between two large pieces of wax paper, parchment paper lightly dusted with flour, or plastic wrap. To help keep the dough from cracking, pound a rolling pin across the dough to flatten it. Next, roll the dough from the center out to the edges, turning the dough until it is 11 to 12 inches (28 to 30 cm) across. Slide onto a parchment-lined baking sheet.

Cover and refrigerate the dough for at least 30 minutes or up to 4 hours.

4. Remove the dough from the refrigerator.
Preheat the oven to 425°F (215°C).

5. Peel the peaches and cut them into ½-inch (12 mm) slices. Cut the apricots into ½-inch (12 mm) slices. (It is not necessary to peel the apricots.) Put in a large bowl.

Add the granulated sugar, brown sugar, flour, and nutmeg and toss to evenly coat.

6. Spoon the peach mixture into the chilled dough in the pie plate.

7. **MAKE A CUT-OUT CRUST:** Using a cookie cutter of your choice, cut shapes from the remaining rolled dough and arrange them on top of the filling.

RECIPE CONTINUES

8. **MAKE THE EGG WASH:** Whisk together the egg, yolk, and cream in a small bowl. Brush the cut-outs on the top of the pie with the egg wash.

Bake for 15 minutes. Lower the oven temperature to 350°F (175°C) and continue to bake until the filling is tender and the crust is a rich golden brown, 35 to 40 minutes more.

9. Transfer to a wire rack and let cool completely. Cut into slices to serve. Serve with the bourbon ice cream.

No-Churn Hint of Bourbon Ice Cream

I've never been a bourbon drinker, but my wife, Julie, and my son-in-law, Mick, enjoy this spirit, so I always have it in the house. Tuthilltown Distillery in the Hudson Valley makes one with New York corn that is as good for cooking as it is for drinking. Its caramel and vanilla notes infuse this quick ice cream. The flavors perfectly complement the acidity and sweetness of the peaches in the Peach-Apricot Pie (page 255).

Makes 900 grams (a generous 5 cups)

Start to finish:
5 hours

Preparing the pan and ice cream:
1 hour

Freezing the ice cream:
4 hours

Ingredients	Metric	Imperial
sweetened condensed milk	396 g	14-ounce can
bourbon	26 g	1 tablespoon
pure vanilla extract or paste	5 g	1 teaspoon
fine sea salt	pinch	pinch
heavy cream	468 g	2 cups

1. Set a loaf pan in the freezer to chill, ideally for 40 minutes.

2. In a medium to large bowl, whisk together the sweetened condensed milk, bourbon, vanilla, and salt.

3. In the bowl of a stand mixer fitted with the whisk attachment, whisk the cream until stiff peaks form, about 2 minutes on medium to medium-high speed.

4. Working with one-third at a time, fold the whipped cream into the sweetened condensed milk mixture. Position the spatula along an edge of the bowl, bringing it down to the bottom of the bowl and then back up, lifting the sweetened condensed milk mixture into the whipped cream. Turn the bowl and continue to incorporate. It is okay, especially in the beginning, if there are some streaks. Overmixing will deflate the mixture.

5. Spoon into the chilled loaf pan, cover, and return to the freezer. Freeze for at least 4 hours but preferably overnight. Spoon or scoop on a slice of pie or serve on the side.

Blueberry Slab Pie

Now that I'm spending my summers in Maine, I take full advantage of the state's famous blueberries when they come into season. A slab pie fits the bill. This big blueberry dessert is great. Rolling the rectangles of dough takes a little effort, but the result is definitely worth it—a rustic but beautiful pie perfect for a summer barbecue or a holiday get-together.

Makes one
12 by 17-inch
(30 by 43 cm)
slab pie

Start to finish:
about 6½ hours

Gathering ingredients
and making and
refrigerating the
pie dough: 2½ hours

Assembling and baking
the pie: about 3 hours

Cooling: 1 hour

Ingredients	Metric	Imperial
Slab Pie Dough (recipe follows)		
all-purpose flour, for dusting		
blueberries	1.5 kg	3⅓ pounds
sugar	160 g	¾ cup plus 1½ tablespoons
cornstarch	45 g	¼ cup plus 2 tablespoons
ground cinnamon	0.6 g	¼ teaspoon
lemon zest	7 g	1 tablespoon plus 1 teaspoon
fresh lemon juice	60 g	¼ cup
EGG WASH		
whole egg	55 g	1 large egg
egg yolk	18 g	1 large yolk
heavy cream	30 g	2 tablespoons

1. Remove the pie dough from the refrigerator and let it warm up at room temperature for about 30 minutes.

2. Set a half sheet pan (13 by 18 inches / 33 by 45 cm) on the work surface. Unwrap the bottom crust dough and put it between two large pieces of wax paper, parchment paper lightly dusted with flour, or plastic wrap. To help keep the dough from cracking, pound a rolling pin across the dough to flatten it. Next, roll the dough from the center out to the edges, turning the dough until it is 15 to 16 inches by 20 to 22 inches (38 to 41 cm by 51 to 56 cm).

RECIPE CONTINUES

For an apple slab pie,
start with 1.8 kg
(4 pounds) of apples.
Peel and cut the
apples into ¼-inch
(6 mm) slices and put
in a large bowl. Add
112 g (½ cup plus
1½ tablespoons)
granulated sugar, 14 g
(1 tablespoon plus
2¾ teaspoons) tapioca
flour, 9 g (1 tablespoon)
all-purpose flour, and
4 g (2 teaspoons)
ground cinnamon and
toss to evenly coat the
apples. Roll out the
dough as written for
the blueberry slab pie,
using this filling instead.

3. Remove the top piece of paper. Invert the dough, still on the other piece of paper, and lay it across the sheet pan. Using the paper, gently press the dough into the bottom and edges of the pan, smoothing and removing any air bubbles. Carefully peel off the paper, leaving the excess dough extending over the top edges of the sheet pan. Small pieces can be trimmed to patch any thin spots and/or repair any cracks. Cover the dough.

4. Unwrap the top crust dough and put it between two large pieces of wax paper, parchment paper lightly dusted with flour, or plastic wrap. To help keep the dough from cracking, pound a rolling pin across the dough to flatten it. Next, roll the dough from the center out to the edges, turning the dough until it is 13 by 18 inches (33 by 46 cm). Slide onto a parchment-lined baking sheet.

Cover and refrigerate the dough for at least 30 minutes or up to 4 hours.

5. Remove the dough from the refrigerator.

Cut the top crust dough into ½-inch (12 mm) strips. On another parchment-lined half sheet pan, lay half of the strips lengthwise, ½ inch (12 mm) apart. Weave the remaining strips in and out crosswise to create a lattice top, rerolling scraps to make more strips if necessary. Cover with plastic wrap and refrigerate for at least 30 minutes.

6. Position an oven rack in the lower third of the oven and preheat the oven to 425°F (215°C).

Place the blueberries in a large bowl. Add the sugar, cornstarch, cinnamon, lemon zest, and lemon juice and stir gently until the cornstarch has dissolved and the blueberries are evenly coated.

7. Spoon the blueberry mixture into the chilled dough in the sheet pan. Carefully slide the lattice top from the parchment to the pie.

8. Trim the edges of the dough so that it extends ¼ to ½ inch (6 to 12 mm) beyond the rim of the sheet pan. Gently press the top and bottom pieces together. Using a fork, press down along the edge to seal together and make a decorative pattern, if desired.

9. **MAKE THE EGG WASH:** Whisk together the egg, yolk, and cream in a small bowl. Brush the top of the pie with the egg wash.

Bake for 15 minutes. Lower the oven temperature to 350°F (175°C) and continue to bake until the filling is tender and the crust is a rich golden brown, 45 to 50 minutes more.

10. Transfer to a wire rack and let cool completely. Cut into slices to serve.

Slab Pie Dough

Makes enough dough for one double-crust slab pie, on a 13 by 18-inch (33 by 45 cm) baking sheet, traditional or lattice with some extra dough for decorating

Dividing this recipe for the top and bottom crusts makes it easier to have just a bit more for the bottom and will not overwork your mixer by making one large batch.

Ingredients	Metric	Imperial
BOTTOM CRUST		
unsalted butter, cold	330 g	12 ounces / 24 tablespoons
ice water	112 g	¼ cup plus 3½ tablespoons
distilled white vinegar	6 g	1½ teaspoons
all-purpose flour	550 g	4½ cups
fine sea salt	10 g	1¾ teaspoons
TOP CRUST		
unsalted butter, cold	237 g	8 ounces / 16 tablespoons
ice water	78 g	¼ cup plus 1½ tablespoons
distilled white vinegar	4 g	1 teaspoon
all-purpose flour	400 g	3⅓ cups
fine sea salt	7 g	1⅛ teaspoons

1. For the bottom crust, cut the butter into ¼-inch (6 mm) cubes and return to the refrigerator. Add the ice water and the vinegar to a small spouted measuring cup.

RECIPE CONTINUES

2. In the bowl of a stand mixer fitted with the paddle attachment, add the flour and salt. Toss together or mix on the lowest setting for about 30 seconds. Add the cubed butter. Pulse on the lowest speed to begin to incorporate the butter and keep the flour in the bowl. Increase the speed to low, then increase to medium-low to continue to mix and break the butter into smaller pieces until the mixture resembles a coarse meal, about 3 minutes total.

3. With the mixer running on low speed, add the water and vinegar mixture and mix until combined and the dough comes together around the paddle, about 1 minute.

4. Lift the dough from the bowl and form into a 1-inch (2.5 cm) thick rectangle. Wrap individually in beeswax wrap or plastic wrap. Refrigerate the dough for at least 2 hours or up to 2 days. At this point the dough can also be frozen for up to 1 month and thawed in the refrigerator when ready to use.

5. Repeat the process for the top crust.

Swiss Chard–Leek Galette with Ricotta

At Bread Alone, we keep some galette dough in the freezer in order to make savory tart specials at the cafe. Cooked greens like chard, spinach, and kale are often featured, as is goat cheese from Cheval Farmstead Dairy in Stuyvesant or sheep cheese from Acorn Hill Farm in Kerhonkson. And we've been making our own ricotta, with Ronnybrook Farm milk, for years. It couldn't be easier to do, and it gives this particular tart fresh dairy flavor.

Makes one 12-inch (30 cm) galette

Start to finish:
about 5 hours

Preparing the ricotta:
50 minutes

Gathering ingredients and making and refrigerating the galette dough: **2¼ hours**

Assembling and baking the galette: **1½ hours**

Cooling: **10 minutes**

Ingredients	Metric	Imperial
Savory Galette Dough (recipe follows)		
6 large Swiss chard leaves	200 g	7 ounces
2 medium leeks	600 g	1 to 1⅓ pounds
3 medium-large shallots	75 g	2½ ounces
extra-virgin olive oil	20 g	1½ tablespoons
arugula	125 g	4 ounces
all-purpose flour, for dusting		
fine sea salt, to taste		
freshly ground black pepper, to taste		
lemon zest	1 g	½ teaspoon
ricotta cheese, preferably Homemade Ricotta (recipe follows)	220 g	1 cup
1 large egg, lightly beaten, for brushing the dough		
flaky or coarse sea salt, for sprinkling (optional)		
giardiniera or Calabrian chilis, for serving (optional)		

1. Remove the galette dough from the refrigerator and let it warm up at room temperature for about 30 minutes.

2. Meanwhile, prepare the filling. Separate the chard leaves from the stems. Trim and discard the ends from the stems. Dice the smaller, tender pieces of stem and roughly chop the leaves. Trim the leeks.

RECIPE CONTINUES

Large green leaves can be reserved for another use (like stock). Cut the white and light-green portion of the leeks into rounds, about ¼ inch (6 mm) thick. Rinse under cold water. If they are especially dirty, soak in a bowl of cold water, letting the dirt sink to the bottom of the bowl, then lift the rounds out. Thinly slice the shallots.

3. Set a large skillet over medium-high heat. Add the olive oil. Stir in the shallots and cook until fragrant, about 1 minute. Add the leek rounds, stirring to combine. Continue to cook, lowering the heat to medium-low, until the leeks are tender, 6 to 8 minutes. Stir in the chard and arugula just enough to wilt. Season with salt and pepper and transfer to a plate.

4. Preheat the oven to 400°F (200°C).
   While the vegetables are cooling, roll out the dough. Unwrap the dough and put it between two large pieces of parchment paper lightly dusted with flour. To help keep the dough from cracking, pound a rolling pin across the dough to flatten it. Next, roll the dough from the center out to the edges, turning the dough until it is about 14 inches (36 cm) across.
   Slide the entire thing onto a baking sheet and remove the top piece of paper.

5. Stir the lemon zest into the ricotta and season with salt and pepper.
   Spread the ricotta on the dough, leaving a 1½- to 2-inch (4 to 5 cm) border. Arrange the vegetable mixture on top of the ricotta.
   Fold the edges of the dough up and over to make a border. Brush with the egg and sprinkle with the flaky salt, if using.

6. Bake until the crust is a rich golden brown and the mixture is heated through, about 40 minutes.

7. Let cool for about 10 minutes. Cut into wedges and serve with the giardiniera or Calabrian chilis, if using.

RECIPE CONTINUES

Savory Galette Dough

Makes enough dough for one 12-inch (30 cm) galette

Some whole wheat flour gives this pastry an assertive flavor, which stands up well to savory fillings of all types.

Ingredients	Metric	Imperial
unsalted butter, cold	190 g	6½ ounces / 14 tablespoons
ice water	64 g	¼ cup plus 1 teaspoon
distilled white vinegar	13 g	1 tablespoon
all-purpose flour	200 g	1½ cups plus 2½ tablespoons
whole wheat flour	116 g	¾ cup plus 3 tablespoons
fine sea salt	6 g	1 teaspoon

1. Cut the butter into ¼-inch (6 mm) cubes and return to the refrigerator. Add the ice water and vinegar to a small spouted measuring cup.

2. In the bowl of a stand mixer fitted with the paddle attachment, add the all-purpose flour, whole wheat flour, and salt. Toss together or mix on the lowest setting for about 30 seconds. Add the cubed butter. Pulse on the lowest speed to begin to incorporate the butter and keep the flour in the bowl. Increase the speed to low, then increase to medium-low to continue to mix and break the butter into smaller pieces until the mixture resembles a coarse meal, about 3 minutes total.

3. With the mixer running on low speed, add the water and vinegar mixture and mix until combined and the dough comes together around the paddle, about 1 minute.

4. Lift the dough from the bowl and form into a disk. Wrap in beeswax wrap or plastic wrap. Refrigerate the dough for at least 2 hours or up to 2 days. At this point the dough can also be frozen for up to 1 month and thawed in the refrigerator when ready to use.

Homemade Ricotta

Makes 445 grams (2 cups) ricotta

No special equipment or ingredients are required to make your own ricotta, and the result is so superior to store-bought ricotta that you will wonder how you ever lived without it.

Ingredients	Metric	Imperial
whole milk	1.5 kg	6 cups
apple cider vinegar	45 g	3 tablespoons
fine sea salt	pinch	pinch

1. In a large saucepan, bring the milk to just below a simmer over medium heat. There will be some steam rising from the top, and the surface of the milk will have ripples and a few small bubbles.

2. Stir in the vinegar and the salt, but then do not stir again. Keep at a simmer, until there are curds on the surface, 15 to 20 minutes.

3. Remove the pan from the heat and let sit undisturbed for 15 minutes.

4. Meanwhile, line a large fine-mesh strainer or a colander with cheesecloth or a linen towel and set over a large bowl. Using a slotted spoon, lift the curds into the lined strainer, occasionally gently lifting the cheesecloth to let any excess liquid drain into the bowl.

5. The ricotta can be used at this point or covered and refrigerated for up to 2 days. Discard the whey.

TARTS

When I was a young chef, fresh out of the CIA, I took a job at Le Veau d'Or, the Upper East Side bistro that had been serving country French classics like coq au vin and boeuf bourguignon since 1937. The kitchen staff consisted of the chef, two daytime cooks, and two nighttime cooks. Without a pastry chef, or even a special area in the kitchen devoted to pastry, the five of us had to make desserts as well as dinner. I learned to make a small repertoire of simple but classic sweets, like chocolate mousse and crème caramel. But my favorite was the warm apple tart, which could be thrown together in half an hour if necessary. Every so often, we'd make twenty pounds of pâte brisée, wrap it in twelve-ounce portions, and store it in the refrigerator. We'd also keep some almond frangipane in a container in the fridge. Assembling the tart was as easy as peeling and slicing some apples, rolling out the dough, fitting it into the pan, and topping it with almond cream and fruit.

When I'm dining out, I'll always choose a simple tart over a fancy cake or a composed dessert. Tarts make me nostalgic. There is something so immensely satisfying about the combination of golden pastry, cream, and maybe a little fruit. They appeal to every taste—anyone can recognize and appreciate a tart's distinct flavors and textures, and admire how they complement each other.

Tarts are also a solution to the problem of homemade dessert. The dough comes together in minutes and can be refrigerated or frozen for later use. (To this day, I always have pâte brisée in the freezer in case of emergency.) Likewise, fruit and other fillings are easily prepared ahead of time or à la minute. With some planning, a tart can be assembled and baked in under an hour, just in time to serve when dinner is over.

Pâte Sucrée

(SWEET TART DOUGH)

Pâte sucrée is a sweet and crumbly pastry dough used to make dessert tarts. It is something we always have ready and available in the refrigerator (it will keep there for up to 5 days) or the freezer (for up to 1 month) at the bakery. Thaw it in the refrigerator overnight. If we get a delivery of very ripe pears one day, we can use them quickly by baking them in tarts; we might also find ourselves running low on desserts, so we'll grab some pâte sucrée from the freezer, roll it out, fill it, and have the tarts ready in about an hour. In other words, we use this dough as a pantry item, always on hand for convenience and emergencies. It may seem a bit fragile and might crack when you transfer it to the tart pan, but it is forgiving and easily patched with trimmed pieces of the dough. To keep it from shrinking when baking, allow extra time to chill the dough after mixing and then again after rolling and putting into the tart pan.

Makes enough dough for one or two 10-inch (25 cm) tarts

Start to finish:
about 3½ to 4 hours

Gathering ingredients and preparing the dough:
20 to 30 minutes

Rolling and refrigerating:
at least 2½ hours but up to 2 days

Parbaking:
about 20 minutes

Prebaking (optional):
additional 20 minutes

Ingredients	Metric	Imperial	Metric	Imperial
	for 1 tart		for 2 tarts	
unsalted butter, cold	160 g	5½ ounces / 11 tablespoons	320 g	11 ounces / 22 tablespoons
egg yolks	36 g	2 large yolks	72 g	4 large yolks
buttermilk (any fat content) or heavy cream	6 g	1¼ teaspoons	12 g	2½ teaspoons
all-purpose flour	120 g	1 cup, plus more for dusting	240 g	2 cups, plus more for dusting
whole wheat pastry flour	120 g	1⅓ cups	240 g	2⅔ cups
powdered sugar	40 g	¼ cup plus 1½ tablespoons	80 g	½ cup plus 3 tablespoons
granulated sugar	20 g	1 tablespoon plus 2 teaspoons	40 g	3 tablespoons plus 1 teaspoon
fine sea salt	6.5 g	1⅛ teaspoons	13g	2¼ teaspoons

1. Cut the butter into ¼-inch (6 mm) cubes and return to the refrigerator. In a small bowl, whisk together the egg yolks and buttermilk.

RECIPE CONTINUES

2. In the bowl of a stand mixer fitted with the paddle attachment, add the all-purpose flour, pastry flour, powdered sugar, granulated sugar, and salt. Toss together or mix on the lowest setting for 1 minute. Add the cubed butter. Pulse on the lowest speed to begin to incorporate the butter and keep the flour in the bowl. Increase the speed to low, then increase to medium-low to continue to mix and break the butter into smaller pieces until the mixture resembles a coarse meal, about 3 minutes total.

3. With the mixer running on low speed, add the egg mixture and mix until combined and the dough comes together around the paddle, 1 to 2 minutes.

4. Lift the dough from the bowl. For one tart, form into a disk. For two tarts, divide the dough in half and form into two disks. Wrap the disk(s) individually in beeswax wrap or plastic wrap. Refrigerate the dough for at least 2 hours or up to 2 days. At this point the dough can also be frozen for up to 1 month and thawed in the refrigerator when ready to use.

5. Remove the dough from the refrigerator and let it warm up at room temperature for about 30 minutes.

6. Set a 10-inch (25 cm) tart pan on the work surface. Unwrap the dough and put it between two large pieces of wax paper, parchment paper lightly dusted with all-purpose flour, or plastic wrap. To help keep the dough from cracking, pound a rolling pin across the dough to start to flatten it. Next, roll the dough from the center out to the edges, turning the dough until it is 12 to 13 inches (30 to 33 cm) across.

7. Remove the top piece of paper. Invert the dough, still on the other piece of paper, and lay it across the top of the pan. Using the paper, gently press the dough into the bottom and edges of the pan, smoothing and removing any air bubbles. Carefully peel off the paper. Fold the excess dough against the top of the pan. Run the rolling pin over the top of the pan to remove the excess dough and leave a smooth top. Use that excess dough to patch any thin spots and/or repair any cracks. Cover and refrigerate the dough for at least 30 minutes or up to 4 hours. Repeat if making two tart shells.

For Tarte à la Crème (page 281), the unbaked shell is used at this point.

8. For parbaked or prebaked empty tart shells, preheat the oven to 375°F (190°C).

Prick the bottom of the dough with a fork. Line the shell with parchment paper and fill with uncooked beans, rice, or pie weights.

9. Bake until the edges of the dough are a light golden brown, about 15 minutes.

If using this tart shell for a tart that will be baked, carefully remove the beans and paper, return the shell to the oven, and continue baking until just barely colored, about 5 minutes more. Transfer to a wire rack and let cool completely in the pan. Proceed with the recipe calling for a parbaked tart shell.

If using this tart shell for a tart that will not be baked, carefully remove the beans and paper, return the shell to the oven, and continue baking until it is a rich golden brown, 15 to 20 minutes more. Transfer to a wire rack and let cool completely in the pan. Proceed with the recipe calling for a prebaked tart shell.

Chocolate Pâte Sucrée

(CHOCOLATE SWEET TART DOUGH)

This chocolate pâte sucrée is a variation on our original sweet and crumbly pastry dough (like plain pâte sucrée, it can also be refrigerated or frozen until you are ready to use it). Because the dough is a dark cocoa brown even before baking, judging doneness is a little bit more difficult. It is best to rely on time and your nose to determine its doneness. Choose a rich natural cocoa (not Dutch process) like Valrhona poudre de cacao.

Makes enough dough for one or two 10-inch (25 cm) tarts

Start to finish:
about 3½ hours

Gathering ingredients and preparing the dough:
20 to 30 minutes

Rolling and refrigerating:
at least 2½ hours but up to 2 days

Parbaking:
about 20 minutes

Prebaking (optional):
additional 20 minutes

Ingredients	Metric	Imperial	Metric	Imperial
	for 1 tart		**for 2 tarts**	
unsalted butter, cold	160 g	5½ ounces / 11 tablespoons	320 g	11 ounces / 22 tablespoons
egg yolks	36 g	2 large yolks	72 g	4 large yolks
buttermilk (any fat content) or heavy cream	6 g	1¼ teaspoons	12 g	2½ teaspoons
all-purpose flour	108 g	¾ cup plus 2 tablespoons plus 1 teaspoon	216 g	1¾ cups plus 2 teaspoons
whole wheat pastry flour	108 g	1 cup plus 3 tablespoons	216 g	2¼ cups plus 2 tablespoons
natural (not Dutch process) cocoa powder	24 g	¼ cup plus 2 teaspoons	48 g	½ cup plus 1½ tablespoons
powdered sugar	40 g	¼ cup plus 1½ tablespoons	80 g	½ cup plus 3 tablespoons
granulated sugar	20 g	1 tablespoon plus 2 teaspoons	40 g	3 tablespoons plus 1 teaspoon
fine sea salt	6.5 g	1⅛ teaspoons	13 g	2¼ teaspoons

Follow the method for Pâte Sucrée (page 271), adding the cocoa powder to the mixer bowl along with the other dry ingredients.

Cherry Tart

This combination of cherries, chocolate, and pistachios is well suited for the winter months and holidays, but is no less festive when cherries are at peak season. Or freeze some for later in the year. Starting with about 1 kilogram (2.2 pounds) of whole cherries, remove the stems and pits, lay out the cherries in a single layer on a parchment-lined baking sheet, cover, and freeze. Once frozen, transfer to a storage bag or container and store in the freezer for up to 6 months. Alternatively, with the availability of high-quality IQF (individually quick frozen) cherries, this tart can easily be made year-round. If using frozen cherries, thaw in a strainer or colander set over a bowl and then blot well on towels to dry.

Makes one 10-inch (25 cm) tart

Start to finish:
about 6 hours

Gathering ingredients and making, refrigerating, and parbaking the pâte sucrée: **about 3½ hours**

Gathering ingredients and preparing the frangipane: **20 minutes**

Assembling and baking the tart: **about 1 hour**

Cooling: **about 1 hour**

Ingredients	Metric	Imperial
1 parbaked Chocolate Pâte Sucrée shell (page 274)		
Pistachio Frangipane (recipe follows)		
pitted cherries, fresh or frozen (see headnote)	375 g	13 ounces
powdered sugar, for dusting (optional)		
whipped cream, for serving (optional)		

1. Preheat the oven to 375°F (190°C). Set the parbaked chocolate pâte sucrée shell (still in the pan) on the work surface.

2. Spoon the frangipane into a pastry bag with a large round opening and pipe evenly into the shell. Alternatively, the frangipane can be spooned into the shell. Smooth the top of the frangipane.

3. Blot the cherries on paper towels and arrange in concentric circles, pressing gently into the frangipane.

4. Bake until the frangipane has risen around the cherries and is a rich golden brown, 40 to 50 minutes. A skewer inserted in the center should come out clean.

5. Transfer to a wire rack. Once cooled, it is best to serve the tart the day it is made. Dust with powdered sugar before serving, if you like. Cut into slices and dollop with whipped cream, if using.

RECIPE CONTINUES

Pistachio Frangipane

Makes 579 grams (2½ cups), enough for 1 tart

The pistachio frangipane can be made up to a day ahead. If making ahead, allow to come to room temperature and mix again if needed to loosen.

Ingredients	Metric	Imperial
pistachio flour (see headnote, page 234)	143 g	1¼ cups plus ½ tablespoon
whole wheat pastry flour	34 g	¼ cup plus 2 tablespoons
ground cardamom	0.6 g	¼ teaspoon
whole eggs	110 g	2 large eggs
pure vanilla extract or paste	5 g	1 teaspoon
unsalted butter, softened	143 g	5 ounces / 10 tablespoons
sugar	143 g	¾ cup
salt	3 g	¼ teaspoon

1. In a medium bowl, add the pistachio flour, pastry flour, and cardamom and stir to combine. In a small bowl, lightly whisk the eggs and vanilla.

2. In the bowl of a stand mixer fitted with the paddle attachment, add the butter, sugar, and salt and mix on medium-low speed until light and fluffy, 3 to 4 minutes. Stop and scrape the bottom and sides and mix for about 30 seconds more. Reduce the speed to low, and with the mixer running, slowly add the egg mixture. Stop and scrape the bottom and sides again and mix until incorporated, 30 seconds to 1 minute. At this point the mixture will look chunky and broken. Add the dry ingredients. Pulse on the Stir setting to begin to incorporate and then mix on low speed until combined, 1 to 2 minutes.

3. The frangipane is ready to be used or can be refrigerated for up to 2 days. Bring to room temperature before using.

Nut Tart

This nut tart is dense with a mixture of nuts and a touch of corn syrup, butter, and eggs to hold it together. Just a thin slice, a triangle about half the size of a normal slice of pie, will satisfy, especially when served with a small scoop of homemade gelato. Raw pistachios can be difficult to find. If available, roast them along with the other nuts and then lightly salt the combined nuts while still warm.

Makes one 10-inch (25 cm) tart

Start to finish:
about 6½ hours

Gathering ingredients and making, refrigerating, and parbaking the pâte sucrée: **about 4 hours**

Toasting and cooling the nuts: **30 minutes**

Assembling and baking the tart: **about 1 hour**

Cooling:
about 1 hour

Ingredients	Metric	Imperial
walnut halves	250 g	2½ cups
hazelnuts, peeled	250 g	1¾ cups
macadamia nuts	250 g	1¾ cups
roasted and lightly salted pistachios (see headnote)	250 g	2½ cups
1 parbaked Pâte Sucrée shell (page 271)		
light or dark brown sugar	164 g	¾ cup plus 2 tablespoons
all-purpose flour	6 g	2 teaspoons
fine sea salt	2.5 g	½ teaspoon
light corn syrup	147 g	¼ cup plus 3 tablespoons
whole eggs	110 g	½ cup (2 large eggs)
unsalted butter, melted	41 g	1.5 ounces / 3 tablespoons
pure vanilla extract or paste	3 g	¾ teaspoon

1. Preheat the oven to 350°F (175°C).

2. Spread the walnuts, hazelnuts, and macadamia nuts on a baking sheet. Roast until fragrant and a light golden brown, 8 to 10 minutes. Add the pistachios and stir to combine. Set aside to cool.

3. Increase the oven temperature to 375°F (190°C). Set the parbaked pâte sucrée shell (still in the pan) on the work surface. Arrange the nuts in the shell.

RECIPE CONTINUES

4. In the bowl of a stand mixer fitted with the paddle attachment, add the brown sugar, flour, and salt. Stir together or mix on the lowest setting for 30 seconds to 1 minute.

5. In a large spouted liquid measuring cup or in a medium bowl, whisk together the corn syrup, eggs, melted butter, and vanilla. Add to the sugar mixture and mix on medium-low until well blended and smooth. Pour evenly over the nuts.

6. Bake until the center of the pie is set but still has a slight jiggle, about 40 minutes.

7. Transfer to a wire rack. Once cooled, it is best to serve the tart the day it is made. Cut into slices to serve.

Tarte à la Crème

(PASTRY CREAM TART)

Tarte à la crème is a showstopper with its golden-brown top and creamy interior. It is the definition of a timeless classic and will be my go-to dessert until the day I die. It is also surprisingly easy to make. Both the sucrée and the pastry cream are made ahead, and baking the final tart can happen in advance as well.

Makes one 10-inch (25 cm) tart

Start to finish:
about 5½ hours

Gathering ingredients
and making,
refrigerating, and rolling
out the pâte sucrée:
3 hours

Making the pastry
cream: **30 minutes**

Assembling and baking
the tart: **about 1 hour**

Cooling: **about 1 hour**

Ingredients

1 unbaked Pâte Sucrée shell (page 271)

Pastry Cream for Tarts (recipe follows)

1. Position one oven rack in the top third of the oven and one in the center and preheat to 425°F (230°C).

2. Spoon the pastry cream into the unbaked tart shell and smooth the top.

3. Bake on the top rack until some areas on the surface are a rich golden brown, about 20 minutes.
    Carefully move the tart to the center rack and lower the oven temperature to 375°F (190°C). Continue to bake until the pastry cream is just set in the center, 30 to 40 minutes more.

4. Transfer to a wire rack. Once cooled, cut into slices to serve at room temperature. If you prefer, the tart can also be refrigerated and served cold.

RECIPE CONTINUES

Pastry Cream for Tarts

Makes 1 kilogram (a generous 3 cups), enough for one tart

For the tarte à la crème, the pastry cream does not need to be chilled. It will be spooned hot into the unbaked tart shell.

Ingredients	Metric	Imperial
sugar	188 g	¾ cup plus 3½ tablespoons
egg yolks	108 g	6 large yolks
cornstarch	45 g	¼ cup plus 2 tablespoons
whole milk	525 g	2 cups plus 1 tablespoon
heavy cream	188 g	¾ cup plus 1 tablespoon
1 vanilla bean pod, split		

1. In the bowl of a stand mixer fitted with the paddle attachment, add the sugar, egg yolks, and cornstarch. Mix on medium-low speed to combine, about 1 minute. Stop and scrape the bottom and sides and continue to mix, increasing the speed to medium, until the mixture holds a ribbon shape: when the paddle is lifted, the mixture should fall back on itself in a slowly dissolving ribbon.

2. Meanwhile, combine the milk, cream, and split vanilla bean in a medium saucier or other saucepan, preferably with a rounded bottom. Bring to a simmer over medium to medium-high heat.

3. With the mixer running on low speed, add the hot cream a ladleful at a time. Once all is incorporated, stop and scrape down the sides and bottom and mix for a few seconds more.

4. Transfer the mixture to the saucepan. Whisk continuously over low heat until the mixture has thickened to the texture of pudding, about 3 minutes. If it is helpful, move the pan off the heat for a few seconds, continuing to whisk, to keep the pastry cream from cooking too quickly or scorching the bottom.

5. Remove from the heat and let cool slightly. The pastry cream can be warm when spooned into the unbaked tart shell.

Chilled Chocolate Tart

When we are making dessert at home, Julie and I are always going for the minimum amount of time it will take us to get something that will give us the maximum enjoyment. Chocolate tart dough takes 10 minutes to make and can stay in the refrigerator for a few days or in the freezer for weeks. The pastry cream takes another 30 minutes. If you have tart dough in the freezer, the process is even simpler. To put this tart together, all you need to do is scoop the pastry cream into the prebaked shell and wait 6 hours for the pastry cream to set—if you can be that patient! It has a simple elegance thanks to a grating of chocolate on top (see the photo on page 199), or add extra pizzazz with candied oranges, if you like.

Makes one 10-inch (25 cm) tart

Start to finish:
about 10½ hours

Gathering ingredients and making, refrigerating, and prebaking the pâte sucrée: **4 hours**

Making the pastry cream: **30 minutes**

Assembling and refrigerating the tart:
about 6½ hours

Ingredients	Metric	Imperial
sugar	188 g	¾ cup plus 3½ tablespoons
egg yolks	108 g	6 large yolks
cornstarch	45 g	¼ cup plus 2 tablespoons
whole milk	525 g	2 cups plus 1 tablespoon
heavy cream	188 g	¾ cup plus 1 tablespoon
1 vanilla bean pod, split		
semisweet chocolate, 70% cacao, coarsely chopped	175 g	6 ounces
unsalted butter	45 g	1.5 ounces / 3 tablespoons
pure vanilla extract or paste (optional)	6 g	1½ teaspoons
1 prebaked Chocolate Pâte Sucrée shell (page 274)		
Candied Orange Slices (page 288; optional)		
whipped cream, plain or sweetened (optional)		
chocolate, for grating (optional)		

1. In the bowl of a stand mixer fitted with the paddle attachment, add the sugar, egg yolks, and cornstarch. Mix on medium-low speed to combine, about 1 minute. Stop and scrape the bottom and sides and continue to mix, increasing the speed to medium, until the mixture holds a ribbon shape: when the paddle is lifted, the mixture should fall back on itself in a slowly dissolving ribbon.

2. Meanwhile, combine the milk, split vanilla bean, and cream in a medium saucier or other saucepan, preferably with a rounded bottom. Bring to a simmer over medium to medium-high heat.

Traditional vanilla pastry cream (page 282) can also be spooned into a plain or chocolate prebaked shell and then set in the fridge. I especially like topping vanilla pastry cream with fresh berries and then refrigerating for 6 hours to set up.

3. With the mixer running on low speed, add the hot cream a ladleful at a time. Once all is incorporated, stop and scrape down the sides and bottom and mix for a few seconds more.

4. Transfer the mixture to the saucepan. Whisk continuously over low heat until the mixture has thickened to the texture of pudding, about 3 minutes. If it is helpful, move the pan off the heat for a few seconds, continuing to whisk, to keep the pastry cream from cooking too quickly or scorching the bottom. Stir in the chocolate, butter, and vanilla extract, if using, until melted and the pastry cream is smooth. Remove from the heat.

5. Spoon the pastry cream into the prebaked tart shell and smooth the top. Refrigerate until the pastry cream is set, about 6 hours. Serve plain or top with candied orange slices or whipped cream, or use a rasp or fine grater to grate chocolate over the top, if desired.

Blood Orange–Lemon Tart

Living in the Northeast in the middle of the winter, I find this citrus cousin to the Tarte à la Crème (page 281) to be a supremely happy cold-weather dessert when the days are short. I enjoy the color variations each slice of fruit contains, from dark magenta to an almost ruby-red orange. And the flavor of the fruit, more complex and layered than lemon, is superb.

Makes one 10-inch (25 cm) tart

Start to finish:
about 4½ hours

Gathering ingredients and making, refrigerating, and parbaking the pâte sucrée: **3½ hours**

Making the filling:
10 minutes

Making the candied orange slices, if using:
2 hours

Baking:
about 40 minutes

Ingredients	Metric	Imperial
1 parbaked Pâte Sucrée shell (page 271)		
all-purpose flour, for dusting		
whole eggs	385 g	7 large eggs
sugar	240 g	1¼ cups
fresh blood orange juice	60 g	¼ cup
lemon juice	60 g	¼ cup
heavy cream	95 g	¼ cup plus 2½ tablespoons
crème fraîche	83 g	¼ cup plus 2 tablespoons
Candied Orange Slices (recipe follows; optional)		
toasted and chopped nuts (optional)	28 g	2 tablespoons

1. Preheat the oven to 350°F (175°C). Set the parbaked shell, still in the pan, on a baking sheet.

2. In the bowl of a stand mixer fitted with the whisk attachment, add the eggs, sugar, blood orange juice, lemon juice, heavy cream, and crème fraîche. Whisk on low speed until combined, stopping as needed to scrape the sides and bottom, about 2 minutes.
    Let sit for a few minutes and then skim the foam from the top.

3. Fill the shell about halfway. Carefully put in the oven and then add more filling, stopping just below the top. (Since the filling is so loose, this will help keep the top of the tart clean and the filling from spilling over on the way to the oven.) You may not use all the filling. Set aside leftovers for another use.

RECIPE CONTINUES

4. Bake until the filling is set but still has a wobble in the center, 40 to 45 minutes. During the last 10 minutes of baking, carefully lay the candied orange slices, if using, on top.

5. Transfer to a wire rack. Once cooled, cut into slices to serve at room temperature. If you prefer, the tart can also be refrigerated and served cold. Scatter with chopped nuts before serving, if desired.

Candied Orange Slices

Makes 10 to 12 slices

Ingredients	Metric	Imperial
sugar	540 g	2¾ cups
water	440 g	1¾ cups plus 2 tablespoons
2 blood oranges or lemons (or 1 of each)		

1. Combine the sugar and water in a wide saucepan. Bring to a boil, stirring to dissolve the sugar. Lower the heat to medium.

2. Meanwhile, cut the oranges into thin rounds, about ⅛ inch (3 mm) thick.

3. Carefully add the slices to the saucepan one at a time to keep them from sticking. Cook, stirring occasionally and lowering the heat to medium-low as needed, until the peels are translucent, about 25 minutes.

4. Lower the heat to low and continue to cook until the slices are tender but not falling apart, about 10 minutes. Remove the pan from the heat and let the slices sit in the syrup for 10 minutes.

5. Set a wire rack over a baking sheet. Transfer the slices one at a time to the wire rack and let cool completely. Reserve the syrup for another use.

BRIOCHE

I first made brioche as a student at the Culinary Institute of America. I remember dropping the softened butter into the dough at the end of kneading and thinking it was way too much. My classmates and I considered it exotic since none of us had ever heard of it at the time.

It's actually a very straightforward dough to make. I like to raise my brioche with sourdough, which gives the bread some depth of flavor and a longer shelf life. But our regular sourdough is a bit too acidic for my taste. Adding a little sugar to the starter balances the acidity, and in my experience doesn't affect the dough's rise. Critically, it's important to knead the dough for several minutes before adding the butter, to develop its strength. After adding the butter, piece by piece, continue to knead the dough until it is silky, shiny, and very smooth.

It's an incredibly versatile dough. I've included instructions for some of our most popular brioche-based items here—maple sticky buns, hamburger rolls, red pepper and Gruyère pull-apart rolls—to give you an idea of how you might use it.

Sweet Levain Brioche Dough

Makes 1 kilogram
(about 2¼ pounds)

Full recipe makes
enough for
10 hamburger rolls
or 12 red pepper–
Gruyère pull-apart
rolls

Half recipe makes
enough for
1 traditional brioche
loaf, 1 cinnamon-
raisin loaf,
12 mocha-filled
brioche buns, or
10 maple sticky
buns

Start to finish:
13 to 18½ hours

Preparing and proofing
the starter, day one
(Sweet Levain for
Brioche, page 292):
6½ to 8½ hours

Gathering ingredients
and preparing the
dough: **20 minutes**

Proofing and
refrigerating the dough:
6 hours to overnight

VARIATION:
**Red Pepper–
Gruyère Pull-Apart
Rolls**

Ingredients	Metric	Imperial
Sweet Levain for Brioche (recipe follows)		
bread flour	250 g	2 cups plus 1½ tablespoons
all-purpose flour	250 g	2 cups plus 1 tablespoon plus 1 teaspoon
sugar	30 g	2½ tablespoons
fine sea salt	7 g	1⅛ teaspoons
instant dry yeast	5 g	1½ teaspoons
whole milk, at room temperature	200 g	¾ cup plus 1½ teaspoons
whole eggs, lightly beaten, at room temperature	110 g	2 large eggs
unsalted butter, at room temperature	60 g	2 ounces / 4 tablespoons
RED PEPPER–GRUYÈRE PULL-APART ROLLS		
Gruyère cheese, cut into ¼-inch (6 mm) cubes and refrigerated	170 g	6 ounces / 1 cup
crushed red pepper flakes	0.3 g	⅛ teaspoon

1. Very lightly drizzle a tablespoon or two of water into a rectangular plastic storage container with a lid or a large bowl. Brush with a pastry brush to coat.

2. In the bowl of the stand mixer that has the levain, weigh the bread flour, all-purpose flour, sugar, salt, and yeast. Fit the mixer with the dough hook and mix on the lowest setting for 30 seconds to evenly distribute the dry ingredients. Add the milk and the eggs and mix on the Stir setting for about 30 seconds, then increase the speed to low to medium-low until the dough is combined but still shaggy, just being sure there are no dry ingredients at the bottom of the mixer bowl, 3 to 4 minutes.

   If making the sweet levain brioche dough: With the mixer running on medium speed, add the butter about 1 tablespoon (14 g) at a time, letting each piece incorporate before adding the next. Once all the butter is incorporated, continue to mix until the dough is smooth and silky, 8 to 10 minutes more.

If making the brioche dough for red pepper–Gruyère pull-apart rolls (page 306): With the mixer running on medium speed, add the butter about 1 tablespoon (14 g) at a time, letting each piece incorporate before adding the next. Once all the butter is incorporated, continue to mix for 5 minutes. Add the Gruyère cubes and crushed red pepper flakes, then mix until the dough is smooth (with some bumps from the cheese), 3 to 5 minutes more.

3. Transfer the dough to the storage container or the bowl. Cover the container with the lid or the bowl tightly with beeswax wrap. Let sit at room temperature for 2 hours and then refrigerate for 4 hours.

At this point, the dough can be used to begin lamination (see Laminated Sweet Levain Brioche Dough, page 311) or for the Brioche Loaf (page 293), Cinnamon-Raisin Loaf (page 296), Maple Sticky Buns (page 299), or the Mocha-Filled Brioche Buns (page 302). If making the brioche loaf, cinnamon-raisin loaf, maple sticky buns, or the mocha-filled brioche buns, divide the dough in half. Cover the halves with a kitchen towel and continue to the recipe(s). The dough halves can also be wrapped and frozen for up to 3 months.

If continuing to a recipe, finished shaped items can be completed through baking or can be covered and proofed in the refrigerator overnight. If refrigerating overnight, let sit covered at room temperature to warm up for 2 to 3 hours.

RECIPE CONTINUES

Sweet Levain for Brioche

Makes 115 grams (4 ounces)

Start to finish: **6½ to 8½ hours**

Gathering ingredients and preparing the dough: **15 minutes**

Proofing: **6 to 8 hours**

Ingredients	Metric	Imperial
all-purpose flour	50 g	¼ cup plus 2 tablespoons plus 1 teaspoon
water (70° to 78°F / 21° to 25.5°C)	35 g	2½ tablespoons
Sourdough Starter (page 98)	20 g	1 tablespoon
sugar	10 g	2½ teaspoons

In the bowl of a stand mixer, weigh the flour, water, sourdough starter, and sugar. Mix together with either the paddle attachment or a spoon. Cover the bowl tightly, preferably with beeswax wrap. Let sit at room temperature for 6 to 8 hours.

Brioche Loaf

At Bread Alone, we've always made simple brioche loaves for our customers who like to use it in French toast. Once you've had French toast made with brioche, you can't go back. It's also great lightly toasted with sweet butter and strawberry jam.

Makes 1 loaf, about 500 grams (18 ounces)

Preparing the Sweet Levain Brioche Dough (page 290): **13 to 18½ hours**

Start to finish for the Brioche Loaf: **about 3 hours**

Rolling and shaping: **20 to 30 minutes**

Proofing: **2 hours**

Baking: **35 minutes**

Ingredients	Metric	Imperial
vegetable oil, for brushing the loaf pan	14 g	1 tablespoon
½ recipe Sweet Levain Brioche Dough (page 290)	500 g	about 18 ounces
EGG WASH		
whole egg	55 g	1 large egg
egg yolk	18 g	1 large yolk
heavy cream	30 g	2 tablespoons
powdered sugar, for dusting (optional)		

1. Brush a traditional loaf pan, 8½ by 4½ by 2½ inches (21.5 by 10 by 6 cm), with the oil.

2. Set the brioche dough on the work surface. The dough should be chilled but not too cold. If it cracks when gently pressed with the rolling pin, let it warm up for a few minutes at room temperature.

   Gently roll and press the dough into an 8-inch (20 cm) square. Make a groove across the square along its center with the side of your hand and fold the dough over itself, pressing lightly on the edges to seal. With the seam side down, roll the rectangle back and forth on a lightly floured countertop until it is the same length as your loaf pan. Set in the prepared pan. Using a chef's knife, cut it down the center, and then with the knife or scissors, cut it across into thirds.

   MAKE THE EGG WASH: Whisk together the egg, yolk, and cream in a small bowl. Brush the top of the brioche with the egg wash. Cover and refrigerate the remaining egg wash. Cover the pan with an inverted box or plastic tub and let sit at room temperature to proof until the dough is tender and expanded, about 2 hours.

RECIPE CONTINUES

3. Preheat the oven to 350°F (175°C).

4. Carefully brush with the egg wash again and transfer to the oven. Bake until the loaf is golden brown, about 35 minutes.

5. Transfer to a wire rack and let cool completely.

6. Using a small fine-mesh strainer, dust the top of the loaf with powdered sugar, if you like.

Cinnamon–Raisin Loaf

It is easy enough to add a cinnamon-raisin swirl to a brioche loaf, and some of our customers prefer this loaf to plain brioche for their French toast.

Makes 1 loaf,
600 grams
(21 ounces)

Preparing the Sweet
Levain Brioche Dough
(page 290):
13 to 18½ hours

Start to finish for the
Cinnamon-Raisin Loaf:
about 3 hours

Rolling and shaping:
30 minutes

Proofing: **2 hours**

Baking: **35 minutes**

Ingredients	Metric	Imperial
vegetable oil, for brushing the loaf pan	14 g	1 tablespoon
½ recipe Sweet Levain Brioche Dough (page 290)	500 g	about 18 ounces
sugar	36 g	3 tablespoons
ground cinnamon	3.5 g	1¼ teaspoons
raisins	85 g	½ cup plus 1 tablespoon
EGG WASH		
whole egg	55 g	1 large egg
egg yolk	18 g	1 large yolk
heavy cream	30 g	2 tablespoons

1. Brush a traditional loaf pan, 8½ by 4½ by 2½ inches (21.5 by 10 by 6 cm), with the oil.

2. Set the brioche dough on the work surface. The dough should be chilled but not too cold. If it cracks when gently pressed with the rolling pin, let it warm up for a few minutes at room temperature.

3. Gently roll and press the dough into an 8 by 16-inch (20 by 40 cm) rectangle. Combine the sugar and cinnamon in a small bowl and sprinkle over the dough, leaving a ¼-inch (6 mm) border. Sprinkle the raisins evenly over the cinnamon sugar. Starting with a long side, roll the dough up like a jelly roll into a snug log. Pinch the outside edges to seal. Fold the log in half and twist once in the center (giving it a shape like an awareness ribbon). Gently place the folded and twisted dough into the prepared pan, tucking the end under.
   MAKE THE EGG WASH: Whisk together the egg, yolk, and cream in a small bowl and brush the top of the brioche. Cover and refrigerate the

RECIPE CONTINUES

remaining egg wash. Cover the pan with an inverted box or plastic tub and let sit at room temperature to proof until the dough is tender and expanded, about 2 hours.

4. Preheat the oven to 350°F (175°C).

5. Carefully brush with the egg wash again and transfer to the oven. Bake until the loaf is golden brown, about 35 minutes.

6. Transfer to a wire rack and let cool completely.

Maple Sticky Buns

We like to make our sticky buns with New York State maple syrup, to give them some local sweetness and flavor. I prefer a light touch with the glaze, since it's so sweet and sticky. But you may like yours dripping with the mixture. To each their own.

Makes 10 buns

Preparing the Sweet
Levain Brioche Dough
(page 290):
13 to 18½ hours

Start to finish for the
Maple Sticky Buns:
about 4½ hours

Preparing and cooling
the topping: **1½ hours**

Rolling and shaping:
30 minutes

Proofing: **2 hours**

Baking: **35 minutes**

Cooling and glazing:
about 30 minutes

Ingredients	Metric	Imperial
vegetable oil, for brushing the pan	14 g	1 tablespoon
MAPLE GLAZE		
light or dark brown sugar	225 g	1 cup plus 3 tablespoons
light corn syrup	83 g	¼ cup
unsalted butter	75 g	2½ ounces / 5 tablespoons
heavy cream	55 g	3½ tablespoons
maple syrup	30 g	2 tablespoons
water	30 g	2 tablespoons
distilled white vinegar	5 g	1 teaspoon
pure vanilla extract or paste	2 g	½ teaspoon
fine sea salt	1 g	¼ teaspoon
pecan halves, lightly toasted	100 g	1 cup
½ recipe Sweet Levain Brioche Dough (page 290)	500 g	about 18 ounces
Pastry Cream for Tarts (page 282)	100 g	⅓ cup
ground cinnamon	1 g	½ teaspoon

1. Brush a 9-inch (23 cm) round cake pan lightly with the oil.

2. **MAKE THE MAPLE GLAZE:** In a medium saucepan over medium heat, combine the brown sugar, corn syrup, butter, cream, maple syrup, water, vinegar, vanilla, and salt. Cook, stirring continuously, until the butter has melted, the sugar has dissolved, and the mixture is thoroughly combined, about 5 minutes.

RECIPE CONTINUES

Pour into the prepared pan and sprinkle the pecans evenly over the top. Let the mixture cool completely.

3. Set the brioche dough on the work surface. The dough should be chilled but not too cold. If it cracks when gently pressed with the rolling pin, let it warm up for a few minutes at room temperature.

4. Gently roll and press the dough into an 8 by 16-inch (20 by 40 cm) rectangle. Combine the pastry cream and cinnamon in a small bowl and spread over the dough, leaving a ½-inch (1.25 cm) border. Starting with a long side, roll the dough up like a jelly roll into a snug log.

   Find the midpoint of the roll and score it (press gently with a knife, but don't cut all of the way through). Then score each half into five equal pieces, for a total of ten. Cut into ten rolls.

5. Arrange the rolls on top of the cooled maple glaze with pecans: Place one in the center and the remaining nine equidistant around the edge. Press down on the rolls slightly.

6. Cover the pan with an inverted box or plastic tub and let sit at room temperature to proof until the dough is tender and expanded, about 2 hours.

7. Preheat the oven to 350°F (175°C).

   Set the pan on a baking sheet. This will be helpful if some of the glaze bubbles over the top of the pan while baking, which can cause some smoking in the oven.

8. Bake until the buns are golden brown, about 35 minutes.

9. Set a wire rack over a baking sheet.

   Transfer the cake round with the buns to the rack and let sit for about 5 minutes.

10. Carefully invert the pan onto the rack, allowing the glaze and the pecans to sit on the top and drip down the sides. Any topping that pools on the tray beneath can be spread on the buns while it is still hot. Let cool to warm (or completely).

Mocha-Filled Brioche Buns

These brioche buns are made in a 12-cup muffin pan, rather than in traditional fluted brioche molds. They can be served plain, adorned simply with the pearl sugar, or filled with vanilla pastry cream (see Pastry Cream for Snails, page 334) rather than the mocha pastry cream if you prefer.

Makes 12 buns

Preparing the Sweet
Levain Brioche Dough
(page 290):
13 to 18½ hours

Preparing the Mocha
Pastry Cream:
**6½ hours
(or up to 3 days before)**

Start to finish for the
Mocha-Filled Brioche
Buns: **about 5 hours**

Rolling and shaping:
30 minutes

Proofing: **2 hours**

Baking: **25 minutes**

Cooling: **1½ hours**

Filling the buns:
30 minutes

Ingredients	Metric	Imperial
vegetable oil, for brushing the pan		
½ recipe Sweet Levain Brioche Dough (page 290)	500 g	about 18 ounces
EGG WASH		
whole egg	55 g	1 large egg
egg yolk	18 g	1 large yolk
heavy cream	30 g	2 tablespoons
pearl sugar, for sprinkling		
Mocha Pastry Cream (recipe follows)		

1. Lightly brush the cups of a 12-cup traditional muffin pan with oil.

2. Divide the brioche dough into twelve equal pieces.
    Cup your fingers around one piece of dough. Roll against the work surface to form a ball. (Once you become proficient, you can roll two at a time, one in each hand.) Set each in a prepared muffin cup.

3. **MAKE THE EGG WASH:** Whisk together the egg, yolk, and cream in a small bowl. Brush the tops of the buns with the egg wash. Cover and refrigerate the remaining egg wash. Cover the pan with an inverted box or plastic tub and let sit at room temperature to proof until the dough is tender and expanded, about 2 hours.

4. Preheat the oven to 350°F (175°C).

5. Carefully brush the buns with the egg wash again, sprinkle with pearl sugar, and transfer to the oven.

RECIPE CONTINUES

Bake until the rolls are golden brown, about 25 minutes, rotating once during baking.

6. Transfer to a wire rack and let cool completely.

7. To fill the buns, spoon the mocha pastry cream into a piping bag fitted with a medium plain or star tip.

8. Cut the buns in half horizontally. Pipe individual rosettes or rounds onto the cut side of the bottom half of each bun and gently set the tops on the pastry cream.

Mocha Pastry Cream

Makes about 572 grams (1½ cups)

The espresso flavor will develop as the pastry cream sits, so it needs the full 6 hours in the refrigerator.

Ingredients	Metric	Imperial
bittersweet chocolate, coarsely chopped	40 g	1½ ounces
espresso powder	4 g	1 tablespoon
sugar	94 g	¼ cup plus 3½ tablespoons
egg yolks	54 g	3 large yolks
cornstarch	23 g	3 tablespoons
whole milk	263 g	1 cup plus 1 tablespoon
heavy cream	94 g	¼ cup plus 2½ tablespoons
pure vanilla extract or paste	2 g	½ teaspoon

1. Put the chocolate and the espresso powder in a medium heatproof storage container and set near the stovetop.

2. In the bowl of a stand mixer fitted with the paddle attachment, add the sugar, egg yolks, and cornstarch. Mix on medium-low speed to combine, about 1 minute. Stop and scrape the bottom and sides and continue to mix, increasing the speed to medium, until the mixture holds a ribbon shape: when the paddle is lifted, the mixture should fall back on itself in a slowly dissolving ribbon.

3. Meanwhile, combine the milk and heavy cream in a medium saucier or other saucepan, preferably with a rounded bottom. Bring to a simmer over medium to medium-high heat. Stir in the vanilla.

4. With the mixer running on low speed, add the hot cream a ladleful at a time. Once all is incorporated, stop and scrape down the sides and bottom and mix for a few seconds more. (Keep the saucepan handy.)

5. Transfer the mixture to the saucepan. Whisk continuously over low heat until the mixture has thickened to the texture of pudding, 2 to 3 minutes. If it is helpful, move the pan off the heat for a few seconds, continuing to whisk, to keep the pastry cream from cooking too quickly or scorching the bottom.

6. Pour over the chocolate and espresso powder in the storage container, stirring until the chocolate has melted and combined. Let cool for 5 to 10 minutes. To avoid a skin forming on the top of the pastry cream, press a piece of plastic wrap directly on the surface. Let cool and then refrigerate for at least 6 hours or up to 3 days.

Red Pepper–Gruyère Pull–Apart Rolls

This recipe demonstrates the versatility of brioche dough. Use it as a template to create flavored pull-apart rolls with sautéed onions or shallots instead of the red pepper; substitute Cheddar for the Gruyère; add herbs.

Makes 12 rolls

Preparing the Sweet Levain Brioche Dough (page 290):
13 to 18½ hours

Start to finish for the Red Pepper–Gruyère Pull-Apart Rolls:
about 3 hours

Rolling and shaping:
30 minutes

Proofing: **2 hours**

Baking:
25 to 30 minutes

Ingredients	Metric	Imperial
Sweet Levain Brioche Dough, variation for Red Pepper-Gruyère Pull-Apart Rolls (page 290)	1.17 kg	2½ pounds
EGG WASH		
whole egg	55 g	1 large egg
egg yolk	18 g	1 large yolk
heavy cream	30 g	2 tablespoons

coarse or flaky sea salt, for sprinkling

1. Line a small baking sheet with parchment paper.

2. Divide the dough into twelve equal pieces.

3. Cup your fingers around one piece of dough. Roll against the work surface to form a ball. (Once you become proficient, you can roll two at a time, one in each hand.) Arrange the rolls three by four in the pan.

4. **MAKE THE EGG WASH:** Whisk together the egg, yolk, and cream and brush over the rolls. Cover the pan with an inverted box or plastic tub and let sit at room temperature until the dough is expanded, about 2 hours.

5. Preheat the oven to 350°F (175°C).

6. Carefully brush the rolls with the egg wash again, sprinkle with the coarse salt, and bake until the rolls are golden brown, 25 to 30 minutes.

7. Transfer to a wire rack and let cool until warm (or completely).

Hamburger Rolls

Brioche rolls are scrumptious when toasted on the grill for a barbecue dinner. Their light sweetness makes a wonderful contrast to savory burgers and toppings.

Makes 10 rolls

Preparing the Sweet Levain Brioche Dough (page 290):
13 to 18½ hours

Start to finish for the Hamburger Rolls:
about 3 hours

Rolling and shaping:
30 minutes

Proofing: **2 hours**

Baking:
25 to 30 minutes

VARIATION: SANDWICH ROLLS

After pressing the dough into a 3-inch (7 cm) round, brush the dough with the egg wash, and then let proof as directed. Brush again with the egg wash and sprinkle with the seeds. Because the rounds are not rolled with the rolling pin to the larger size, they will bake into taller, rounder rolls.

Ingredients	Metric	Imperial
Sweet Levain Brioche Dough (page 290)	1 kg	about 2¼ pounds
all-purpose flour, for dusting		
EGG WASH		
whole egg	55 g	1 large egg
egg yolk	18 g	1 large yolk
heavy cream	30 g	2 tablespoons
sesame and/or poppy seeds (optional)	5 to 10 g	½ to 1 tablespoon

1. Line two baking sheets with parchment paper.

2. Divide the dough into ten equal pieces.
   Cup your fingers around one piece of dough. Roll against the work surface to form a ball. (Once you become proficient, you can roll two at a time, one in each hand.)

3. Adding flour only as needed, press the dough into rounds about 3 inches (7 cm) across. Using a rolling pin, gently roll the rounds out to about 4 inches (10 cm). Arrange five on each baking sheet (in a pattern like a playing card).
   MAKE THE EGG WASH: Whisk together the egg, yolk, and cream in a small bowl. Brush the tops of the rolls with the egg wash. Cover and refrigerate the remaining egg wash. Cover the pan with an inverted box or plastic tub and let sit at room temperature to proof until the dough is tender and expanded, about 2 hours.

RECIPE CONTINUES

4. Position the oven racks in the upper and lower thirds of the oven. Preheat the oven to 350°F (175°C).

5. Carefully brush the rolls with the egg wash again, sprinkle with the seeds, if using, and transfer to the oven.

Bake until the rolls are golden brown, 25 to 30 minutes, switching the pans between the shelves and rotating once during baking.

6. Transfer to a wire rack and let cool completely.

Laminated Sweet Levain Brioche Dough

If you think that brioche is the ultimate enriched bread, then you haven't tried laminated brioche. Incorporating a butter block into the dough and then folding it results in an incredibly light and rich bread that is, in my opinion, the ultimate brioche.

Makes 1.2 kg (about 2⅔ pounds), enough for 2 loaves

Preparing the Sweet Levain Brioche Dough (page 290):
13 to 18½ hours

Start to finish for the Laminated Sweet Levain Brioche Dough:
13 to 15½ hours

Making and refrigerating the butter block: 8½ to 10½ hours

Rolling, turning for lamination, and finishing the dough:
4½ to 5 hours

Ingredients	Metric	Imperial
Sweet Levain Brioche Dough (page 290)	1 kg	about 2¼ pounds
Brioche Butter Block (recipe follows)	200 g	7 ounces / 14 tablespoons
all-purpose flour, for dusting		

Follow the steps for making the sweet levain brioche dough and the butter block, refrigerating both, then proceed to rolling (page 312).

Brioche Butter Block

Making the block: 30 minutes

Refrigerating: 8 to 10 hours (This only needs to be done an hour ahead, but making it in conjunction with the dough will ensure it's all ready to go.)

It is best to make the butter block with a European-style butter because of its higher fat content (meaning less water). Making a uniform rectangle of butter is easiest if you start with the butter in one piece (many brands can be purchased in 227-gram/half-pound blocks or 453-gram/1-pound blocks), but if unavailable, sticks will work (see step 2).

Ingredients	Metric	Imperial
unsalted butter, cold	200 g	14 tablespoons / 7 ounces
all-purpose flour, for dusting		

1. Set the butter in the center of a large piece of parchment paper. Lay another piece of parchment paper on top. Using a rolling pin, pound

RECIPE CONTINUES

across the butter to begin to flatten it. Turn the butter and pound across it in the opposite direction. Straighten out the parchment paper where it is sticking to the butter.

Next begin to roll the butter into a rectangular shape, turning the block and flipping it over to keep it even in thickness. Continue until flattened to a 7 by 8-inch (18 by 20 cm) rectangle.

2. Remove the top piece of parchment paper. Wrap the butter block tightly in the other piece of parchment paper. Refrigerate overnight.

Alternatively, using sticks of butter, set the butter in the center of a large piece of parchment paper and let soften to a moldable consistency. Top with another piece of parchment paper and form into a rough rectangle with no visible breaks. If at any point the butter gets too soft, refrigerate for about 20 minutes. Continue to roll and shape into the desired 7 by 8-inch (18 by 20 cm) rectangle, wrap in parchment paper until cold, and proceed as written.

Rolling the Brioche Dough and Locking In the Butter Block

Start to finish: **30 minutes to 1 hour**

Rolling and locking in the butter: **20 to 30 minutes**

Freezing or refrigerating (optional): **10 to 30 minutes**

The key to successful layers in laminated brioche is making sure the butter and the dough are at the same consistency. Meaning, once the butter is folded into the dough ("locked in") and the rolling begins, you want the butter and the dough to roll together to have even layers of butter and dough as you go. If the butter is too cold, it can break inside the dough and sometimes tear it. If the butter is too warm, it can slide inside the dough and leave gaps with no butter. Properly evaluating the correct temperature of the butter will come with practice. A good way to test if the butter is ready is if it bends without breaking. At this point, take out the dough, and then in about 5 minutes you should be ready to go.

1. Remove the butter block and the dough from the refrigerator. Lightly flour the work surface and a rolling pin.

Using a bowl scraper, carefully release the brioche dough from the container or bowl onto the work surface. Lightly flour the top of the dough. Starting in the center, roll the dough outward, turning often and flipping it over, to roll out evenly into a 7 by 16-inch (18 by 40 cm) rectangle, adding flour only as needed to the dough and rolling pin to keep it from sticking. At this point, the dough should not crack. If it does, it is too cold and should sit at room temperature for a few minutes.

2. Position the dough so that the long edges are facing you.

Unwrap the butter and gently set it in the center of the dough so that the butter fills the width of the dough and there are even amounts of dough on either side. Stretch and fold the two sides of the dough over the butter so they meet in the center and cover the butter. Pinch together to seal. You will still see butter on the sides. Pinch those edges together as well. Using the rolling pin, press down on the dough across the seam, moving from the top to the bottom, just to begin to flatten the dough.

At this point, you can continue the rolling and folding for turn one, or if the dough and butter seem to have warmed, wrap securely in parchment paper and/or plastic wrap, set on a baking sheet, and put in the freezer for 10 minutes or the refrigerator for 30 minutes.

Turn One

Start to finish: **1½ hours**

Rolling and folding: **10 to 30 minutes**

Refrigerating: **1 hour**

1. Dust the work surface and rolling pin only if needed. Position the dough on the work surface with the seam running from top to bottom in front of you with a short end facing you. Using the rolling pin, press down on the dough across the seam, moving from the top to the bottom, just to begin to flatten the dough. At this point, the dough should not crack. If it does, it is too cold and should sit at room temperature for a few minutes.

Roll the dough, adding flour only as needed, but flipping the dough to roll both the top and the bottom, until the length has expanded to about 20 inches (about 50 cm). The width should be 8 inches (20 cm). If not, turn the dough and roll the width a bit more. If the dough

RECIPE CONTINUES

becomes difficult to roll any larger and shrinks back, cover it and let it rest for about 15 minutes.

2. Turn the dough as needed to have a short end facing you again. Brush off any excess flour. Fold up the bottom third of the dough's length, as if you were folding a letter. Next, fold down the top third of the dough to cover the bottom third.

3. Rotate the block of dough 90 degrees so the rounded end is on the left and the open end is on the right. Think of it like a book with the spine to the left side. Brush off any excess flour. Using a chef's knife, slice along the rounded edge to open up the left side. (There are two reasons for this: to keep the consistency of the dough uniform and to create a more distinct lamination.)

If you like, to keep track of the turns, press your finger into a corner to make an indentation signifying the first turn.

4. Wrap the dough block securely in parchment paper and/or plastic wrap, set on a baking sheet, and refrigerate for 1 hour.

Turn Two

Start to finish: **1½ hours**
Rolling and folding: **10 to 30 minutes**
Refrigerating: **1 hour**

1. Dust the work surface and rolling pin only if needed. Unwrap the dough and position on the work surface with the short end facing you. Using the rolling pin, press down on the dough across the seam, moving from the top to the bottom, just to begin to flatten the dough. At this point, the dough should not crack. If it does, it is too cold and should sit at room temperature for a few minutes.

Roll the dough, adding flour only as needed, but flipping the dough to roll both the top and the bottom, until the length has expanded to 18 to 20 inches (45 to 50 cm). The width should be 8 to 9 inches (20 to 23 cm). If not, turn the dough and roll the width a bit more. If the dough becomes difficult to roll any larger and shrinks back, cover and let rest for about 15 minutes.

2. Turn the dough as needed to have a short end facing you again. Brush off any excess flour. Fold up the bottom of the dough to meet the top, folding the dough in half.

3. Rotate the block of dough 90 degrees so the rounded end is on the left and the open end is on the right. Think of it like a book with the spine to the left side. Brush off any excess flour. Using a chef's knife, slice along the rounded edge to open up the left side.

If you like, to keep track of the turns, press your finger into a corner to make two indentations signifying the second turn.

4. Wrap the dough block securely in parchment paper and/or plastic wrap, set on a baking sheet, and refrigerate for 1 hour.

Finishing the Dough

Start to finish: 30 minutes to 1 hour
Rolling: about 10 minutes
Freezing or refrigerating: 10 to 30 minutes

1. Line a clean baking sheet with parchment paper. Lightly dust the work surface with flour.

2. Unwrap the dough block and set it on the work surface with the side that was cut to the left and the opening to the right. Lightly dust the top of the dough block with flour.

3. Roll the dough, adding flour only as needed, but flipping the dough to roll both the top and the bottom, until the length has expanded to 20 inches (50 cm). The width should be 8 inches (20 cm). If not, turn the dough and roll the width a bit more.

4. Using a bench scraper or a chef's knife, cut the dough in half, making two 10 by 8-inch (25 by 20 cm) rectangles. Transfer to the prepared baking sheet, putting a piece of parchment paper between them. Wrap the top of the baking sheet.

RECIPE CONTINUES

Put in the freezer for 10 minutes or the refrigerator for 30 minutes to firm up the dough.

At this point, the dough can be refrigerated overnight, frozen for up to 1 month, or used for the layered brioche loaves (see below). If the dough is frozen, before using, transfer to the refrigerator to thaw overnight and continue with the desired recipe with no additional freezing.

Working with one piece at a time, continue to the recipe for the layered brioche loaves. The piece not being used should be wrapped securely in parchment paper and/or plastic wrap and refrigerated.

Pull–Apart Laminated Brioche Loaves

Makes 2 loaves, each 600 grams (21 ounces)

Preparing the Laminated Sweet Levain Brioche Dough:
26 to 34 hours

Start to finish for the Pull-Apart Laminated Brioche Loaves:
about 5 hours

Rolling and shaping:
30 minutes

Proofing: **2 hours**

Baking:
45 to 50 minutes

Cooling: **1½ hours**

Ingredients	Metric	Imperial
vegetable oil, for brushing the pans		
Laminated Sweet Levain Brioche Dough (page 311)	1.2 kg	2½ pounds
EGG WASH		
whole egg	55 g	1 large egg
egg yolk	18 g	1 large yolk
heavy cream	30 g	2 tablespoons
pearl sugar, for sprinkling (optional)		

1. Brush two traditional loaf pans, 8½ by 4½ by 2½ inches (21.5 by 10 by 6 cm), lightly with oil.

2. Set one half of the brioche dough on the work surface. The dough should be chilled but not too cold. If it cracks when gently pressed with the rolling pin, let it warm up for a few minutes at room temperature.

3. Roll the dough into a narrow 6 by 24-inch (15 by 60 cm) rectangle.
   Using a chef's knife, cut the dough in half lengthwise into two 3 by 24-inch (7.5 by 60 cm) strips.
   Working with one piece at a time, cut each strip into three smaller strips, 3 by 8 inches (7.5 by 20 cm) each. Roll these three strips into spirals and set in one of the prepared pans with the cut sides facing up and down. Repeat with the other half of the dough and pan.

4. **MAKE THE EGG WASH:** Whisk together the egg, yolk, and cream in a small bowl. Brush the tops of the loaves with the egg wash. Cover and refrigerate the remaining egg wash. Cover the pans with an inverted

RECIPE CONTINUES

box or plastic tub and let sit at room temperature to proof until the dough is tender and expanded, about 2 hours.

5. Preheat the oven to 350°F (175°C).

Set the loaf pans on a baking sheet. Baking the loaves on a sheet pan will be helpful if some of the butter leaches out over the top of the pan while baking, which can cause some smoking in the oven.

Carefully brush the tops of the loaves again with egg wash, sprinkle with the pearl sugar, if desired, and transfer to the oven.

Bake until the loaves are a rich golden brown, 45 to 50 minutes.

CROISSANTS

On a recent trip to Paris, I met up with my friend (and Nels's mother-in-law) Katherine, who grew up there and spends a part of every year in the city. We took a meandering walk from her apartment near the Arc de Triomphe, as she pointed out the Esplanade des Invalides, an elegant and beautiful green space bordered by some of the grandest buildings in the city. She shared childhood memories of what it was like to visit friends here, and pointed out the wonderful boutiques that line Rue Saint-Dominique. Our destination was Boulangerie Liberté, at number 58 on that historic and charming street. I had become friendly with its owner, Mickael Benichou, on a previous trip. He welcomed us warmly and sat us at a sidewalk table on the picture-perfect September day. The sun was shining and it was 65°F (18°C). A plate of pains aux raisins and a couple of croissants appeared.

I took a bite of a croissant and noted its gentle and flaky crust, in contrast with its melting, brioche-like interior. There was the wonderful richness and flavor of French butter with a hint of tangy levain. It was just so perfect in its balance and simplicity. I actually felt my eyes prickle with tears. Katherine became alarmed. "Are you sad? Are you crying?" I explained that beautifully made pastry made me emotional, and she nodded in sympathy. If you are a novice baker, you might not have had this type of reaction to baked goods yet. But once you spend some time working with dough and becoming sensitive to its development at every stage, you may feel similarly moved by an expertly crafted croissant.

The croissant is timeless. Like a great piece of music that can be enjoyed over and over again, played by various maestros each with their own interpretation, the well-made croissant never fails to please. This is why croissants have never gone out of style in Paris. Even as young Parisian bakers experiment with new shapes and flavors, they continue to respect the technique that is so essential to producing both classic croissants and the wildest variations. Croissants have

always been in my baking repertoire, and I'll never tire of tinkering with my recipe to see how I can improve it or use it in new ways.

Croissant styles have changed over time. Many of today's Instagram-perfect croissants, bisected, will have visibly separate and relatively dry leaves of dough. When you bite into one of these, the crust shatters, your shirt and the table immediately showered with flakes of pastry. And if this is the type of croissant that you like, that's great. But my ideal croissant, and this is purely a matter of taste and aesthetics, hearkens back to the first examples I devoured as a young cook traveling to France for the first time. On the spectrum of laminated pastries that runs from crispiest puff pastry to tenderest Danish, my favorite croissants definitely fall closer to Danish in richness and pillowy texture. I expect a few crumbs from the crisp exterior to fall as I'm eating one, but I also want to experience the softness as well as some chew and resistance from a contrasting interior. To get this dual texture, I prefer a soft, rich dough with a little more butter and milk than you'd need for a more obviously layered result.

Lamination is never going to be quick, but it is a very straightforward, simple, and satisfying skill to master. There are no real shortcuts, in my opinion, when you want to create multiple layers of butter and pastry. But like crafting a sourdough loaf, making croissants is more wait than work. The process of removing your dough from the refrigerator, dusting the counter with flour, rolling out the dough, folding it, wrapping it, and refrigerating it again takes 10 minutes. But the dough does have to rest in the refrigerator for an hour between folds. With a little bit of planning and organization, you can get plenty of errands done, or plenty of rest and relaxation, while you wait. Folding techniques vary. Some bakers do three 3-folds (letter folds); some one 3-fold (a letter fold), and then one 4-fold (a book fold); and then some do two 4-folds (book folds). I like to do three 3-folds. If you are not experienced, it's a little more straightforward than the 4-fold method. It will also give you more layers in the end—fifty-five layers as opposed to twenty-five or thirty-three. More layers is my personal preference.

I've formulated my recipe so you'll get 1.25 kilograms of dough. If you are going to go to the trouble of making your own croissant dough, you'll want to make enough to enjoy it and use it for a couple of weeks. I recommend dividing the folded dough into three portions and freezing two of them. Each of the recipes below calls for a generous 0.5 kilogram of dough. When the first batch of pastries has been eaten (this won't take long, you can be sure), you can thaw another portion of dough to bake another batch.

TIMELINE FOR MAKING CROISSANTS

DAY 1: In the morning to afternoon, make the sweet levain.

Late afternoon, make the croissant dough and the butter block. And, if making snails with pastry cream, make the pastry cream as well. Let the dough sit at room temperature for 4 hours and then refrigerate overnight.

DAY 2: Roll out the dough, lock in the butter, do three turns, and complete the final roll of the dough. Divide the dough in half.

Cut the dough into portions and shape traditional croissants or snails. Put in the freezer to partially freeze and then proof the croissants overnight.

DAY 3: Bake the croissants.

Sourdough Croissant Dough

Years ago, we started putting a little liquid levain in our croissant dough. This evolved into a sweet levain, with a little added sugar, for a nice sweet-and-sour balance. Adding a gram of instant yeast is optional. Not using it won't make a difference in fermentation time in warmer weather, but in the cooler months, the dough might need some extra time in the morning to fully proof.

Makes
1.25 kilograms
(2¾ pounds),
enough for
16 traditional
croissants or
20 snails, or a
combination of
8 traditional
croissants and
10 snails

Start to finish:
about 30 hours

Preparing and proofing
the Sweet Levain for
Croissants (recipe
follows): 6½ to 8½ hours

Gathering ingredients
and preparing the
dough: 15 minutes

Proofing and
refrigerating:
12 to 14 hours

Making and
refrigerating the butter
block: 8½ to 10½ hours

Rolling, turning for
lamination, and finishing
the dough:
6 to 6½ hours

Ingredients	Metric	Imperial
vegetable oil, for greasing		
Sweet Levain for Croissants (recipe follows)		
bread flour	300 g	2½ cups
all-purpose flour	200 g	1½ cups plus 2 tablespoons plus 1 teaspoon
sugar	35 g	3 tablespoons
fine sea salt	12 g	2 teaspoons
instant dry yeast (optional)	1 g	½ teaspoon
water (70° to 78°F / 21° to 25.5°C)	165 g	½ cup plus 3½ tablespoons
whole milk	150 g	½ cup plus 1½ tablespoons
unsalted butter, melted and cooled	50 g	1¾ ounces / 3½ tablespoons
Croissant Butter Block (recipe follows)	250 g	8¾ ounces / 17½ tablespoons

1. Lightly brush a 2-quart (2-liter) glass storage container with a lid or a large bowl with oil.

2. In the bowl of the stand mixer that has the sweet levain, add the bread flour, all-purpose flour, sugar, salt, and yeast, if using. Fit the mixer with the dough hook and mix on the lowest setting for 30 seconds to evenly distribute the dry ingredients. Add the water, milk, and melted butter. Mix on the Stir setting for about 30 seconds, then increase the speed to low to medium-low until the dough is combined and smooth, about 5 minutes.

3. Transfer the dough to the container or bowl. Cover the container with the lid or the bowl tightly with beeswax wrap. Let sit at room temperature for 4 hours and then refrigerate overnight, 8 to 10 hours. Make the butter block (opposite), then proceed to rolling (page 326).

Sweet Levain for Croissants

Makes 115 grams (4 ounces)

Ingredients	Metric	Imperial
all-purpose flour	50 g	¼ cup plus 2 tablespoons plus 1 teaspoon
sugar	10 g	2½ teaspoons
water (70° to 78°F / 21° to 25.5°C)	35 g	2½ tablespoons
Sourdough Starter (page 98)	20 g	1 tablespoon

In the bowl of a stand mixer, add the flour, sugar, water, and sourdough starter. Mix together with either the paddle attachment or a spoon. Cover the top tightly, preferably with beeswax wrap. Let sit at room temperature for 6 to 8 hours.

Croissant Butter Block

Making the block: 30 minutes

Refrigerating: 8 to 10 hours (This only needs to be done an hour ahead, but making it in conjunction with the dough will ensure it's all ready to go.)

It is best to make the butter block with a European-style butter because of its higher fat content (meaning less water). Making a uniform rectangle of butter is easiest if you start with the butter in one piece (many brands can be purchased in 453-gram / 1-pound blocks), but if unavailable, sticks will work (see step 2).

Ingredients	Metric	Imperial
unsalted butter, cold	250 g	8¾ ounces / 17½ tablespoons
all-purpose flour, for dusting		

1. Set the butter in the center of a large piece of parchment paper. Lay another piece of parchment paper on top. Using a rolling pin, pound across the butter to begin to flatten it. Turn the butter and pound across it in the opposite direction. Straighten out the parchment paper where it is sticking to the butter.

Next begin to roll the butter into a rectangular shape, turning the block, and flipping it over to keep it even in thickness. Continue until flattened to a 7 by 8-inch (18 by 20 cm) rectangle.

RECIPE CONTINUES

2. Remove the top piece of parchment paper. Wrap the butter block tightly in the other piece of parchment paper. Refrigerate overnight.

Alternatively, using sticks of butter, set the butter in the center of a large piece of parchment paper and let soften to a moldable consistency. Top with another piece of parchment paper and form into a rough rectangle with no visible breaks. If at any point the butter gets too soft, refrigerate for about 20 minutes. Continue to roll and shape in the desired 7 by 8-inch (18 by 20 cm) rectangle, wrap in parchment paper until cold, and proceed as written.

Rolling the Croissant Dough and Locking In the Butter Block

Start to finish: 30 minutes to 1 hour
Rolling and locking in the butter: 20 to 30 minutes
Freezing or refrigerating (optional): 10 to 30 minutes

The key to successful layers in croissants is making sure the butter and the dough are at the same consistency. Meaning, once the butter is folded into the dough ("locked in") and the rolling begins, you want the butter and the dough to roll together to have even layers of butter and dough as you go. If the butter is too cold, it can break inside the dough and sometimes tear it. If the butter is too warm, it can slide inside the dough and leave gaps with no butter. Properly evaluating the correct temperature of the butter will come with practice. A good way to test if the butter is ready is if it bends without breaking. At this point, take out the dough, and then in about 5 minutes you should be ready to go.

1. Remove the butter block and the dough from the refrigerator. Lightly flour the work surface and a rolling pin.

Using a bowl scraper, carefully release the croissant dough from the container or bowl onto the work surface. Lightly flour the top of the dough. Starting in the center, roll the dough outward, turning often and flipping it over, to roll out evenly into a 7 by 16-inch (18 by 40 cm) rectangle, adding flour only as needed to the dough and rolling pin to keep it from sticking. At this point, the dough should not crack. If it does, it is too cold and should sit at room temperature for a few minutes.

2. Position the dough so that a long edge is facing you.

Unwrap the butter and gently set it in the center of the dough so that the butter fills the width of the dough and there are even amounts of dough on either side. Stretch and fold the two sides of the dough over the butter so they meet in the center and cover the butter. Pinch together to seal. You will still see butter on the sides. Pinch those edges together as well. Using the rolling pin, press down on the dough across the seam, moving from the top to the bottom, just to begin to flatten the dough.

At this point, you can continue the rolling and folding for turn one, or if the dough and butter seem to have warmed, wrap securely in parchment paper and/or plastic wrap, set on a baking sheet, and put in the freezer for 10 minutes or the refrigerator for 30 minutes.

Turn One

Start to finish: 1½ hours
Rolling and folding: 10 to 15 minutes
Refrigerating: 1 hour

1. Dust the work surface and rolling pin only if needed. Position the dough on the work surface with the seam running from top to bottom in front of you with a short end facing you. Using the rolling pin, press down on the dough across the seam, moving from the top to the bottom, just to begin to flatten the dough. At this point, the dough should not crack. If it does, it is too cold and should sit at room temperature for a few minutes.

Roll the dough, adding flour only as needed, but flipping the dough to roll both the top and the bottom, until the length has expanded to 20 to 22 inches (50 to 55 cm). The width should be 8 to 9 inches (20 to 23 cm). If not, turn the dough and roll the width a bit more.

2. Turn the dough as needed to have a short end facing you again. Brush off any excess flour. Fold up the bottom third of the dough's length, as if you were folding a letter. Next, fold down the top third of the dough to cover the bottom third.

RECIPE CONTINUES

3. Rotate the block of dough 90 degrees so the rounded end is on the left and the open end is on the right. Think of it like a book with the spine to the left side. Brush off any excess flour. Using a chef's knife, slice open the rounded edge to open up the left side. (There are two reasons for this: to keep the consistency of the dough uniform and to create a more distinct lamination.)

If you like, to keep track of the turns, press your finger into a corner to make an indentation signifying the first turn.

4. Wrap the dough block securely in parchment paper and/or plastic wrap, set on a baking sheet, and refrigerate for 1 hour.

Turn Two

Start to finish: 1½ hours
Rolling and folding: about 10 to 15 minutes
Refrigerating: 1 hour

1. Lightly dust the work surface and the rolling pin with flour.

2. Unwrap the dough block and set it on the work surface with the side that was cut to the left and the opening to the right. Lightly dust the top of the dough block with flour. Using the rolling pin, press down on the dough across the seam, moving from the top to the bottom, just to begin to flatten the dough. At this point, the dough should not crack. If it does, it is too cold and should sit at room temperature for a few minutes.

3. Roll the dough, adding flour only as needed, but flipping the dough to roll both the top and the bottom, until the length has expanded to 20 to 22 inches (50 to 55 cm). The width should be 8 to 9 inches (20 to 23 cm). If not, turn the dough and roll the width a bit more.

4. Turn the dough as needed to have a short end facing you again. Brush off any excess flour. Fold up the bottom third of the dough's length, then fold down the top third to cover the bottom third, as you did before.

5. Rotate the block of dough 90 degrees so the rounded end is on the left and the open end is on the right. Using a chef's knife, slice along the rounded edge to open up the left side.

If you like, to keep track of the turns, press your finger into a corner to make two indentations signifying the second turn.

6. Wrap the dough block securely in parchment paper and/or plastic wrap, set on a baking sheet, and refrigerate for 1 hour.

Turn Three

Start to finish: 1½ hours
Rolling and folding: about 10 to 15 minutes
Refrigerating: 1 hour

1. Repeat all the steps for turn two, marking the dough with three indentations, if you like.

Finishing the Dough

Start to finish: 30 minutes to 1 hour
Rolling: about 10 minutes
Freezing or refrigerating: 10 to 30 minutes

1. Line a clean baking sheet with parchment paper. Lightly dust the work surface with flour.

2. Unwrap the dough block and set it on the work surface with the side that was cut to the left and the opening to the right. Lightly dust the top of the dough block with flour.

3. Roll the dough, adding flour only as needed, but flipping the dough to roll both the top and the bottom, until the length has expanded to 24 inches (60 cm). The width should be 8 to 9 inches (20 to 23 cm). If not, turn the dough and roll the width a bit more.

4. Using a bench scraper or a chef's knife, cut the dough in half, making two rectangles each 12 inches long by 8 to 9 inches wide

RECIPE CONTINUES

(30 cm long by 20 to 23 cm wide). Transfer to the prepared baking sheet, putting a piece of parchment paper between them. Wrap the top of the baking sheet.

Put in the freezer for 10 minutes or the refrigerator for 30 minutes to firm up the dough.

At this point, the dough can be refrigerated overnight, frozen for up to 1 month, or used for traditional croissants or snails (see below). If the dough is frozen, before using, transfer to the refrigerator to thaw overnight and continue with the desired recipe with no additional freezing.

Working with one piece at a time, continue to the recipe for traditional croissants and/or snails. The piece not being used should be wrapped securely in parchment paper and/or plastic wrap and refrigerated.

Proofing Box at Home for Croissants

Setting up a proofing box at home is very straightforward and can be done in the oven, in the microwave, or even on the counter. The goal is to create a closed, warm area with some humidity.

IN THE OVEN: Position one oven rack on the lowest rung and another in the center of the oven. Set the croissants on the center rack. Pour 2 to 3 cups of boiling water into a loaf pan and set on the bottom rack. Close the door and do not open until morning.

If you have only one oven, transfer to the counter and cover with an inverted box or tub while preheating.

IN THE MICROWAVE: Most microwaves will not accommodate a baking sheet, but if you're only baking a few croissants, it is a good option. Set the croissants in the microwave, ideally to one side. Find a liquid measuring cup or a bowl that will fit next to them. Pour 1 to 3 cups of boiling water into the measuring cup. Close the door and do not open until morning.

ON THE COUNTER: Set the croissants on the baking sheet and position a loaf pan, liquid measuring cup, or a bowl next to them. Choose an inverted box or tub that will fit over both. Pour 2 to 3 cups of boiling water in the pan and cover with the box. This option is not quite as effective as the oven or microwave because it isn't an insulated, sealed environment.

Traditional Croissants

Makes 8 croissants

Preparing the
Sourdough Croissant
Dough: **about 30 hours**

Start to finish for
Traditional Croissants:
about 11½ hours

Rolling and shaping:
20 to 30 minutes

Freezing: **1 hour**

Proofing: **overnight**

Baking:
35 to 45 minutes

Cooling: **20 minutes**

Ingredients	Metric	Imperial
all-purpose flour, for dusting		
½ recipe Sourdough Croissant Dough (page 324)	625 g	1⅓ pounds
EGG WASH		
whole egg	55 g	1 large egg
egg yolk	18 g	1 large yolk
heavy cream	30 g	2 tablespoons

1. Line a baking sheet with parchment paper. Lightly dust the work surface and the rolling pin with flour.

2. Set the croissant dough on the work surface. The dough should be chilled but not too cold. If it cracks when gently pressed with the pin, let it warm up for a few minutes at room temperature.
   Roll the length of the dough to 16 inches (40 cm).

3. Using a ruler as needed, score the dough (press gently with a knife, but don't cut all the way through) every 4 inches (10 cm), from top to bottom, to mark four even rectangles. Then, cut into the rectangles, trimming the two outside edges as needed. Set the trimmings to the side.
   Cut across each rectangle to make a total of eight triangles.

4. Line the triangles up so that the bases/shortest sides of the triangles are facing you. Working with one triangle at a time, make a small (⅜-inch / 1 cm) slit in the center of each base.

5. Lift one triangle from the work surface, brushing off any excess flour. Hold the base with one hand and use the fingertips from the other to gently stretch the dough to about 12 inches (30 cm).
   Return it to the work surface. Fold the two sides of the base from the

RECIPE CONTINUES

slit outward, and then roll the triangle up from the wide end all the way to the tip. As you roll, gently pull and stretch from the point end. Set on the prepared baking sheet with the small tip/tail of dough underneath. Press down slightly just to keep from rolling.

6. Repeat the stretching and rolling with the remaining seven triangles, setting them on the baking sheet. Roll the trimmings together, then into a spiral, and set on the baking sheet as well.

7. Freeze on the baking sheet for 1 hour, just to partially freeze.

   At this point the croissants can also be wrapped well and frozen completely for up to 1 month (see note on freezing, page 335).

   MAKE THE EGG WASH: Whisk together the egg, yolk, and cream in a small bowl. Brush the croissants with the egg wash. Cover and refrigerate the remaining egg wash. Set the croissants in the oven with a loaf pan filled halfway with boiling water or cover the baking sheet with an inverted box or plastic tub with a loaf pan filled halfway with boiling water (see Proofing Box at Home for Croissants, page 330).

   Let proof at room temperature until the dough is tender and expanded, overnight.

8. The next morning, if proofed in the oven, remove the tray from the oven and carefully cover it.

9. Preheat the oven to 350°F (175°C).

10. Carefully brush the croissants with the egg wash again and transfer to the oven.

    Bake until the croissants are a rich golden brown, 35 to 45 minutes.

11. Transfer to a wire rack and let cool completely.

SNAILS

We've always made croissants and pain au chocolat at Bread Alone, but over the years we've made countless other products, including snails and muffins, using croissant dough as a foundation. Spiral, snail-shaped croissants lend themselves to both sweet and savory fillings. One of my favorite Parisian bakeries, Du Pain et des Idées, has become famous for its creative "escargot" variations, with fillings such as praline, chocolate and banana, berries and cream cheese, and so on. At Bread Alone, we tend to think seasonally, making apple snails in the fall, pesto snails in the summer. Once you get the hang of it, you can come up with your own flavorings.

Pastry Cream for Snails

This is more pastry cream than you will need for ten snails, but it has many other delicious uses, such as filling donuts, mini tart shells, and eclairs. The pastry cream needs to be made ahead and refrigerated for at least 6 hours or up to 3 days. Plan on making it either on the day you mix the dough or the next, possibly between turns. Once the ingredients are prepped and weighed, it comes together very quickly. A high-quality pure vanilla extract or vanilla paste works well here, but you can also use a vanilla bean. Cut the vanilla bean in half, then scrape out the seeds and add both the seeds and the pod to the pan. Discard the pod before mixing.

Makes about
532 grams (1¼ cups)

Start to finish:
about 7 hours

Gathering ingredients
and preparing the
pastry cream:
20 minutes

Cooling and
refrigerating:
**6½ hours or
up to 3 days**

Ingredients	Metric	Imperial
sugar	94 g	¼ cup plus 3½ tablespoons
egg yolks	54 g	3 large yolks
cornstarch	23 g	3 tablespoons
whole milk	263 g	1 cup plus 1 tablespoon
heavy cream	94 g	¼ cup plus 2½ tablespoons
pure vanilla extract or paste	4 g	½ teaspoon

1. In the bowl of a stand mixer fitted with the paddle attachment, add the sugar, egg yolks, and cornstarch. Mix on medium-low speed to combine, about 1 minute. Stop and scrape the bottom and sides and continue to mix, increasing the speed to medium, until the mixture holds a ribbon shape: when the paddle is lifted, the mixture should fall back on itself in a slowly dissolving ribbon.

2. Meanwhile, combine the milk and cream in a medium saucier or other saucepan, preferably with a rounded bottom. Bring to a simmer over medium to medium-high heat. Stir in the vanilla.

3. With the mixer running on low speed, add the hot cream a ladleful at a time. Once all is incorporated, stop and scrape down the sides and bottom and mix for a few seconds more.

4. Transfer the mixture to the saucepan. Whisk continuously over low heat until the mixture has thickened to the texture of pudding, 2 to 3 minutes. If it is helpful, move the pan off the heat for a few seconds,

continuing to whisk, to keep from cooking too quickly or scorching the bottom.

5. Transfer to a storage container and let cool for 5 to 10 minutes. To avoid a skin forming on the top of the pastry cream, press a piece of plastic wrap directly on the surface. Let cool and then refrigerate for at least 6 hours or up to 3 days.

Freezing Snails and Croissants

Once snails or traditional croissants are formed, they can be frozen, if well wrapped, for up to 1 month.

Lay a piece of parchment paper over the snails or croissants and then wrap the whole baking sheet securely with plastic wrap. Set on a level spot in the freezer until completely frozen, about 8 hours. Ideally, the snails or croissants will remain on the baking sheet ready to go, but if space is needed, they can be quickly and carefully transferred to an airtight storage container or bag and returned to the freezer.

The night before you plan to enjoy the snails or croissants, return them to a lined baking sheet (or sheets) as needed and spaced for baking (eight traditional croissants per sheet, five snails per sheet). Remove the plastic wrap around the baking sheet(s) as well as the top piece of parchment paper. Drape new plastic wrap over the top of the baking sheet(s). The snails or croissants should all be covered but no longer tightly wrapped. Transfer to the refrigerator overnight.

The morning of, set the baking sheet(s) on the work surface and remove the plastic wrap. Brush the snails or croissants with the egg wash. Cover the baking sheet(s) with an inverted box or plastic tub and let proof at room temperature until the dough is tender and expanded, about 2 hours.

Meanwhile, preheat the oven to 350°F (175°C).

Carefully brush the snails or croissants with the egg wash again and transfer to the oven.

Bake until the snails or croissants are a rich golden brown, 30 to 45 minutes.

Transfer to a wire rack and let cool completely.

Pains aux Raisins

When it comes to snails, pains aux raisins are the classic and the benchmark. They are just that delicious! A thin layer of vanilla pastry cream is spread on the dough and then topped with plump raisins. I like to use the smaller Zante currants instead to be sure to have them evenly distributed for some in every bite. If the currants are a bit hard, put them in a bowl, pour boiling water over them, let sit for about 30 minutes, drain, and dry well.

Makes 10 pains aux raisins

Start to finish:
10 to 15 hours*

Rolling and shaping, day one: **20 to 30 minutes**

Freezing: **30 minutes**

Proofing: **overnight**

Baking, day two: **30 to 35 minutes**

Cooling: **20 minutes**

*Note: This start-to-finish time is based on the croissant dough and pastry cream being made before assembly of the snails. See the notes under the respective recipes for the preparation times needed.

Ingredients	Metric	Imperial
all-purpose flour, for dusting		
½ recipe Sourdough Croissant Dough (page 324)	625 g	1⅓ pounds
Pastry Cream for Snails (page 334)	100 to 125 g	⅓ to ⅓ cup plus 2½ tablespoons
raisins or Zante currants	100 g	¾ cup
EGG WASH		
whole egg	55 g	1 large egg
egg yolk	18 g	1 large yolk
heavy cream	30 g	2 tablespoons

1. Line two baking sheets with parchment paper. Lightly dust the work surface and the rolling pin with flour.

2. Set the croissant dough on the work surface. The dough should be chilled but not too cold. If it cracks when gently pressed with the pin, let it warm up for a few minutes at room temperature.

    Roll the length of the dough to 18 inches (45 cm). Position the dough so a long end is facing you.

3. Spread the pastry cream evenly over the dough and sprinkle with the raisins.

4. Starting at the bottom, lift the lower edge of the dough and gently fold it over until it turns on itself. Continue rolling, lifting the dough up

RECIPE CONTINUES

Pesto Snails,
PAGE 343

Pains
aux
Raisins

Apple Snails,
PAGE 339

**Chocolate-
Hazelnut.**
Combine 85 g (¼ cup)
pastry cream and 40 g
(2½ tablespoons)
hazelnut paste. Spread
on the dough and
sprinkle with 60 g
(2 ounces) finely
chopped bittersweet
chocolate and 40 g
(3½ tablespoons)
chopped hazelnuts.

Pistachio-Apricot.
Combine 75 g
(3½ tablespoons)
pastry cream and 50 g
(3 tablespoons)
pistachio paste.
Spread on the dough
and sprinkle with 50 g
(7 to 8) chopped dried
apricots and 50 g
(⅓ cup) roasted and
salted pistachios.

and over as you go, until you complete the full roll. Finish with the seam facing down.

5. Measure the dough. It should be approximately 18 inches (45 cm). It's okay if it has expanded slightly or even shrunk back during the rolling process.

Find the midpoint of the roll and score it (press gently with a knife, but don't cut all the way through). Then score each half into five equal pieces, for a total of ten. Cut into ten rounds, trimming the edges as needed. Set any trimmings to the side.

6. Divide the snails between the prepared baking sheets, five per sheet.

Roll the trimmings together, then into a pinwheel and set on one of the baking sheets as well.

7. Freeze on the baking sheets for 30 minutes, just to partially freeze.

At this point, the snails can also be wrapped well and frozen completely for up to 1 month (see note on freezing, page 335).

MAKE THE EGG WASH: Whisk together the egg, yolk, and cream in a small bowl. Brush the snails with the egg wash. Cover and refrigerate the remaining egg wash. Set the snails in the oven with a loaf pan filled halfway with boiling water or cover the baking sheets with an inverted box or plastic tub with a loaf pan filled halfway with boiling water (see Proofing Box at Home, page 330).

Let proof at room temperature until the dough is tender and expanded, overnight.

8. The next morning, if proofed in the oven, remove the trays from the oven and carefully cover them.

9. Arrange the oven racks in the top and bottom thirds of the oven. Preheat the oven to 350°F (175°C).

10. Carefully brush the snails with the egg wash again and transfer to the oven.

Bake, switching the shelf position of the pans and rotating once during baking, until the snails are a rich golden brown, 30 to 35 minutes.

11. Transfer to a wire rack and let cool completely.

Apple Snails

Makes 10 snails

Start to finish:
10 to 15 hours
(see Note on page 336)

Preparing the apple
butter and cooked
apples (includes cooling),
day one: 1½ hours

Rolling and shaping:
20 to 30 minutes

Freezing: 30 minutes

Proofing: overnight

Baking, day two:
30 to 35 minutes

Cooling: 20 minutes

Ingredients	Metric	Imperial
all-purpose flour, for dusting		
½ recipe Sourdough Croissant Dough (page 324)	625 g	1⅓ pounds
Apple Butter (recipe follows)	100 to 125 g	¼ cup plus 2 tablespoons to ¼ cup plus 3½ tablespoons
Cooked Apples (recipe follows)	150 g	1 cup
EGG WASH		
whole egg	55 g	1 large egg
egg yolk	18 g	1 large yolk
heavy cream	30 g	2 tablespoons

1. Line two baking sheets with parchment paper. Lightly dust the work surface and the rolling pin with flour.

2. Set the croissant dough on the work surface. The dough should be chilled but not too cold. If it cracks when gently pressed with the pin, let it warm up for a few minutes at room temperature.

   Roll the length of the dough to 18 inches (45 cm). Position the dough so a long end is facing you.

3. Spread the apple butter evenly over the dough and sprinkle with the cooked apples.

4. Starting at the bottom, lift the lower edge of the dough and gently fold it over until it turns on itself. Continue rolling, lifting the dough up and over as you go, until you complete the full roll. Finish with the seam facing down.

5. Measure the dough. It should be approximately 18 inches (45 cm). It's okay if it has expanded slightly or even shrunk back during the rolling process.

RECIPE CONTINUES

Find the midpoint of the roll and score it (press gently with a knife, but don't cut all of the way through). Then score each half into five equal pieces, for a total of ten. Cut into ten rounds, trimming the edges as needed. Set any trimmings to the side.

6. Divide the snails between the prepared baking sheets, five per sheet.

Roll the trimmings together, then into a pinwheel, and set on one of the baking sheets as well.

7. Freeze on the baking sheets for 30 minutes, just to partially freeze.

At this point, the snails can also be wrapped well and frozen completely for up to 1 month (see note on freezing, page 335).

MAKE THE EGG WASH: Whisk together the egg, yolk, and cream in a small bowl. Brush the snails with the egg wash. Cover and refrigerate the remaining egg wash mixture. Set the snails in the oven with a loaf pan filled halfway with boiling water or cover the baking sheets with an inverted box or plastic tub with a loaf pan filled halfway with boiling water (see Proofing Box at Home, page 330).

Let proof at room temperature until the dough is tender and expanded, overnight.

8. The next morning, if proofed in the oven, remove the trays from the oven and carefully cover them.

9. Arrange the oven racks in the top and bottom thirds of the oven. Preheat the oven to 350°F (175°C).

10. Carefully brush the snails with the egg wash again and transfer to the oven.

Bake, switching the shelf position of the pans and rotating once during baking, until the snails are a rich golden brown, 30 to 35 minutes.

11. Transfer to a wire rack and let cool completely.

Apple Butter and Cooked Apples for Snails

Makes about 625 grams (2¼ cups) apple butter and
150 grams (1 cup) cooked apples

This is more apple butter than you will need for ten snails, but it is delicious spread on a thick slice of toast. I like to use apple juice to control the amount of spice, but apple cider can also be used. Taste a little. You may want to skip the cinnamon in the apple butter. Both the apple butter and cooked apples will need to be cooled before spreading on the dough for the snails, so allow 45 minutes for them to cool or make them ahead.

Ingredients	Metric	Imperial
APPLE BUTTER		
apples, peeled and cut into ½-inch (1.25 cm) pieces	1 kg	2¼ pounds
apple juice or water	100 to 125 g	¼ cup plus 3 tablespoons to ½ cup plus 1½ teaspoons
granulated sugar	100 g	½ cup plus 1 teaspoon
light or dark brown sugar	60 g	¼ cup plus 1 tablespoon
fresh lemon juice	13 g	2½ teaspoons
ground cinnamon	0.5 g	¼ teaspoon
fine sea salt	1 g	¼ teaspoon
COOKED APPLES		
unsalted butter	15 g	½ ounce / 1 tablespoon
1 medium apple, peeled and cut into very small dice	150 to 175 g	5 to 6 ounces

1. **MAKE THE APPLE BUTTER:** In a large saucepan over medium heat, combine the apples, 100 g (¼ cup plus 3 tablespoons) of the apple juice, the granulated sugar, brown sugar, lemon juice, cinnamon, and salt. Cook, stirring and mashing the apples as they break down (a potato masher works well here) and adding an additional 1½ tablespoons apple juice as needed if the mixture gets too dry. Adjust the heat as needed, cooking until the apple mixture is very soft, about 30 minutes. Remove from the heat.

2. Mash and stir by hand until a smooth consistency is achieved or transfer to a blender or food processor and blend until smooth. Let sit

RECIPE CONTINUES

at room temperature until completely cooled, about 45 minutes. The apple butter can also be stored in an airtight container in the refrigerator for up to 3 days.

3. **MAKE THE COOKED APPLES:** In a medium skillet over medium heat, melt the butter. Add the apples and cook, shaking the pan or stirring often, until the apple pieces are a light golden brown, 3 to 5 minutes. Remove from the heat and let cool.

Pesto Snails

Croissants swirled with pesto are equally at home for breakfast and brunch as they are for lunch or an evening meal with salad or soup.

Start to finish:
10 to 15 hours
(see Note on page 330)

Preparing the pesto, day one: 30 minutes

Rolling and shaping:
20 to 30 minutes

Freezing: 30 minutes

Proofing: overnight

Baking, day two:
30 to 35 minutes

Cooling: 20 minutes

VARIATION: GOAT CHEESE-HONEY

In a medium bowl, mix together 100 g (3½ ounces) of softened goat cheese, 50 g (1¾ ounces) of softened cream cheese, and 20 g (2½ teaspoons) of honey until well incorporated and smooth. Then mix in 15 g (1 tablespoon) of heavy cream to make the mixture more spreadable.

Ingredients	Metric	Imperial
all-purpose flour, for dusting		
½ recipe Sourdough Croissant Dough (page 324)	625 g	1⅓ pounds
Basil Pesto for Snails (recipe follows)	150 g	½ cup plus 2 tablespoons
Grana Padano or Parmigiano-Reggiano, grated	50 g	⅓ cup plus 1 tablespoon
EGG WASH		
whole egg	55 g	1 large egg
egg yolk	18 g	1 large yolk
heavy cream	30 g	2 tablespoons

1. Line two baking sheets with parchment paper. Lightly dust the work surface and the rolling pin with flour.

2. Set the croissant dough on the work surface. The dough should be chilled but not too cold. If it cracks when gently pressed with the pin, let it warm up for a few minutes at room temperature.

   Roll the length of the dough to 18 inches (45 cm). Position the dough so a long end is facing you.

3. Spread the pesto evenly over the dough and sprinkle with the cheese.

4. Starting at the bottom, lift the lower edge of the dough and gently fold it over until it turns on itself. Continue rolling, lifting the dough up and over as you go, until you complete the full roll. Finish with the seam facing down.

RECIPE CONTINUES

5. Measure the dough. It should be approximately 18 inches (45 cm). It's okay if it has expanded slightly or even shrunk back during the rolling process.

Find the midpoint of the roll and score it (press gently with a knife, but don't cut all the way through). Then score each half into five equal pieces, for a total of ten. Cut into ten rounds, trimming the edges as needed. Set any trimmings to the side.

6. Divide the snails between the baking sheets, five per sheet.

Roll the trimmings together, then into a pinwheel, and set on one of the baking sheets as well.

7. Freeze on the baking sheets for 30 minutes, just to partially freeze.

At this point the snails can also be wrapped well and frozen completely for up to 1 month (see note on freezing, page 335).

MAKE THE EGG WASH: Whisk together the egg, yolk, and cream in a small bowl. Brush the snails with the egg wash. Cover and refrigerate the remaining egg wash. Set the snails in the oven with a loaf pan filled halfway with boiling water or cover the baking sheets with an inverted box or plastic tub with a loaf pan filled halfway with boiling water (see Proofing Box at Home, page 330).

Let proof at room temperature until the dough is tender and expanded, overnight.

8. The next morning, if proofed in the oven, remove the trays from the oven and carefully cover them.

9. Arrange the oven racks in the top and bottom thirds of the oven. Preheat the oven to 350°F (175°C).

10. Carefully brush the snails with the egg wash again and transfer to the oven.

Bake, switching the shelf position of the pans and rotating once during baking, until the snails are a rich golden brown, 30 to 35 minutes.

11. Transfer to a wire rack and let cool completely.

Basil Pesto for Snails

Makes 150 grams (½ cup plus 2 tablespoons), enough for 10 snails

This simple method for pesto makes just the right amount for a generous layer in the dough for ten snails. Don't skip blanching the basil. It really locks in the bright green color. For this application, I leave out the garlic, but add a coarsely chopped clove with the seeds if you like. I use pumpkin seeds, but traditional pine nuts or other nuts like walnuts or pistachios will work well too.

Ingredients	Metric	Imperial
basil leaves	75 g	4 to 5 cups, loosely packed
pumpkin seeds, roasted and lightly salted	50 g	⅓ cup
extra-virgin olive oil	25 g	2 tablespoons
fine sea salt, to taste		

1. Bring a large saucepan of water to a boil. Fill a medium bowl with ice water.

2. Add the basil leaves to the boiling water and blanch for about 30 seconds. Immediately immerse the hot basil in the ice water to stop the cooking process, reserving about ¼ cup of the basil blanching water.

3. Once cooled, drain the basil and dry it well. Put in the jar of a high-powered blender with the pumpkin seeds. Pulse to chop, scraping the sides and repeating as needed. Then, slowly, with the blender running, stream in the olive oil. For the croissants, the pesto should be thick but spreadable. Stream in a little of the basil blanching water, if needed. Season with sea salt to taste.

WHEAT

IN THE

WORLD

T HROUGHOUT MY CAREER, AND LONG BEFORE it became trendy, I have valued and championed the local. We opened Bread Alone to serve the local community, and our most loyal customers have been our Catskills neighbors. We have always bought our fruit and produce from nearby farmers. We are proud to be part of the New York grainshed movement. As a student and an educator

I sought out local baking traditions across Europe, and even wrote a book called *Local Breads*, to recognize and honor the specificity of certain loaves like *tourte de seigle* from the Auvergne in France and dark Silesian rye from the Czech Republic. In my last book, *Living Bread*, I spent time with Italian wheat scientists, growers, millers, and bakers to understand a unique system for preserving Italian wheat seeds, growing heritage wheat on small farms, milling it nearby, and distributing it to microbakeries in the area in order to feed the local population.

I was flattered when soil scientist David Guerena got in touch with me after reading *Living Bread* to tell me about his work at the International Maize and Wheat Improvement Center (CIMMYT), in Texcoco, about twenty-five miles northeast of Mexico City. But I wasn't sure how my baking and research related to CIMMYT, a global organization interested in big-picture issues like slowing climate change through sustainable farming practices, experimenting with new crosses to obtain disease-resistant and more nutritious wheat, and supplying farmers in locations halfway around the world from the Hudson Valley with new wheat germplasm matched to growing conditions in those areas.

The Seed Bank

CIMMYT has a gargantuan wheat seed bank that David wanted me to see. The organization was established by the Mexican government and the Rockefeller Foundation in the 1940s with the aim of raising crop productivity in Mexico and abroad. Of course, I had heard of CIMMYT's first wheat breeder, Norman Borlaug, who won the Nobel Peace Prize in 1970 for his work on the selective breeding of wheat varieties for disease resistance and stable yields to stave off famine in developing countries. Borlaug's "green revolution" has been credited with averting starvation for billions of people and reducing poverty.

It has also been blamed for the industrialization of food and seed systems, the worsening of diet quality, the decrease in plant diversity, the decrease in water quality, and the degradation or loss of ecosystem services.

I was curious to learn how CIMMYT's extensive and sometimes controversial mission of "improving" wheat overlapped with both what my friends in Italy and my neighbors in the Northeast US were doing to reestablish local grain economies. After a long phone conversation with David about wheat farming and climate change, water and ecosystem quality, biodiversity, and nutrition, he invited me to spend a week at CIMMYT, to tour its wheat seed bank, walk the test plots of the wheat lines designed to grow in different parts of the world, observe lab tests that could determine the success of hybridization, and make bread in CIMMYT's test bakery. I learned how CIMMYT's breeding and field management programs have evolved since the days of the green revolution. Now there is an emphasis on selecting plants more resistant to pathogens, so that farmers can cut down or eliminate the use of pesticides and fungicides. Today CIMMYT's wheat breeders select wheat lines for drought resistance, so farmers need less water to grow wheat.

On my first day in Texcoco, I was awed by the size and scope of CIMMYT's seed bank, adjacent to its office building but really a world of its own. A security code is required for entrance to the vast concrete vault that protects their prized seed collection. The temperature is kept strictly near 0°F (–18°C).

Before entering we were required to put on thick blue winter jackets, wool hats, and gloves. The vault contains nearly 150,000 accessions of wheat from all around the world (more than one hundred times the number stored in the seed bank I visited in Sicily), representing twenty thousand years of wheat cultivation by humans. In its organization, the vault is comparable to an old-fashioned library. Rolling shelving units run on tracks in the floor and can be pushed to the left or right or turned around for easy access. Each unit is about eight feet tall and twenty feet wide, with eight shelves. Each shelf holds thirty boxes, each one labeled with a bunch of barcodes. Inside each box are dozens of seed envelopes. A barcode, along with a variety name, on each envelope identifies the seeds inside. A scan of the barcode will pull up the complete genetic profile of the wheat. Each seed sample has undergone genetic testing to identify its characteristics and aid in crop breeding for specific traits. Careful records are kept of color, kernel size, protein content, nutritional value, flavor, and more. And of course the history and provenance of every variety are noted. Using a computer catalog, researchers looking for Paigambari wheat seeds, grown for forty-five hundred years in western and central India, might be directed to carousel 93, shelf 2, box 5, envelope 20.

Maintenance is an ongoing and extraordinary effort. All samples have to be checked periodically for viability. Lab techs work in a sprouting room, wrapping seeds in damp paper towels and placing them in humidified cabinets to evaluate sprouting ability. If a sample doesn't meet the standard, other seeds are planted in a test plot in the field to produce a new supply so the bank can be re-stocked with more vibrant samples.

This vault might seem like the ultimate resource for both ancient and modern wheat varieties. And it is true that the collection is a remarkable feat of preservation. But this vast archive of both antique and contemporary wheat seeds is much more than a museum or a safeguard in case an apocalyptic event wipes out the world's wheat fields (CIMMYT is affiliated and shares its seeds with the so-called doomsday vault in Spitsbergen, Norway, which does in fact exist to protect the planet's agricultural resources from threats and catastrophes big and small).

CIMMYT's collection of genetic resources is integral to the organization's mission today to supply farmers across the world with new varieties that will grow well in their particular microclimates, as flooding, droughts, and heat waves—all the result of climate change—are already beginning to adversely affect crops. The scientific community has long recognized what the wider world is just recently beginning to understand, that the world's food security depends not only on far-flung industrial farms but on alternative local sources. When Russia invaded Ukraine in 2022, a crucial part of the world's wheat crop was blocked from leaving the Black Sea, leaving twenty-five African countries that rely on Russian and Ukrainian wheat without a steady supply of a vital food. It was in anticipation of a catastrophe

like this that CIMMYT has been supplying sub-Saharan Africa with high-yielding wheat varieties bred to thrive in the agro-ecologies of that region. If both big and small farmers are to meet the world's demand for wheat, many of them are going to need seeds genetically predisposed to thrive under new and sometimes extreme environmental conditions. Using the genetic material from different seeds, grain scientists grow plants that they hope will flourish in all the nooks and crannies of our changing planet.

Breeding with Purpose

As Maria Itria Ibba, head of CIMMYT's flour testing lab, explained to me, responsible, environmentally sensitive farming of bread wheat isn't simply a matter of going back to the way it used to be done before industrialization. Climate change and the appearance of new pests and diseases demand at the very least that heirloom varieties be studied and improved through selective breeding to thrive under today's conditions. But the main focus at CIMMYT is developing climate-resilient, nutritious, high-yielding, disease-resistant, and pest-tolerant wheat lines by improving wheat genetic diversity through either classical breeding (crossing between wheat lines) or by creating new synthetic wheat (meaning it was hybridized in a lab). Grain scientists identify important crop traits, search the genomic profiles of plants for desirable genes, and experiment with plant breeding. These "synthesized" wheats are a rich source of enhanced and novel ge-

netic diversity used for wheat improvement worldwide. There is art to it as well as science. Alison Bentley, head of CIMMYT's Global Wheat Program, likened the program's ongoing breeding processes to painting with oils. On her palette were colors from a myriad of plants. Which wheat might lend her new cross a resistance to Septoria leaf blotch or Hessian flies? Which might contribute heat tolerance or vitamin content?

After my thrilling visit to the seed bank, I flew to CIMMYT's test fields in Obregón, in southern Sonora, where much of the work of wheat crossing and selection takes place. This work is labor-intensive, intricate, and seems quite primitive at first glance. Heads of wheat are self-pollinating, meaning that each head has both male and female spikes. To cross two varieties, variety 1 is demasculated, its male spikes removed when it reaches a certain point of maturity. Then pollen from the male spikes of variety 2 are sprinkled on the female spikes of variety 1. Each female spike is carefully covered with a little cloth sock to prevent fertilization by errant pollen from another plant. It's an amazing sight, to see multiple covered wheat spikes blowing in the breeze. They'll remain covered until the new seeds are hand harvested, examined, and analyzed. Then the plants are allowed to self-pollinate for five generations, to establish and ensure the genetic stability of the line. This is not Frankenscience. It is controlled breeding with very specific goals.

I expected CIMMYT's test plots to look like the ones I saw in Italy—small squares of different varieties of wheat grown side by side under the same conditions. Instead, I saw multiple plots of the same wheat, each plot designed to mimic different growing conditions. To test drought resistance, one plot is fully watered, another is under half-drought conditions, and yet another simulates full-drought conditions. To test for disease resistance, leaf rust is introduced to a plot of a wheat variety that is known to be susceptible, planted next to varieties where susceptibility is unknown. Scientists observe the spread of the fungi to determine the varieties' susceptibility. The idea is to create environmental stresses that wheat might encounter in different places in the world. I was surprised by some of the results. I was describing the potentially hot, humid, and wet growing conditions on upstate New York farms to Karim Ammar, a durum wheat breeder originally from Tunisia who has worked extensively to identify and breed drought- and disease-resistant Mediterranean landrace wheats. He described several bread wheat varieties popular with central Texas farmers that he thought might do well in upstate New York. "But our climates are completely different," I argued. "Yes," he said, "but this particular variety has thrived during periods of extreme flooding, so I'm guessing that it can withstand the damp conditions you describe."

A successful wheat's nutritional and baking qualities must be tested in CIMMYT's rigorous and advanced flour lab and test bakery. The lab receives forty, fifty, and sometimes one hundred bags of wheat berries a day, all of different varieties. Workers use mesh screens placed on top of wooden boxes to sort through the berries, removing bugs and debris. Then the berries are milled in a small test mill and put through a barrage of tests to evaluate moisture content, gluten strength and quality, extensibility (to test the stretchiness of dough made with this flour), ash content (to determine the amount and type of minerals in each sample), and falling number (which tests the structural integrity of starch chains). Finally, each flour sample is used to bake tiny pan loaves, which are then judged for volume, color, and texture, using guidelines from the Cereals & Grains Association (formerly known as the American Association of Cereal Chemists International [AACCI]). I had brought some of my sourdough starter from home and used it to bake small loaves with three different kinds of flour milled in the lab. My loaf made with Borlaug 100 (named after CIMMYT's original wheat breeder to commemorate his hundredth birthday) produced a well-risen and stable loaf that withstood a twenty-four-hour cool ferment and had a lovely flavor and texture. Drought-, heat-, and leaf rust—resistant, this new variety has yielded up to 30 percent better than other popular varieties in locations as various as Australia and Nepal.

When CIMMYT breeders sign off on a new wheat variety, after it has been tested in the field, the mill, and the bakery, they'll take a certain amount of seed and grow out some volume, so it can be distributed for free around the world for testing on loca-tion. The amount of work that goes into getting these seeds ready for shipping is unbelievable. First, the seeds must be hand cleaned, and then passed through a dishwasher-like machine for washing. Seeds are then spread, a kilogram at a time, onto screens, where they are sterilized and then dried so they won't germinate in transit. They are inspected for pathogens before being packed in 75-gram envelopes for shipping to other research facilities and breeding institutions. Say a certain variety has been bred specifically to be grown in the Punjab province of Pakistan, a region where new climate-change scenarios already threaten wheat production, with the immediate goal of obtaining a higher yield than current varieties and the ultimate goal of helping the country reach wheat self-sufficiency. Seed deemed likely to succeed must be shipped to Pakistani research stations. After it is successfully grown in test plots for several generations, it will enter a seed multiplication program so it can be distributed in large quantities to local farmers.

Sustainable Wheat and Bread

This experience made me think long and hard about the privileged and ultimately untenable position of quite a few boutique growers, millers, and bakers in the US, who for now have the luxury of choosing single-source, less-productive (and thus more expensive) wheat, solely for its baking characteristics and, let's face it, charming pedigree. The most practical and successful small wheat farmers and millers in the US recognize the need to grow and mill wheat varieties not just for their flavor and glamorous heritage but to supply the greatest number of buyers for a reasonable price.

Greg Russo, my colleague and neighbor at Farmer Ground Flour, told me that his mill doesn't focus as much on niche varieties as other regional mills, sticking mostly with Glenn wheat (a hard winter wheat variety developed in North Dakota and released in 2005) and Warthog wheat (another modern variety that does well in the Northeast) in their flour blend, so they can sell their local flour efficiently and affordably. "In my personal experience," Greg says, "maybe at a very high level some professional bakers will notice different flavor notes in single-variety flours, but the vast majority of consumers are simply looking for organically grown, freshly milled flour that will make good bread."

To focus on old-timey names over the reality of local growing conditions isn't the best long-term strategy. Peter Martens, one of the Hudson Valley's most successful organic wheat farmers and the owner of Seneca Grain & Bean in the Finger Lakes, looked not to the local past or to the Midwest when seeking wheat varieties for his fields, but to Europe, where climate conditions more closely resemble those of New York State. He plants Renan, a soft red winter wheat developed in the 1980s in France. Renan has a buttery flavor, says Peter, and makes beautiful loaves because, even though it has a rela-

tively low protein content (about 9 percent), it develops unusually long gluten strands. "Here in the eastern US, wheat farmers tend to look at a lot of research coming out of Purdue or Ohio State. But it might make more sense to look at France or Germany. That's the direction we're taking, looking into northern European varieties." Martens is currently seeking certification from the US Department of Agriculture for his Renan seed. Such certification will officially recognize its genetic purity and identity, and allow him to establish production fields in order to produce his own Renan seeds for use on his farm and to sell to others in the area.

If we want to feed the entire population while preserving the environment, we are going to have to ask wheat breeders and seed suppliers to offer varieties that are productive, can be sustainably grown, and contain the quality protein necessary for baking. And then we are going to have to convince farmers to grow these varieties, and bakers to bake with them. Last but not least, we are going to have to educate consumers about the state of wheat farming and convince them of the importance of these best practices, for their health and the health of the planet. This sounds like a tall order, but after visiting CIMMYT and learning about the work of Greg, Peter, Aaron MacLeod and Harmonie Bettenhausen at Hartwick's Wheat Innovation Center, June Russell at Glynwood, and many others closer to home, I am more optimistic than I have ever been about the future of wheat farming and about both commercial and home craft baking.

APPENDIX

Equipment Resources

Here are some resources for the equipment needed to make the breads in this book. Some items—a KitchenAid mixer, a baking stone—are essential, while others—rattan proofing baskets from Germany—are nice to have but not absolutely necessary.

BROD & TAYLOR: This baking supply company sells a compact dough sheeter for the home kitchen, as well as proofing boxes and a sourdough warmer similar to the one made by Sourhouse.
brodandtaylor.com

CHALLENGER: This shallow cast-iron bread pan with a cover has become all the rage among home bakers, for good reason. Its low sides make it safe and easy for transferring loaves, and its large size accommodates most shapes. In addition, Challenger stocks a full range of artisan baking equipment.
challengerbreadware.com

COOPÉRATIVE VANNERIE DE VILLAINES: Resource for the highest-quality French bannetons and baskets. Expensive but worth it.
vannerie.com

HERBERT BIRNBAUM: Beautiful rattan and plastic proofing baskets in all shapes and sizes, made in Germany.
herbert-birnbaum.de/en

KING ARTHUR BAKING COMPANY: King Arthur sells a wide range of equipment as well as ingredients. A reliable source for the KitchenAid Pro Line stand mixer used to test the recipes in this book, it also stocks bread knives, lames, pizza wheels, pastry brushes, bannetons, baking steels, brioche pans, and dough-rising containers.
kingarthurbaking.com

PLEASANT HILL GRAIN: An outstanding resource and one-stop shop, with knowledgeable and helpful staff. Baking stones, proofing baskets, bread dough scoring lames, bench and bowl scrapers, digital scales, baking peels, cast-iron skillets and loaf pans, and Dutch ovens. It also sells the Brod & Taylor proofer, which will keep your dough at whatever temperature you'd like in a moist environment. A good source for Mockmill and other home mills, it stocks a good selection of triple-cleaned grain for home milling and sprouting. Pleasant Hill Grain also sells ingredients, including barley malt syrup and instant dry yeast.
pleasanthillgrain.com

SOURHOUSE: This innovative company makes a wonderful new gadget, the Goldie by Sourhouse, a countertop sourdough warmer that reliably and quickly ferments my starter whenever I need it. **sourhouse.co**

Flour Resources

If you want to bake with supermarket flour, your best bets are organic untreated flours from national brands King Arthur, Bob's Red Mill, and Arrowhead Mills. I do strongly encourage you to make the extra effort to visit your local mill or its website to experience baking with noncommodity flours. Here are some of my favorites, state by state.

ALABAMA
To Your Health, Fitzpatrick, AL, **healthyflour.com**

ALASKA
Alaska Flour Company, Delta Junction, AK, **alaskaflourcompany.com**

ARIZONA
BKW Grains, Marana, AZ, **bkwazgrown.com**

Hayden Flour Mills, Gilbert, AZ, **haydenflourmills.com**

ARKANSAS
War Eagle Mill, Rogers, AR, **wareaglemill.com**

CALIFORNIA
Capay Mills, Rumsey, CA, **capaymills.com**

Early Bird Farm & Mill, Wilseyville, CA, **earlybirdnc.com**

Grist & Toll, Pasadena, CA, **gristandtoll.com**

Honoré Farm and Mill, Marin County, CA, **honoremill.org**

COLORADO
Dry Storage Co., Boulder, CO, **drystorageco.com**

Grains from the Plains, Hugo, CO, **grainsfromtheplains.com**

FLORIDA
Honeycomb Bakers, Winter Haven, FL, **honeycombbread.com**

GEORGIA
Dayspring Farms, Danielsville, GA, **dayspringfarmsga.com**

IDAHO
Hillside Grain, Bellevue, ID, **hillsidegrain.com**

ILLINOIS
Breslin Farms, Ottawa, IL, **breslinfarms.com**

Brian Severson Farms, Dwight, IL, **qualityorganic.net**

Funks Grove Heritage Fruits and Grains, Urbana, IL, **funksgrovehfg.com**

Hazzard Free Farm, Pecatonica, IL, **hazzardfreefarm.com**

Janie's Mill, Ashkum, IL, **janiesmill.com**

INDIANA
Bridgeton Mill, Bridgeton, IN,
bridgetonmill.net

IOWA
Early Morning Harvest, Panora, IA,
earlymorningharvest.com

KANSAS
Farmer Direct Foods, New Cambria, KS,
farmerdirectfoods.com

Heartland Mill, Marienthal, KS,
heartlandmill.com

KENTUCKY
Weisenberger Mills, Midway, KY,
weisenberger.com

MAINE
Aurora Mills & Farm, Linnaeus, ME,
auroramillsandfarm.com

Maine Grains, Skowhegan, ME,
mainegrains.com

Misty Brook Farm, Albion, ME,
mistybrook.com

Songbird Farm, Unity, ME,
songbirdorganicfarm.com

MASSACHUSETTS
Ground Up Grain, Hadley, MA,
groundupgrain.com

Plimoth Grist Mill, Plymouth, MA,
plimoth.org

MICHIGAN
Grand Traverse Culinary Oils,
Traverse City, MI
**localdifference.org/partner
/grand-traverse-culinary-oils-flours**

New Mission Milling, Zeeland, MI,
newmissionmilling.com

Westwind Milling, Swartz Creek, MI,
westwindmilling.com

MINNESOTA
Natural Way Mills, Middle River, MN,
naturalwaymills.com

Sunrise Flour Mill, North Branch, MN,
sunriseflourmill.com

Swany White Flour Mills, Freeport, MN,
swanywhiteflour.com

Whole Grain Milling, Welcome, MN,
wholegrainmilling.net

MISSOURI
Neighbor's Mill Bakery & Café,
Springfield, MO,
neighborsmill.com

MONTANA
Conservation Grains, Choteau, MT,
conservationgrains.com

NEW JERSEY
River Valley Community Grains,
Long Valley, NJ,
rivervalleycommunitygrains.com

NEW MEXICO
**Navajo Agricultural Products Industry
(NAPI),** Farmington, NM,
napi.navajopride.com

NEW YORK
The Birkett Mills, Penn Yan, NY,
thebirkettmills.com

Farmer Ground Flour, Trumansburg, NY,
farmergroundflour.com

Gianforte Farm, Cazenovia, NY,
gianfortefarm.com

Hawthorne Valley Farm, Ghent, NY,
farm.hawthornevalley.org

Middle Brook Mill, Jefferson, NY,
middlebrookmill.com

Milestone Mill, Hurley, NY,
milestonemill.com

Wild Hive Farm, Clinton Corners, NY,
wildhivefarm.com

NORTH CAROLINA
Carolina Ground Flour, Hendersonville, NC,
carolinaground.com

Lindley Mills, Graham, NC,
lindleymills.com

Red Tail Grains, Orange County, NC,
redtailgrains.com

OHIO
Bear's Mill, Greenville, OH,
bearsmill.org

Shagbark Seed & Mill, Athens, OH,
shagbarkmill.com

OKLAHOMA
Chisholm Trail Milling, Enid, OK,
chisholmtrailmilling.com

John's Farm, Fairview, OK,
johnsfarm.com

OREGON
Camas Country Mill, Eugene, OR,
camascountrymill.com

Lonesome Whistle Farm, Junction City, OR,
lonesome-whistle.com

PENNSYLVANIA
Castle Valley Mill, Doylestown, PA,
castlevalleymill.com

Small Valley Milling, Halifax, PA,
smallvalleymilling.com

Weatherbury Farm, Avella, PA,
weatherburyfarm.com

RHODE ISLAND
Kenyon's Grist Mill, West Kingston, RI,
kenyonsgristmill.com

SOUTH CAROLINA
Anson Mills, Columbia, SC,
ansonmills.com

Marsh Hen Milling, Edisto Island, SC,
marshhenmill.com

SOUTH DAKOTA
Belle Valley Ancient Grains, Newell, SD,
bellevalleyancientgrains.com

TENNESSEE
Valentine Mills, Dandridge, TN,
facebook.com/valentinemill

TEXAS
Barton Springs Mill, Dripping Springs, TX,
bartonspringsmill.com

Homestead Gristmill, Waco, TX,
homesteadgristmill.com

UTAH
Central Milling, Logan, UT,
centralmilling.com

VERMONT
Nitty Gritty Grain Co., Charlotte, VT,
nittygrittygrain.com

Rogers Farmstead, Berlin, VT,
rogersfarmstead.com

VIRGINIA
Deep Roots Milling, Roseland, VA,
deeprootsmilling.com

Locke's Mill, Berryville, VA,
lockesmillgrains.com

Wade's Mill, Raphine, VA,
wadesmill.com

WASHINGTON
Bluebird Grain Farms, Winthrop, WA,
bluebirdgrainfarms.com

Cairnspring Mills, Burlington, WA,
cairnspring.com

Palouse Colony Farm, Endicott, WA,
palouseheritage.com

Shepherd's Grain, Edmonds, WA,
shepherdsgrain.com

Small's Family Farm, Walla Walla, WA,
smallsfamilyfarm.com

WISCONSIN
Great River Organic Milling, Fountain City,
WI, **greatrivermilling.com**

Meadowlark Community Mill,
Ridgeway, WI, **meadowlarkorganics.com**

WYOMING
Wyoming Heritage Grains, Ralston, WY,
wyomingheritagegrains.com

ACKNOWLEDGMENTS

I have many people to thank:

First and foremost, Nels Leader and Sharon Burns-Leader for allowing me to retire with such grace.

My family: Chloe, Otto, Liv, Mick, Leila, Noah, Alex.

My coauthors Lauren Chattman and Amy Vogler.

Photographers Joerg Lehmann, Lisa Nagahama, Kate Devine, Alfonso Cortes, Alekz Pacheco, Mark Antman.

My longtime agent, Janis Donnaud.

The team at Avery: Anne Kosmoski, Farin Schlussel, Suzy Swartz, Ashley Tucker, Lucia Watson.

In France: Pascal Achar, Mikael Benichou, Joël Defives, Basile Fourmont, Bertrand Girardeau, Vincent Maudet, Olivia Polsky, Eric Verthy, and a special thanks to Katherine Weisberg.

At Les Ambassadeurs du Pain: Thomas Planchot.

Paul Lebeau at Mockmill.

At CIMMYT: Karim Ammar, Alison Bentley, Jason Donovan, Susanne Dreisigacker, Simon Fonteyne, Bram Govaerts, Velu Govindan, David Guerena, Maria Itria Ibba, Francisco Piñera, Matthew Reynolds, Carolina Rivera, Carolina Saint Pierre, Carolina Sansaloni, Ravi Singh, Nele Verhulst.

Bakers Arnd Erbel, Didier Rosada, Mike Smetak, Natalya Syanova.

Mentors and inspirations: Edward Espe Brown, Fabrice Guéry, Nicky Giusto, Nancy Harmon Jenkins, Basil Kamir, Jean LeFleur, André Lefort, Hy Lerner, Scott and Helen Nearing, Jules and Helen Rabin, Paul Rea, Steve Sullivan.

Millers: Robert Beauchemin, Neil Johnston, Amber Lambke, Peter Martens, Thor Oechsner, Greg Russo, Eric Smith.

From the Maine Grain Alliance: Tristan Noyes, Kayla Starr.

Harmonie Bettenhausen, Aimee Hill, Aaron MacLeod, Darren Reisberg, June Russell.

INDEX

Note: Italicized page numbers indicate material in photographs or illustrations.